D1107786

By the Political Sea

By the Political Sea

by

Katie Scofield Louchheim

1970
DOUBLEDAY & COMPANY, INC.
GARDEN CITY, NEW YORK

Designed by Wilma Robin

*This book is dedicated
to my husband and my daughters
who lived through it all*

This book owes its existence to Ken McCormick, Evelyn Petersen Metzger, and my own compulsion for making notes. It was difficult to harness the Niagara of my journals but Evelyn did succeed. Anne W. Corrigan and Ralph Backlund, each in turn, encouraged my sometimes discouragement, turned my eliptical poetic phrases into comprehensible paragraphs. The practiced eye of *Newsweek*'s Ken Crawford redirected many a reverse flow. Verda Morgan put up with daily disorder, retyped, and reminded me of the dates of my self-imposed deadlines. Virginia Gunner sacrificed weekends to type up the manuscript.

Friends in the Senate and in the House, researchers at the Democratic and Republican National Committees, photographers, co-workers, members of the Association of American Foreign Service Women, the Democratic Congressional Wives Forum gave me their advice, their opinions, and their time. Among those I want to express special thanks to are: William McCormick Blair, Rose Conway, D. B. Hardeman, Betty Hahn, Beverly Knowles, William Lewis, Louis Martin, George Packard, W. B. Ragsdale, Jo Rauh, Christine Sadler, and Geraldine Sohle. And to Stephen Mitchell and his accomplices, successors, and sometime enemies, my thanks for giving me lessons in that inexact science, the art of the possible, most frequently described as politics.

Contents

PROLOGUE

One afternoon in the summer of 1964, congressional helpers
and friends had been invited to the family floor of the White House
to mingle with the wives of the Organization of American States.
The President made one of his unexpected entrances. The chatting
faded away and all eyes turned toward him. He first walked to the
sofa where Bird sat between Latin American leaders' wives, placed
a kiss on her brow. He then went around the room shaking hands.
At one point he reached over heads and hands to bestow a kiss on
Phyllis Dillon (Douglas Dillon was still Secretary of the Treasury)
and Betty Fulbright, wife of the Chairman of the Foreign Relations Committee of the Senate. Senator Eugene McCarthy's wife
and I stood next in his path. He shook hands with us.

In a later recounting of the scene, I said that Phyllis Dillon
got a good-bye kiss (Dillon had tendered his resignation), Betty
Fulbright, a longtime friendship kiss, Abigail McCarthy, a "don't
count on your husband as Vice Presidential candidate" shake.
"And you?" I was asked. "I was in the wrong pew," I replied.

There was only one reassurance, one poultice to be applied after
a royal rebuff had been administered . . . When I got the shrug
or the "who-are-you" look, I recalled the unexpected autographed
pictures and the many appearances he made for me—as vice chairman of the Democratic National Committee—at functions unimportant to him but vital to the party. Or more recent proof positive, the appointment as Permanent Delegate to the Executive
Board of UNESCO, an office with the personal rank of Ambassador, a six-year sinecure the Republicans (when President Nixon

took over in January of '69) immediately demanded I relinquish.

I can even go back to the time when the slight was on my side, though unintentional. In the summer of 1960 I gave a dinner for an old friend and reluctant candidate for the Senate in New Jersey, Thorn Lord. Thorn was perhaps the most admired political pro the party could boast of; he had elected Governor Meyner and completely revised state political procedures.

Earl Mazo, an appreciative friend of Thorn's, (now with *Reader's Digest* then with the New York *Herald Tribune*) helped make up the list of the ten newspaper men present. After the coffee, someone suggested we take a straw poll on who the Democratic candidate would be. Kennedy won easily. Symington, Stevenson, and the then majority leader, Lyndon Baines Johnson, each got one vote or two votes. It was understood that such dinners were off the record. Reporters were present only as guests.

The very next day Thorn, in his capacity as state chairman, met candidate Johnson to escort him on a New Jersey tour. Lying on the floor of the car was a copy of the Newark *News* with large headlines telling of Kennedy's victory sweep at a Georgetown dinner and of Johnson's one-vote support. Candidate Johnson read on; the hostess was named in small print. "I thought Katie was my friend," he remarked wryly.

I was and still am President Johnson's friend. Politics teaches one that public figures hurt more easily than the rest of us but appreciate more visibly . . . hence the cordial autographs one acquires.

Who You Are

IF I HAD LIVED ANY PLACE BUT WASHINGTON, I WOULD HAVE RUN FOR Congress. In the nation's capital, which still has no elected representatives—or any self-government—I turned instead to helping others get elected.

My husband, who is a bird watcher, likens me to a ruddy turnstone, a shore bird that runs along the beach at low tide, turning over every shell looking for sustenance. Like the turnstone, I never gave up. Not everything turns out to be useful but one finds a lot that is interesting. Over the years the unexpected has lighted up my every day, added wisdom to the commonplace and meaning to the political process.

To explain one's motivations is never easy and always suspect. This much I know: I have a compulsion about working, participating, and making notes. I like hard work as much as I dislike not being in on what's going on. For me work has made ambition bearable.

My husband has always understood this and encouraged me along the way. When my spirits sink, he will remind me of what the White Queen said to Alice: "Turn out your toes, and remember who you are."

I not only remember who I am but how I got that way. I inherited my ability to persist from my mother; hers was a world of limited opportunities for women but she made the best of them. I have always had an overdeveloped instinct for trying to achieve the difficult, if not the impossible. I acquired it as a child.

All About Me

AS AN ONLY CHILD IN A TALL, GLOOMY NEW YORK HOUSE, I NEVER
dreamed I would meet and associate and trade favors with names
in the news. I lived in a world of make believe; some days I was
going to be an actress, on others a ballet dancer.

I played alone in a large nursery on the top floor that had in it
all the playthings a little girl could wish for: a dollhouse twice my
size that had been especially constructed for my mother, a white
and gold theater with a red velvet curtain, a grocery store with
scales and shelves of miniature staples, and an array of dolls, each
with its own wardrobe.

In childhood the truth seems oversize and preposterous and the
imagined appears to be real. Looking back, I find very little that
is real and a lot that I made up. I strung up buttons to act on my
theater stage and played all the parts; in my infinitely rich treasure
of hand-me-downs, veils, scarves, high-heeled slippers, and dresses,
I was the mother and the tutor of all my dolls. Occasionally some
reality would creep into my repertoire; when my mother consulted
a decorator about the pug-dog-embroidered velvet furniture in our
parlor, I undertook the rearrangement of the dollhouse furniture,
speaking with the voice of W. & J. Sloane.

My father took me on nature walks in Central Park where we
fed the squirrels. Soon thereafter I was found crouched on my
knees, in a corner of my playroom, calling gently, "Here, bunny,
bunny, here, bunny."

Turn-of-the-century children were smothered in affection,

shielded, overdressed, and overprotected. Photographs of me at age two depict an inordinate number of bows, laces, tucks, and frills. I was coddled, chastised, supervised, and suppressed. The world was somewhere outside three pairs of window curtains: a layer of net, another of lace, and still another of velvet or taffeta depending on the room. Everything rustled, everyone was—so one was led to believe—well behaved and well brought up.

On rainy or snowy days I would steal down to the basement where the smells were heavenly, hoping the cook's son would be there to play with me. Lottie, a German maid who belonged originally to my great-grandmother, taught me to read. Louisa Michaux, who despised Lottie, a sentiment vigorously reciprocated, was my mother's maid, who curled my curls and pressed my bows. Louisa came from Luxembourg, Lottie from Bremen. Seniority swished in Lottie's black taffeta apron where she kept the household keys. The putting-to-bed rituals were properly in Louisa's keeping. Lottie would manage to keep watch; as soon as the starched petticoats of Louisa had swooshed their way down the hall, Lottie would steal in, sit on the bed, and in a heavy German accent read *Little Nemo*, the latest episode in *The Katzenjammer Kids* (the funny papers), or Grimm's fairy tales from a battered book with pop-up pictures.

Inevitably a loud quarrel broke out between my two guardians. Lottie wept, Louisa stormed. Rights and wrongs were submitted to a higher tribunal, that of my mother and my maiden aunt. My aunt, only nine years my senior, alternately tormented and spoiled me. My mother, outraged, would remonstrate with her on both scores. There was never peace; quarrels were built upon one another, no one remembered how they originated. I knew they were temporarily concluded when doors slammed and I was summoned.

Most of my time was spent in the adult world. Surrounded by temperamental and uninhibited relatives, my grandfather, my mother, bachelor uncle, and spinster aunt, I soon majored in accommodation. Perhaps that was what led me later into politics.

I learned early that wars, games, and bestowed affections could be lost as well as won. Before feelings between people were described as "interpersonal," I knew that I could best escape the hurts and the tempests by making believe I was a creature in a toy store, a doll that no one wanted, a madame in a veil at the grocer's, or an obliging maid at the door admitting Prince Charming.

While my grandmother lived, I loved and was loved back with a fairy-tale "forever after" fervor. Grandma found my fabrications adorable. I was forbidden to ride in our elevator alone; when caught, I invented errands for Grandma, and the latter never betrayed me. We made periodic excursions down Fifth Avenue. Riding in a polished Renault with a speaking tube and jump seats, I was reminded to keep my white shoes beneath the seat lest their freshly powdered surfaces come in contact with her voluminous black skirt. The first stop was always at F. A. O. Schwarz where smiling salesladies recognized a generous client. Since I inevitably chose a small toy, a miniature doll, a tiny dollhouse rug, Grandma would have anticipated my embarrassing taste. On entering the store she would purchase an extravagance which I never touched, and which stayed safely boxed in the toy closet. We feasted afterward at Maillard's. Grandma, who was forbidden sweets, later recited in elaborate detail what "that child" had consumed. It was understood that I did not see her eat and that my mother would ask no questions.

Before she died, she lay for many weeks propped against huge square pillows with one foot extended, while I rubbed her big toe, a sensation she described as beneficial. Early that December we celebrated Hanukkah, the feast of lights, together. I cried a lot when Mother explained she had gone to heaven. For several days thereafter I put large amounts of lump sugar on the window sill; how else would Grandmother be sure to have enough sugar in her heavenly tea?

My family were moderate Republicans and nominal Jews. Neither subject was ever explored or discussed. While my grandmother lived she would take me to temple, where I cringed at the bellows of the rabbi, delivered in what I was certain were the tones of Judgment Day reproaches. My grandfather, who was sentimental and worshiped my grandmother, kept certain rituals alive for her sake. On Friday nights, he would mumble blessings over the bread,[1] while all the uncles and aunts, summoned from their own family disputes, would sit impatiently waiting to strike the first blow in this larger arena. After dinner, bored with one another, the uncles, like overgrown boys, would escape to my nursery to smoke their forbidden cigars. (Sabbath smoking was not permitted.)

After my grandmother's death, no one went to temple except on the high holidays, Rosh Hashonoh and Yom Kippur. My private lessons in Hebrew came to an end, a great relief to a child avoiding the then unlabeled defect of halitosis. (My piano teacher's instructions in counting afforded a proximity I also found unbearable. Both lady instructors were single; I remember imagining that this ailment must belong only to spinsters. Early on, I resolved to avoid this state.)

Later, when the opulence of my childhood was replaced by the language of economy, a language my mother never cared to understand, and her fragile marriage sank in a stormy sea of disappointments, my mother became a Christian Scientist. There is no doubt, as I look back, that she felt the need for spiritual answers to worldly questions and the solace of a practitioner who would listen and assure her that God is love and the fullness of that love precludes mortal error. My father, in turn, became a Unitarian. Quite simply, his was an escape conversion; he despised being Jewish. He felt, as did hundreds of other Jews, like tearing down the fence around him. At the outset of World War I he also changed his name from Shoenfeld to Scofield, an anglicizing that he claimed converted the unpopular German sound to a true-blue American one.

My mother was small, exquisite, and demanding. The five-story house at 47 West Eighty-sixth Street was amply supplied with

[1] Translated from the Hebrew, the blessing reads: "Blessed art Thou, O Lord, our God, King of the Universe who brings forth bread from the earth."

bells which she kept well exercised. Our affluence bloomed in an era when affluence could be measured in numbers of servants, courses at meals, and hats on hatstands. My father, a handsome, tall, graceful man, plied me with mechanical toys which only he enjoyed. Later he taught me to skate, dance, play tennis, and walk at a fast clip. A shadowy figure, a non-participant, he remained above the daily battles—or out of reach.

Early in his marriage my father lost all Mother's money in business; my grandfather, though highly respected as head of Armour & Company in New York, could not afford the overabundance my mother's inclinations dictated. We were funded, munificently until his export-import firm failed, by my mother's youngest brother, the bachelor uncle of my childhood. Taking over from my grandmother, he would carry me off to shopping expeditions and Saturday matinees. At fourteen I went to boarding school, unaware that I was one of a few Jewish girls accepted by Rosemary Hall, that my uncle was paying the tuition, that I had been raised in a matriarchy, and that as a new girl I would be tested and tried, and would weep bitterly after the Christmas holidays, begging not to return. My mother dominated. I went back. Eventually I made friends and was elected to minor school offices. As ice hockey captain, I innovated. Boys I grew up with had taught me to play in Central Park; I challenged a boys' school in Greenwich. Most of my team, including the captain, landed in the infirmary. As mistress of dramatics, I was in charge of the Nativity play, which took place in the chapel on the school grounds. After clothing the Virgin, attendant angels, and shepherds from the cheesecloth rags available in the "Shakespeare closet" (our spring ritual included a Shakespeare play in the orchard), I rented costumes for the three kings. Caroline Rutz-Rees, mistress and founder of Rosemary Hall (in 1890), chided me; pacing her cottage floor, crunching large quantities of lump sugar into her coffee cup, she detained me after class. "Scofield"—we were addressed according to English public school custom by our last names—"we stay with the Shakespeare closet, tradition has its due place in this school."

I did not know then that in 1920 Miss Rutz-Rees had been elected Democratic National Committeewoman for Connecticut, or that later, she, too, would innovate, demanding that women be appointed to the all-powerful Executive Committee of the party hierarchy. The thought of kings in cheesecloth, however, remains abhorrent and I am still a confirmed tradition smasher.

Rosemary, justifiably, had the reputation of being scholastically excellent. Fortunately for me, this proved to be true, for it was all the formal education I ever got. Patterned on spartan English models, and guided by the innovative Miss Rutz-Rees, self-government, the honor system, the classics, and ardent competitive sportsmanship were added to the mix of starched stiff collars, scratchy uniforms, daily chapel, and impersonal formidable teachers who demanded excellence and obedience. Among other skills acquired in my three years' attendance, I learned to compete and to lose. My mother, fortunately, was not at hand to raise hob when I did. At earlier stages she had reproached elementary teachers for indications of favoritism toward others at my expense.

I never did get to Smith College where I had been duly entered and accepted. The cash to send me to college was nowhere to be found. My uncle had his firm's insolvency to reckon with, and so my mother, my aunt, and I were shipped abroad where living was cheaper. My recognition of the realities of family finances occurred late; I was seventeen when we traveled by train from Holland to Germany. I wept when my mother bestowed an extravagant dollar bill on the German conductor. He, too, cried for different reasons.

In those years my mother and father met only to quarrel, but remained together to play out the social game's rules. My mother suspected that divorce might interfere with her ultimate objective —to see me properly married and settled down, a popular formula that summed up the respectability and security a young woman required.

In Germany I learned to speak the language, studied piano, and watched with increasing astonishment the moral decay of a society that could cope neither with inflation nor with the collapse of its military gods, its hierarchies, and its worship of law and order.

My ancestors were Germans, with an Austrian strain belonging to the great-grandmother who had spoiled my mother as my grandmother had spoiled me. Both my grandmother and great-grandmother, though long deceased, lived on in portraits and predilections. My mother cited their dictums, copied their extravagant generous dictates. My great-grandfather, a considerable person in his own right, came through my mother's account only as a handsome successful businessman. Despite his devotion to my mother, the matriarchal side claimed all my mother's fealty. Great-great-grandparents had been titled by the Austrian court. The title served as a compensation (I had always suspected) to moneylending Jews who kept the monarchy afloat.

My great-grandfather came to this country in 1848. He had enlisted as a soldier in his native Bavaria in a rebellion against the Duke of Baden and was forced to flee when the Duke was victorious. He managed to acquire a fortune, a Fifth Avenue house on the corner of Eighty-fourth Street, opposite the Metropolitan Museum, a retinue of servants, hangers-on, works of art, and two children, one of whom was my maternal grandmother. Some years ago a newly founded livestock museum in Laramie, Wyoming, wrote asking for the papers of my grandfather and great-grandfather, both of whom were successful pioneers in the industry.

My father's family were North Germans, cold, impersonal, and formidable. My paternal grandfather was passionately pro-German and remained so during the First World War. He and my maternal grandfather, who despised everything German, staged noisy quarrels at the frequent family gatherings my mother insisted upon. I can remember Grandfather Joseph (Mother's father) inveighing against the Kaiser, winding up his peroration with a homemade invective that never failed to startle his listeners: "I'd like to see that fella, that bum, standing on Brooklyn

Bridge on the coldest day of the coldest winter, wearing a linen
duster and selling matches."

My Shoenfeld grandfather became one of the founders of the
Ethical Culture Society. After his death his widow lived abroad,
traveling from spa to spa. No one ever knew what she thought or
whom she liked. In her housekeeping days she kept everything
under lock and key, including a litter of kittens (they might
destroy her silk chairs and lace curtains) and the cake, of which
she always ate the center, carefully cut out around a teacup.

Eventually, my mother and father were divorced. I'm not certain I ever understood my father; he had an impersonal veneer
that was hard to crack. Perhaps he developed a protective covering
that enabled him to survive the turbulence that my mother's family
stirred up. Mother never gave up, but Father had long since resigned himself to the part of a bit player in my life and in the lives
of others. It was from my mother that I learned the lessons of persistence, of innovation, of doing what she dearly loved to call
the "right thing," be it a kindness or launching a cause. Included in her formidable character were strong streaks of open-
mindedness. She turned fighting liberal in later life and no convert
was ever a more fierce believer. She was an avid learner and course-
taker; I grew up to whole pages, read aloud, of Henry Adams'
Mont St. Michel and Chartres. Armed with a purpose and a plan,
she would attack the paintings in the Prado, Grandfather's diabetic
diets, the search for a wife for her widowed brother, a family quarrel, or a benefit. In her day, women were not called "doers," but
my mother more than qualified for the title. She founded more
institutions, staged more fund-raising events, and sought out more
cultural sources than most of her wealthier contemporaries. I can
see her still in her box at the New York Symphony concert, listening to Mozart, casting an occasional eye on my posture (aged
seven, I had to sit still and straight, my white-gloved hands in my
lap), concentrating on Walter Damrosch's graceful concession to
the necessary motions of conducting.

She did not approve of young women working, but I was determined to give it a try. Back in New York, I took a morning secretarial course, held jobs in the afternoon. The German baron in the antique store liked to talk but disliked the United States. He was fond of saying: *"Die Vögel singen nicht und die Mädchen lachen nicht* [The birds don't sing and the girls don't laugh]," a curse he believed he could not survive.

From antiques I went on to decorators, to publishers. The last was a man called Harold Vinal, editor of *Voices*, an accepted poetry quarterly. His mother sent him his clean underwear and homemade goodies every week; I had to unwrap the package. Poetry, then as now, did not pay the rent. His business venture consisted of sharing publication costs with unknown authors in hopes of selling pungent plots to the movies. These were the twenties, and the movies survived on the theory that everyone could write. Involuntarily I learned speed reading as I galloped through the muck and mire of hundreds of manuscripts.

Eventually we sold our New York house. My grandfather retired, my bachelor uncle had married as had my mother's younger sister, my teasing aunt. After a year in Los Angeles we moved into a New York apartment where our overproportioned furniture looked not unlike dinosaurs wedged in telephone booths.

My grandfather, whose entire life had been devoted to the daily competitive forces of a burgeoning industry (he had lost his first fortune in the Chicago fire and acquired his second by the time of his marriage), found retirement intolerable. His business cronies haunted him, his pinochle games ceased to divert him, and his health began to give way. In the spring of 1926 we sailed for Europe, Mother, Grandfather, and I, presumably for an indefinite stay.

Ten days after we landed in Hamburg, Germany, Walter Louchheim and I were married by a Justice of the Peace who shouted his way through the ceremony. Like all those who fear they will not be understood (Walter's German was neither fluent nor current), the J.P. raised his voice. We caused him further consternation

when we refused to exchange rings. One wedding ring would suffice—it still does.

Walter was then on the floor of the New York Stock Exchange
and a partner in his father's successful brokerage house. The mutual friend who had originally introduced us described me as
pretty but dumb. I admired Walter's philosophy library and he,
in turn, found me agreeable and educable. He later loaned me
several books. I claim he married me to get them back; he has
always been loath to lend a book.

We lived through the crash and the depression; no one had to
tell us that the New Deal had some if not all the answers. We were
living in Shrewsbury, New Jersey, when we read of the formation
of the Securities and Exchange Commission. Walter had abandoned Wall Street, returning to the philosophic studies he had
relinquished at his father's urging. He had long preached Stock
Exchange reform—why not, I asked, put his talents at the disposal
of this new agency created to cure some of the ills he bemoaned?
He never did complete his Ph.D. thesis on the Aristotelian theories
of time and space. He was immediately offered a position on the
Securities and Exchange Commission, the Chairman of which was
Joseph P. Kennedy.

In October of 1934, I put a quilt on the piano and closed the
Shrewsbury house. With one daughter in my arms and the other,
aged three, clinging to my coat, I walked down the Washington
station platform. My thoughts were certainly not of politics, campaigns, or public life. In the long cab ride to the Wardman Park
Hotel where we had taken rooms, I recall appreciating the trees,
wide avenues, marble buildings, and the low taxi fare.

I spent a lot of time, those first weeks, riding around Washington in an open LaSalle, figuratively fitting our household into
various neighborhoods. I came home one evening to tell Walter
that I had found the place where we were going to live: "It's
called Georgetown, it's unique. Every house has a personality, and
the bricks are all old." A year later we moved to Georgetown—
with us came all the possessions my mother prized (she had given

up housekeeping), the treasures acquired by the great-grandmother for whom I was named. Her portrait and that of her handsome husband hang in my room; she has the fine features that my mother and grandmother inherited—and I missed. Her eyes follow me about, asking questions: she wants to know why I ever went to work and I'm still trying to answer her. Possessions can be most upsetting; they stay on, but the guardians leave one.

Up from Nowhere

MY SENSE OF IMPERMANENCE, THAT FIRST WINTER IN THE NATION'S capital, came through clearly in an interview with the headmistress of Beauvoir, the National Cathedral School kindergarten. Would she accept my three-year-old daughter for a few weeks? Fourteen years later, when my daughter graduated, the same woman twitted me: "That was a mighty long few weeks!"

Our home in Shrewsbury, New Jersey, had stood on Sycamore Avenue, an appropriately tree-lined thoroughfare. Washington streets in the 1930s could be described as "alphabet-lined." I would catch myself eavesdropping on conversations before I plunged in; I had to be certain they were talking about recovery when they said NRA (National Recovery Act), and that FCC referred to the Federal Communications Commission, and not to FTC, the Federal Trade Commission, or SEC, the Securities and Exchange Commission, where my husband worked.

Daytimes I haunted the galleries of the House and the Senate, the solemnity of vast marble hearing rooms, the sanctuary quiet of the dark, delicately proportioned Supreme Court chamber, still lodged in what had been the Senate in the days of the founding fathers.

But I soon grew tired of talking and weary of watching: the monotony of the Senate floor always astonishes gallery visitors. Senator Copeland,[1] wearing his habitual red carnation, reading his paper, and filing his nails; the conservative from Virginia,

1 Senator Royal Samuel Copeland, New York, 1922–38.

Senator Harry Byrd; the archdemagogue, Huey Long; and the fiery segregationist, Senator Bilbo—all became familiar faces to gallery-goers like myself.

But I wanted action, and what is currently referred to as participation. Friends introduced me to Dorothy McAllister, the persuasive and enthusiastic Director of Women's Activities for the Democratic National Committee. Dorothy turned a know-nothing volunteer into a permanent fixture. Licking stamps and sealing envelopes were part of one's training. It took the postage meter, Hubert Humphrey once remarked, to liberate women volunteers. Dorothy wisely fed us bits and pieces of research work when our interest flagged, while Virginia Rishel, who edited the *Democratic Digest*, let us suggest ideas for articles and, later, allowed me to write one or two.

In 1940, as was the custom in Roosevelt campaigns, the main headquarters moved to New York City. Dorothy moved along with the pros, leaving Mrs. James (Libby) Rowe to run the research end of the Women's Division. Brainy volunteers were put to work compiling Republican voting records. Taking leave of absence from the office of a young Congressman (then in his third term), Dorothy Nichols typed up the output. The Congressman, Lyndon B. Johnson, borrowed his secretary back, admired and distributed the voting records (he was then Chairman of the Congressional Campaign Committee), and sent Libby Rowe[2] thank-you orchids.

Funds were always low, and when they reached zero, some of us went round with hopeful smiles and tin cups. Heady with modest response, I transferred my fund raising to New York, where I tackled bankers and brokers with what I thought was some success. When one of them whipped out his checkbook and asked me to name a sum, I was flustered and muttered five hundred dollars. As he handed me the check I realized how much I had underestimated him. I discovered that what it takes to get money from one rich man is another rich man.

[2] Named by President Kennedy Chairman of the National Capital Planning Commission in 1961.

A few nights after the 1940 victory, the entire Women's Division was invited by Mrs. Roosevelt to the White House. Twenty-seven excited females and one office boy, in rented dinner jacket and red bow tie, waited in line to shake hands with the President. He was seated in the Red Room in a wheel chair, one in which he could propel himself about. Mrs. Roosevelt stood at his side.

As we approached, I realized that Helen Todd, the historian and author of *A Man Named Grant*, was behind me in the line. Helen, another polio victim, was also propelling herself along in a wheel chair. As the distance narrowed between us and the President, I grew tense. What would the President say? After my handshake, I turned to overhear him remark in that wonderfully attention-engaging voice: "Let me have a look at that model. Might be better than mine." When he laughed, he gave all of us within earshot the sensation of having shared a private joke. Helen, a faithful, gifted volunteer, took her moment of glory with proper pride; she and the President conversed in low tones before she wheeled on.

After we had been greeted by the President, Mrs. Roosevelt took us on a tour of the East Room where a new grand piano had just been uncrated. "The President," she told us in half-laughing tones, "was only interested in the eagles." She pointed to the gilded legs. "As an ornithologist, he wanted to be certain they were correct, right down to the last feather."

Although my fund-raising efforts had not satisfied me, they apparently were considered worthy of recognition. Walter and I were bidden to the White House for the 1941 inaugural luncheon. The crowd, small enough considering the importance of the occasion, milled in the main hall after lunch, waiting for the President to emerge from the Red Room. Suddenly the doors were opened, an aisle was cleared, and a fascinated silence gripped us. Out trotted Fala, the President's Scotch terrier, just as certain of his audience as any prima donna. A swaggering dog can make even White House guests laugh. A moment later the President emerged on the arm of his son James, followed by Princess Martha of Norway.

President Roosevelt came through to most Americans as a mellifluous voice on radio, or a distant hero glimpsed in newsreels. Until these recent opportunities to see him close up, he had been for me no more than a remote figure at large White House receptions. Two things now struck me. The character of the man could be read in an instant: his face, his look, told what he was—indifferent to scorn or opprobrium, an aristocrat with an ample supply of irony (he balanced irony with empathy), and a quick communicator, as he had been with Helen Todd. Secondly, you could tell he had suffered. Hardships, particularly physical handicaps, held no terror for him. Walking on the arm of his son must have been painful as well as awkward, as he was vain and liked looking his best. So his face carried the message, as if he had made up his mind long ago that Lincoln was right: every man after forty is responsible for his face.

He had long since learned what I then discovered for myself: the decisive moments in one's life are seldom announced by engraved invitations or diplomas, or handed to one on a silver platter. The big one for me came on a warm spring day at Johns Hopkins Hospital in Baltimore. The internist who had put me through weeks of tests for a recurring intestinal infection sat looking Olympian on the edge of my bed. His advice added up to my leading a semi-invalid's life. "But, Doctor," I said, "what would you tell me if I *had* to earn a living?" He looked shocked, as though I had mentioned the unmentionable. Repeating his cautions about what I might eat, how much I must rest, and how little of life's improvised departures from routine I might participate in, he did his best to sound fatherly and friendly.

When I described the scene to my husband, I realized how much I owed to that stern doctor and his deadly remedies. After all, I had at least two thirds of my allotted life span still ahead of me! "I'm going to work," I announced.

The problem with the doctor's advice was that I did not want to live that way. Leading a restricted life, eating lightly, taking lots of rest would undoubtedly have agreed with me—I still feel better under such a regime. But at that time I would have diagnosed my condition as suffering from too much doctoring and too little of interest to do. So I ignored the kindly doctor's advice.

Michael Straight, then editor of the *New Republic*, hired me on the recommendation of friends. I was to be paid space rates. By then I had already spent a winter as a volunteer at the National League of Women Voters, doing research for a pamphlet entitled "The Awkward Age in Civil Service." On Pearl Harbor Sunday I had engaged a young violinist to come and practice piano and violin sonatas with me, Sunday being the one day we were both free. She never came, and I never went back to serious ensemble playing. Instead, I spent that afternoon sewing insignia on a friend's[3] uniform.

World War II liberated women like me. The war effort needed everyone, even those of us who still had to write "housewife" on an application form. We squirmed over the blank spaces and hoped no one would look too closely when we wrote "volunteer work for the National League of Women Voters" or described other endeavors we had faithfully sustained. We had begun to despise the word "volunteer," an activity that sounded more like therapy than a job.

My friends in government began offering me real jobs, but the civil service regulations excluded women lacking a college degree from a "P" (Professional) rating. Although because of my political experience I qualified for a Congressional liaison post in OPA, I was entitled only to a file clerk's or secretary's slot. In December of 1942, I joined the staff of OFRRO, the Office of Foreign Relief and Rehabilitation Operations (located in the State Department), the United States predecessor of UNRRA,[4] one of the first attempts at international cooperation. Herbert Lehman, twice Governor of New York and later Senator[5] from that state, was Director General of UNRRA. At a dinner he and his wife

---

[3] Henry Ehrlich, now senior editor of *Look* magazine.
[4] United Nations Relief and Rehabilitation Administration.
[5] Term November 9, 1949, to January 3, 1957.

Edith gave in 1954 he described me as one of UNRRA's "main-stays," but he confessed that he never knew how I happened to join his organization. "Because Charles Darlington, an old friend then about to become OFRRO's Executive Director, came to supper," I told him. We were going to a concert. Charles mentioned that he had five thousand letters to answer and no one to help him. I offered my services. When I went to get my coat, Charles asked my husband, "Is Katie pulling my leg?" Walter explained that after months of job hunting I remained frustrated and unemployed. The very next day I filled in a Form 57, noting that I would accept the lowest clerical salary.

In 1961, almost twenty years later, Charles Darlington came to my brand-new rectangular office in the Department of State to ask my help. After we had exchanged preliminaries he pounced: "What has Chester Bowles got against me?" Charles had requested a French-speaking African Embassy; his language skill was above par, he wanted very much to end his career by serving his country once again. In the intervening years he had been in business. That noon I did not have the answer to Charles's question, but I had a cause. I owed Charles a debt. It was my turn to help him get the job he wanted.

Bowles's rather determined reluctance reduced Charles to "a stuffed shirt. Probably never really would go out and get his feet dirty." I knew that Charles would be a prodigious worker, as would his talented wife. He really could not help his height, his unmistakably upper-class appearance. I said so and Bowles appeared to listen.

When Charles next appeared I gave him my diagnosis: "I think I know what Chet Bowles has against you—your forebears and your watch chain." I recommended he dress less like a diplomat. A day later he arrived at my office. "See, no vest, no chain. Button-down shirt, bow tie. A salesman's look, don't you think?" He got the post, served with distinction in Gabon, shook hands with every tribal chief on his home ground, and later wrote a book with his wife Alice called *African Betrayal.*

UNRRA finally came into being in December 1943 in Atlantic City. Some forty-four nations were represented. Dean Acheson, then Assistant Secretary of State, led the U.S. delegation. The Russians arrived late, laden with vodka and caviar and two men called Sergeiev, one the chief of the delegation, the other an underling. Our problem throughout that meeting was to make sure we were dealing with the right Sergeiev! Mike Pearson, later to be Canadian Prime Minister but then Canadian Ambassador to the U.S., Jan Masaryk of Czechoslovakia, and other international celebrities electrified the meeting rooms with their verbal pyrotechnics, but Dean Acheson more than took their measure.

Because the Public Affairs Officer (the name by which bureaucracy even then disguised its press agents) was frequently found in a fairly liquid state, I took over for him. Working with the press afforded me a brand-new experience. The Washington press corps is sharp, high-powered, competitive, and clannish. You soon learn not to underestimate them, not to lie to them, and to remember that if there's a story they'll find it, no matter how many false trails you leave. Most of them are generous, tireless, dedicated, and forgiving. They make wonderful friends and great teachers.

For the next three years I wrote press releases describing UNRRA's relief activities, answered direct inquiries from the press, and helped run UNRRA council meetings in Montreal and London. Once I had to call the Coast Guard for permission to photograph UNRRA wheat shipments as they left the dock. The officer in charge, Lieutenant Alex Chopin, turned out to be the son of my French governess; I had spent many a rainy day with him battling at boys' games. When last seen, I recalled, he was wearing the then fashionable small boy's sailor suit. Permission was quickly granted.

My work often took me through an impasse others had failed to resolve. Clearing cables on strategic matters with our Soviet Deputy Menshikov proved just such a project; his reactions could be counted on, they were negative. After many calls and exchanges, we might record a yes. When Mr. Menshikov, some years later, turned up in Washington as the Soviet Ambassador, I once remarked to him that in the UNRRA days he practically never smiled. "There was nothing to smile about," he replied.

At UNRRA council meetings it fell to my lot to assign the thank-you speeches customary at the conclusion of such sessions. The more important the country, the more prestigious the assignment; thanking the Chairman, the Committee Chairman, the Executive Secretary were plums invariably assigned to the United States, Canada, Great Britain, the Soviet Union, China (then mainland), and France. When it came to thanking the local police, the hotel staff, and other functionaries, the small countries would grudgingly agree to accept these chores. Because a certain independent Ambassador despised these lowly—for him—appreciative sentences, he inevitably made a scene. "He's all yours," my colleagues would remark as they sent me off. I have a vivid recollection of his stamping his foot before he capitulated.

I learned other lessons in national pride. Struggling at Montreal for an appointed hour to arrange a group photograph of the "great powers," I encountered a wall of unwillingness to be the country to agree to any other great power's fixed time. My ordeal lasted for several days before I discovered that I had to assure each great power (some were touchier than others) that it was the first to choose ten-thirty, two days hence. I treasure the final result; a group picture with no one looking pleased.

We had our crises with Congress, with correspondents, and with our own returning relief workers, some of whom could always be depended upon to blast the conditions of the country where they had served. It fell to my lot to try and talk them out of telling all. On various occasions I failed. Their intransigence taught me that in every effort there are those who must defect and tell. More of these defectors are today finding their way into print. The public's appetite for their disclosures, true or half true, appears to be insatiable.

When the head of Public Affairs went abroad, he left with me a magazine article ghosted for Governor Lehman's signature on the displaced persons camps that were just burgeoning into news. The text was replete with statements on the illegitimate children bred in these confines, physical violence, and the breakdown of morale. I knew Governor Lehman, by then, well enough to be certain he would not sign the article. Caught in a cross fire between the irate Governor and the uninhibited magazine editor with a commitment in hand, I tried to effect a compromise. All I got was fiery remonstrances and severe upbraidings. That evening Governor Lehman called to say how sorry he was he had lost his temper, thereby displaying a magnanimity and a compassion for underlings that others whom I worked with did not always possess.

After I had rewritten the article to the satisfaction of both parties, I had developed an oversized interest in the displaced persons camps.

In July of 1945, in return for faithful service and on the assurance that I would turn up in London to help run the upcoming annual UNRRA council meeting, I was sent overseas to set up an information program in the displaced persons camps in Germany. Since no one knew what a displaced persons specialist was, I wrote my own job description. The mysterious labyrinths of bureaucracy have held no terrors for me since.

Although my WAC uniform and the rank of major made it easier, finding a bed to sleep in, a place to eat, or a means of getting about consumed almost all of my energies. In the once handsome city of Frankfurt, rats and rubble had taken over. Outside the city, in the former I. G. Farben building, General Eisenhower ran an orderly show at Supreme Headquarters, Allied Expeditionary Forces. You could see yourself in the mirrored gloss of the paratroopers' boots standing guard at the entrance.

No one had told me in predeparture briefings that I would need a bedroll. I landed in Frankfurt not only without a billet, but without sheets, blankets, or pillows. The great meeting place at SHAEF was the deck on which meals were served in good weather. By the end of the first evening meal, I had borrowed bed-

ding and rediscovered old friends, in reverse order. When travel
orders finally came through, two UNRRA officers and I, in a
SHAEF command car with a corporal at the wheel, set off on an
inspection tour. We spent the first night in Augsburg in a hotel
half destroyed. I sat up most of the night watching rats race round
the cinder deck outside my window. The former yachting editor of
a well-known daily, then in army public affairs, kept urging us to
turn round and head for Frankfurt and billets that were still
standing.

There were days on the road when I wondered why we did not
take his advice. The solid craters on the former autobahn matched
the scenery; damaged Luftwaffe planes hid behind the scorched
pines. At Heilbronn two Polish DPs had just stolen a German cow
and slaughtered it; in return, German farmers were shooting at
anyone who looked like a Pole. The Russian DPs on the day of
their departure for home had done a thorough job of destroying
the Heilbronn camp; they had slashed mattresses, burned plumb-
ing and lighting fixtures. All that remained for a highly cheerful
Red Cross worker to show off were a nursery of twelve homemade cribs and one cracked mirror.

At Feldafing, outside Munich, where Dachau survivors were still
wandering around in their extermination prison garb, I first heard
talk of a "kibbutz" and a homeland in Palestine. Trying to remain
sensible, take notes, and avoid the terrible looks of hope that lit
up the eyes of refugees whenever an American came into view
proved at times more than I could manage. Where was the miracle?
their eyes asked. Don't you Americans have manna in your pock-
ets? Coming back into Munich, we passed an open army truck
with our military baseball team singing and hollering as they
waved. *Their* war was over.

At the Munich Rathaus, as at every stop, German cleaning
women were washing down the stone steps. Even if a building was
left half standing, and the rest had been carried off and heaped up
in neat piles in the streets, the cleansing process proceeded in its
ordered round. Up in the ladies' toilet, two of these caretakers

accosted me. Had I seen Hitler dead, did he really die, had I been to Berlin to his bunker? Had I spat on him, as they would have? Mindful of the confiscated Nazi literature they had neatly assembled into toilet paper squares, I wondered what their sentiments had been in the Fuehrer's heyday.

We rolled into Frankfurt late the next night. My billet was on the top floor of an apartment house; if you turned on the light downstairs and raced up the four flights, you might make it to the top before the light went out automatically. (Functional economy was always a German specialty.) Exhausted, I lit a lamp. My blankets were gone! Back down I went. It was too cold to try the coverless comfort of a sleeping pill. I ran two blocks, climbed another set of stairs, and there were my blankets. Fortunately the officer who had lent them to me was out. In the vernacular of war, I simply liberated them.

The next morning I heard a voice call up the stairway: "How about breakfast?" How did he know I was back? I called down. "There's only one blanket thief in the whole ETO," he replied.

When I inspected a camp at Wiesbaden, I found the remains of a once elegant set of subterranean mineral baths in one of the still standing hotels. The water ran tepidly warm. Armed with a month's mail, I took an hour to soak up my first warm water and my first home-front news. It wasn't till late in the hour that I discovered strange male faces staring out of a window across the courtyard. The next time I bathed I did so in hothouse temperatures, all windows closed and curtains drawn.

At Wiesbaden I also put my own precautionary plan for photographic coverage into effect. Knowing UNRRA had no funds, I had drafted an exchange of letters signed by Governor Lehman and appropriate Generals, permitting the UNRRA public affairs staff to make use of available Signal Corps photographers. In Wiesbaden I found just such an asset, complete with his own jeep. Now that I had transportation, I began to bathe more frequently and carry more stills to waiting press men. I became part of the "families" of displaced persons at the camp. I never failed to be moved by their heartbreaking attempts at leading a normal life. The Lithuanians, Latvians, and Estonians kept flowers in their rooms, arranged concerts in the dining hall, and held classes in the drafty basement. They were going to go right on being educators and agronomists and physicists and, even, musicians. And what could you do for them but listen?

I left Germany with a bad conscience; here were people who had suffered incarceration, the death of relatives, the nightmares of permanent exile—and all we could do was feed and house them. At the take-off of our London-bound plane, the pilot confided that he was overloaded and the tail would drag getting up. The description fitted my mood.

In London Jan Masaryk, elected to the rotating chairmanship of the UNRRA council meeting, was already being harassed by Soviet demands to force the DPs to return to their homeland. Here at last was a tangible problem we could do something about. With the help of our Allies, we managed to outvote the Communist countries, leaving the DPs free, at least, to determine their own fate. One night at dinner some of us questioned Masaryk about his powerful neighbors, the Soviets. Was it wise for him to return to Czechoslovakia? He held us spellbound with a long, for him, account of his passionate love for his people, his devotion to the principles of his father (who had liberated the Czechs), and his determination to take the necessary risk. Because he was both a cynic and a fatalist, he ended his peroration with a question of his own: "What choice have I? I cannot abandon my people who wait for me. As for the Russians . . . did any of you ever hear of a mouse raping an elephant?"

In London on VJ Day, I could look out my hotel window and see the people dancing in the streets. With my newspaper friends, I fought the crowd to a standing post where, by holding a mirror above my head, I could get a view of the official procession entering Westminster Abbey for a solemn prayer of thanksgiving. Getting back to my hotel was another story; my companions and I got separated and I discovered how high the iron grilles around the parks really were. Strange friendly arms helped me climb over a fence and set me down on the other side, where I caught glimpses of the King and Queen waving from the balcony of Buckingham Palace. That night I joined the dancers and the queues; we waited our turn to ride the underground to the London docks where the real celebration, so we were told, would take place. Sitting in a pub called The Prospect of Whitby, I became convinced, at last, that I was seeing the genuine dockside London: sailors, soldiers, singing, dancing in place. All of a sudden I noticed the BBC newsreel crew giving reality that extra prompting that only film directors understand.

In March of 1946 I resigned. Fiorello LaGuardia had replaced Governor Lehman, whom I had come to regard as a dedicated public servant, often selfless, and always kind. Besides it was time —I could tell by the looks my family gave me—to go back to being a housewife and, I hoped, a writer. Over the next years I tried; my files are still full of neatly stacked rejection slips. I wrote a novel in letter form about my summer overseas among the DP camps, a difficult subject and a more difficult technique—letter writing is in itself an art, though a gradually disappearing one. An interview with Ilya Ehrenburg became a cover story for the *New Republic;* several publishers wrote asking to see any other work I had in process. But none liked the letters about DP camps, although the turndowns were always encouraging.

Free-lance writers, I soon discovered, could not live on hope, even with a husband like mine to underwrite them. Tracking down a story on the GI Bill of Rights, I made another discovery: what I could not bring to life in prose came through for me in a poem. The sight of GIs walking through Harvard Yard bolted me to the pavement. I stared; I wanted their youth, their spirits, their enthusiasm, like the frieze on Keats's Grecian urn, to stand still, live on for the ages. But each time I tried to write the story it sounded like a rosary made out of statistics. I tore up all my drafts and hammered out a poem:

HARVARD YARD 1946[6]

Youth grown older than the ivy
carries thought under the trees,
tall with years past their remembering.

Walking fast across the landmark,
you there, with the wings and ribbons,
in what bomb bay did you listen
to the feeble cock of wisdom?
Did your random burst of carnage
spare the heresy of Hegel,
wake the stubborn ghost of Nietzche?

Playing at cards beneath the seas,
did you raise those eyes that judge
to draw an ace and wonder
if the thunder of the depth charge
shook some old Newtonian tree?

What foxhole sent you pink and blushing
to walk and look and talk with books?

Was it too hot for you, the doctor,
was it too still in Buckner Bay?
Did you deliver death too often,
did you always wait for this?

Did Rheims, Ryukyus, Remagen
fill this room with rapt attention?
Did some thirsty will to reason,
even in the mindless bodies
stumbling through the streets of war,
scream a parched and quenchless question?
What is learning, what is law,
but a walk between a war?

After that I pursued my vice in earnest, although the poems were hidden in the back of the desk drawer, except those that were for and about my family, ceremonial and sentimental *vers d'occa-*

---

[6] First published in the *Harvard Alumni Bulletin*.

sion written to amuse my husband and our daughters. Occasionally I sold an article or a book review and in between I wrote plays, short stories, and finally another novel. My generous friend, Christine Sadler, of *McCall's*, alleging that the weekly column for Labor's League for Political Education was more than she could handle, offered to share the writing with me. We signed ourselves Polly Edison, short for Political Education, alternating the anonymous authorship. The column was intended to interest union wives and women union members in a simplified version of current issues. At the end of the three years Joe Keenan, then Secretary Treasurer of the Building and Construction Trades of the AF of L and an adviser to George Meany, decided what LLPE[7] needed was a women's division. Joe, who had become my good friend, asked me to head up the division. The objectives appealed to me, but I feared the union regulars' reaction. Surely someone who had not come up the union ladder would be suspect. Joe argued the opposite; any woman they chose who had a bona fide union affiliation would make all her competitors unhappy; it would be safer to take an outsider.

I had just said yes, I would get started in January of 1954, when my intermittent political activity caught up with me.

---

[7] American Federation of Labor had not yet merged with Congress of Industrial Organizations (CIO). Political education of union workers and their wives is today conducted by COPE—Committee on Political Education.

It Pays to Rise Above Principle

MY RETURN TO POLITICS HAD TAKEN PLACE IN 1948. A FRIEND AD-
vised me to file as a delegate from the District of Columbia to the
Democratic National Convention in Philadelphia. Joe Rauh, a liberal leader and Chairman of ADA's Executive Committee, col-
lected four insurgents, of whom I was one, to file for inclusion
on the official slate of delegates. The local party machine turned us
down. It used as an excuse the fact that our checks to cover the
filing fee had not been certified. Since this same machine had
previously told us certified checks were not necessary, we knew
we'd been had. Joe took our case to court, but the ink on the
legal papers was no sooner dry than the opposition collapsed. Four
brand-new "insurgents" became respectable and joined the party
machine.

The City of Brotherly Love boiled over in July with people, confusion, and hot air, both real and political, which we inhaled with
gusto. Two events, unrecorded by historians, stand out in my
memory. I had been invited to be one of the seconders of Congresswoman Helen Gahagan Douglas' nomination for Vice President and was standing with a friend in the back of the hall drafting
my speech. Suddenly we were butted hard against the wall. We
turned to find a live donkey staring at us with unfriendly eye. Mrs.
Douglas' name was never placed in nomination because too much
time had been consumed by a floor fight over civil rights. The
speech was laid to rest in my scrapbook.

On another night, I listened while friends telephoned Justice William O. Douglas, who was vacationing in the West, to tell him there was a rumor that President Truman might invite him to run for Vice President. Like all grounded legends, the event became part of the folklore of the 1948 convention. For me, these unchronicled moments were heady wine and I was hooked ever after on politics.

In 1952, Daisy Harriman sent for me; she wanted me to run as the alternate Democratic National Committee woman from the District of Columbia. Daisy's wish sounded very much like a command; I accepted. Visions of her endorsement and my easy victory followed me home that afternoon. But the incumbent, Betty Lindley, wife of the columnist Ernest K. Lindley, had no intention of bowing out. Departing for the summer, Daisy waved me a fond good-by but left no public endorsement behind.

The nation's capital, at that time, possessed neither political identification of its own nor any resemblance to political activity elsewhere. For good reason: in 1948, only four hundred citizens voted in a District primary for one list of delegates to the Democratic National Convention. There were no rival slates. Even the place of voting remained secret to all but the most persistent inquirers. Other privileges such as electing one's Mayor, voting for President, or being represented in Congress were denied the anonymous citizens of this sprawling Federal City. I determined to fight for a change.

The primary in 1952 was a good place to begin. The District had no primary laws. Anything could happen and did. Fortunately, the Republicans were in the same fix; the fierce battle between Senator Taft and General Eisenhower for the endorsement of the District's delegates was still reverberating in the press. A good fight gets plenty of attention. Slumbering citizens gradually awoke to the possibility of exercising their right to choose. We Democrats took the assistance offered and went to work.

As there were no polling places, we asked the City Commissioners for permission to use the firehouses. The discovery that there were no firehouses, and thus no fire protection, in the newly-built outlying black areas appalled me; we had to use church and community halls. There were no ballot boxes, so we improvised, buying oversize breadboxes and slitting the top for ballot drops. And as there was no orderly procedure for counting ballots, we instituted a panel of prominent citizens to count the Presidential preference vote in the bitter contest between Averell Harriman and Senator Estes Kefauver.

Our slate had been endorsed by Harriman and won overwhelmingly. The reluctant Averell, having tasted victory, began running for the Presidency in earnest; to his campaign managers he put the question, "Where do we go next?"

There was no question about where I would go next, at least in my mind—Chicago and the Democratic Convention. Meanwhile I had learned the lessons of local politics by heart and would never forget them. Then and there I could have written a primer of do's and don'ts; little did I know that I would be doing just that—and soon.

My friends put me on the 1952 Stevenson campaign train for the last ten days. The importance of my presence can best be estimated by a tongue-in-cheek comment made by Eddie Folliard of the Washington *Post*. From Providence, Rhode Island, he wrote: "Katie Louchheim was charged with procuring cough drops for the candidate." Eddie had not heard me threatening to call the police when a busload of teen-agers wearing "I Like Ike" sweat shirts tried to boo the candidate into silence. Nor was he around when a woman with a child in her arms stepped up to thank me and said, "They are corrupting our young people. They pay them to do this." Since then heckling has become a habit, one might even call it an occupation, though an unsalaried one.

On September 15, 1953, as duly elected alternate Democratic National Committeewoman for the District of Columbia, I attended a meeting of the Democratic National Committee at the Conrad Hilton Hotel in Chicago. As alternate, it was my duty to take the place of my good friend Daisy, who could not be present. When I first received notice of the meeting, I saw no reason to go all the way to Chicago for a post-defeat wake, since Adlai Stevenson had lost the 1952 election. My friends and coworkers on the Democratic Central Committee of the District of Columbia let me know that I had better show up. "Why do you think we elected you?" they asked in peevish tones.

After the meeting was adjourned, I stood in the Conrad Hilton hallway waiting for an elevator. Stevenson's choice for National Committee Chairman, Steve Mitchell, suddenly loomed up at my side. What was I doing? he asked. Before I could reply, he went on: "What are your future plans?" I told him about the LLPE commitment. "Don't do anything of the kind," he admonished me, "at least not until after you hear from me." When we reached the hotel lobby he moved away to talk to someone else. Coming home in the plane, I puzzled over his remark. Did he think I would give up the excitement of a brand-new endeavor for some subsidiary role at his headquarters?

A fortnight later Steve telephoned about ten in the evening to inquire if he could come round to my house. Walter was already in bed reading, but I insisted he get dressed and come downstairs. When Steve arrived, he, too, had brought a witness and an ally, his friend and deputy from the Democratic National Committee, Hy Raskin. He told me that India Edwards, Vice Chairman of the Democratic National Committee, had resigned as Director of Women's Activities in order to leave Washington with her husband. She would temporarily retain her title as Vice Chairman, but how would I like to become Director of Women's Activities for the party? With Walter's smiling assent, I accepted with delight, provided Steve would square it with Joe Keenan and George Meany.

Thus began my seven-year political stretch on the national level.

And so I made the big move to headquarters, a title, and a staff. Shortly after my installation, I found myself out on the speaking circuit. Dean Acheson gave me the most instructive introduction I had yet had. "I gave her some advice," he said. "Eat a tumbler of ground glass every morning."

I could look out my window at the busy intersection of K Street and Connecticut Avenue, and I could think about General Eisenhower's popularity, and the low state of our Democratic National Committee funds, or the reason why so many women got under the skins of so many men in politics.

I concentrated on the latter problem, drew down the venetian blinds, and thought and thought. I knew why most men went into politics; it was from a need to be liked and admired (beyond the hearth) and to give expression to their convictions. That was just as true of women. But some men were possessed of an inner drive that had to be given political expression and became leaders. Why was it that power was becoming to men? Although women's motivation was often the same, power wasn't really becoming to them. There were exceptions—Eleanor Roosevelt, Queen Elizabeth II, Indira Gandhi, and Senator Margaret Chase Smith, to mention a few. But I wasn't dealing with them, I was dealing with those who tended to be aggressive, who waved the feminist banner, and who wore tight lace dresses and too much make-up. They were conspicuously at a disadvantage in politics. Their insecurity showed; like a slip, it spoiled their appearance.

When I reached the speech-making stage, I told a suburban audience: "In politics women are on trial, they are forever being pictured as jealous, petty, ambitious, and their faults are debated and examined in secret—by men. Men are also ambitious, petty, and jealous, but there are more of them, and except for candidates, politics is not their only activity. They belong to a whole other world, a fraternal business organization, that keeps them faithful to one another—a world that has its stag rites, whose doors read 'Men Only.'" What could I do to change this painful situation? I discarded a few of my more impulsive ideas, such as a contest for The *Impossible* Woman of the Year. The nomination would carry with it a one-way ticket to the Kingdom of the Impossible, the place all women go when men have hurt their feelings or underestimated them. Too risky, I decided—there would be too many candidates to choose from.

Things became serious when my husband, forced to say a few words at a political breakfast, remarked, "My only regret is that I have but one wife to give to my party." Could it be that I was about to be turned in for a homebody?

So I drew up a three-point plan: (1) make political participation for women more interesting, more effective and inviting; (2) identify women with money raising on a national level (nothing could do more to enhance their importance and change their image); and (3) develop more women in public service and in party councils. (In most communities the women leaders, whatever their party, put politics last. I hoped to change this habit.)

I introduced satire into our material; a favorite was a skit called "How to Rile a Reporter," illustrating the ineptitude with which some women dealt with the press. Another known as "Alice in Demoland" satirized the various familiar female types—Old Faithful, the chairwoman whose hands are gnarled from stuffing envelopes; the Sprinter, always late, disorganized (she's locked the car keys inside the car); the Title Holder, Miss Encyclopedia (her statistics scared the average worker); and Appassionata, the bandwagon girl, who loves politics because "It's better than the League of Women Voters, there are men in it."

We put out "Campaign Kits for Women Leaders," we even told them how to use county and state fairs to advantage. We issued "Tips on Suburban Vote Getting," "Election Day Victory Plans," "Cues for Candidates," and lots of come-ons for newcomers, including "How to Build Precinct Strength," which told about the women who watched the moving vans and went calling.

Meanwhile, I was learning about women from our own, the Democratic National Committeewomen from the states. They came in all shapes, sizes, and types; I remember the breast-beater whom I held prisoner in the ladies' room to keep her from returning to the meeting and introducing an absurd resolution. And the lady with a big hat and mink earrings who disappeared upstairs (in my home). "My dear," she said when she came down, "I never really feel I know anybody till I've been through their house."

For some, gracing the green baize table was sufficient: they liked Occasions, at which they could demonstrate their sweet soprano; there were others who could barely wait for the first tense moment to wave the feminist shirt. And there were those, thank heavens, whose wisdom, wit, and friendship I could count on.

Another recurrent and perhaps less curable problem for us was the dedicated woman liberal, adamant, readier to lose than to compromise her ideal. On one occasion I warned a friend that a vote for X would be wasting her ballot (in a primary contest), for Y, also a liberal, would win. On election day she wired me that she had taken my advice. When Y won, I wired back: "It always pays to rise above principle."

When Paul Butler replaced Steve Mitchell as National Chairman in 1954, he imported women assistants who looked like female impersonators. The first one wore soft-soled shoes (the better to snoop with?). She banished the vital coffeepot we kept on the filing cabinet and threatened to seal up the door between us and the Chairman's outer office, thereby cutting off our access to visitors. At her command, all the thousands of invitations to a fund-raising dinner were written by hand.

At times Paul reminded me of a reincarnated Napoleon disguised in a Billy Graham mask. He came complete with the latest in mood switches; in a matter of seconds he could project convincing manifestations of charm, wit, tragedy, or wrath. His first concerns were the loitering in the switchboard room, too much eavesdropping, and too many long-distance calls. Memos went out ordering silence, less communication, and no listening. Nothing changed.

Among his schemes for the 1956 Democratic National Convention was a corps of pages chosen from among young persons who had sold the most *Democratic Digests* (a monthly magazine), and the substitution of real sheriffs for the patronage appointees who previously had served as sergeant-at-arms. The House and Senate controlled the pages and the sergeant-at-arms the choice of his aides. But Paul was bent on by-passing patronage, plucking power from those who really held it. Meanwhile he was busy insuring the loyalty of National Committeemen and -women; he set up new rules permitting their attendance at fund-raising dinners for free. (The prerogatives of party officials were many, but it was understood they would be able to pay their travel and other expenses themselves.)

When, after the 1956 defeat, Paul Butler set up a political workshop program to be run by men—to train both men and women—he was moving into my territory. He was also acknowledging that the new look in political participation had attracted new groups of women and that I was accomplishing one of my objectives. Matthew McCloskey, the cheerful party Treasurer, did not get along with Chairman Butler. He would inquire when my birthday was. "Too bad it's past," he would say, "I was going to give you Butler for your birthday." But Butler ruled while Matt joked. The Chairman had his admirers, plaudits for the Democratic Advisory Council he established are still heard in liberal circles.[1] Another plus of his regime was the first meeting of black leaders from all over the U.S., held in 1958. My office had prepared a list of elected officials who then totaled eighty. Partly as a result of President Johnson's Civil Rights Act of 1965, today more than twelve hundred blacks hold political office.[2]

Though we never did climb out of our financial hole, women by that time *were* raising money. In 1954 I was already daydreaming of the thousands of dollars I would produce in the name of women. In September of that year we held a Dollar Day in the nation's capital, not exactly a fair testing ground since Washington has more than its share of talented women. Hundreds of attractive women with hatboxes stood at popular street corners asking passers-by to "Put a Dollar in the Hat, Help Elect a Democrat."

[1] The Democratic National Committee in 1970 adopted Butler's formula and set up a Democratic Policy Council.

[2] Steve Mitchell and I fought successful battles for integrated meetings in then segregated cities such as New Orleans, Dallas, Nashville, and others.

The count exceeded eighteen thousand dollars and the expenses, what's more, were limited to labels pasted over old hatboxes.

The big money, of course, awaited in the big cities, and in them, alas, lay my defeat. The unapproachable boss of Brooklyn, a tall, wide-shouldered, husky-voiced man, laughed at me: "Ask them for a dollar—why, we give them a dollar." In Chicago the authorities assured me the money would be stolen on its way back to local headquarters.

A kindly pro finally lectured me about the basic flaws of my scheme. City bosses had their own ways of raising funds; the word was passed down through the hierarchical line, thus insuring control at the top. Why would they try a crazy headquarters scheme like mine which, if it worked—and he conceded that it might—would cut his life line?

But I didn't give up: my next gimmick was called "Teas for TV," a latter-day version of the old chain letter. Each hostess invited ten women to watch a political broadcast. Each guest gave a dollar and, hopefully, agreed to give an identical "Tea for TV" for ten other guests. California used the idea statewide and raised more than fifty thousand dollars.

The trouble with previous national fund-raising schemes (one in 1952, and again in 1956) was their dependence on five-dollar booklets, items which all too often never got into the hands of workers at precinct levels. Printing and shipping and distribution mounted into real money. Women used to combatting polio by raising nickels and dimes could and did organize fund raising block by block. I still believe that Dollar Days, one for Republicans and one for Democrats, are a natural and were made to order for women organizers. The man who gives his dollar is apt to follow it up on election day with a vote.

One hot summer day in 1959 at Democratic National Committee Headquarters I was interrupted by the arrival of a process server; in the name of some of our creditors he was about to attach the furniture, and I was the only officer on the premises. "Tell him I have disappeared, tell him I've slid down a tightly knotted ladder made of old bills, and that we're out of everything else." The kind man standing outside my door could be heard laughing, and disappearing.

For all the seven years of my incumbency, I fought hard against the common political myths, trying to debunk the obvious ones that kept women on the side lines. Every time I was interviewed, televised, even coverized (Claire Williams of the Republican National Committee and I once shared the cover of *U. S. News and World Report*), I would proclaim there was no such thing as a woman's vote, nor were there women's issues. Women tended to vote as did men, according to their region, economic interest, and personal bias, but not as a bloc.[3]

We once took a poll of county chairmen and chairwomen, offering them twenty issues from among which to choose the top ten. Both women and men chose the identical issues. It wasn't true, I would point out, that women would not vote for other women or that they were more influenced by intuition than by facts. In the 1960 campaign I was constantly asked whether women were not for Kennedy because of his looks. My reply took the form of a question: "Were looks what made Eleanor Roosevelt and Mahatma Gandhi so beloved?" Despite my remonstrances, when it came to pre-convention news stories, my Republican counterpart, Bertha Adkins, and I were asked more questions about our wardrobes than anything else. Our differences were displayed in materials, Bertha's wool suit for cooler San Francisco and my cotton for hot Chicago. We did manage an appearance on CBS' *The Leading Question* on which Bertha got to talk about integrity, thrift, and peace, and I about the part-time Republican President (Eisenhower's heart attack required him to take it easy).

Early on, during a Steve Mitchell (Democratic National Committee Chairman) and Len Hall (Republican National Com-

---

[3] During the Eisenhower years polls appeared regularly maintaining that the women elected Ike. They failed to point out that there are (a) more women voters than men and (b) more voters in the upper income brackets, and (c) that the latter are largely Republican.

mittee Chairman) debate, I learned how important it is to have
friends in the audience. That night the young people at Georgetown University seemed overwhelmingly Republican. As the evening went on, I made a discovery; one person could create a mood
simply by starting the laughter, the applause, or the booing. It
worked every time. When Paul Butler took over from Steve as
Chairman of the Democratic National Committee, a repeat debate
was scheduled. Len Hall remarked to Paul, "I don't mind you and
I didn't mind Mitchell, but that Katie Louchheim, she's a men-
ace." I enjoyed sparring with opponents, and accepted Len Hall's
compliment as it was meant. We joke about "my powers" when we
meet.

In one of those endless interviews about women, I grew impa-
tient and remarked acidly: "Brains have no sex." Once the laughter had died away, the interviewer retorted in acid tones: "You
mean sex has no brains?"

I definitely deferred to him for the last laugh line. But there
were times when not even a ready quip could solve my problems.
The advertising agency that was handling the Democratic
National Committee account in 1956 insisted that we put all of
our Democratic Congresswomen on an afternoon convention program to catch the housewife.[4] In a kind of ritualistic procession,
each representative told her story. The networks cut us off right
after my introduction. The distaff side of the press, quite properly,
blasted us and the Congresswomen themselves were deeply
offended. Even the millinery unions joined the criticism; they
were offended because the Congresswomen had not worn hats.
I realized all too late that advertising men think in terms of stunts,
and this parade of women fitted their formulas.

The all-time horror in the stunt line must go to the 1948 convention in Philadelphia. Someone dreamed up a Liberty Bell made

[4] The ten Democratic women members of Congress were: Iris Blitch,
Georgia; Gracie Pfost, Idaho; Martha Griffiths, Michigan; Coya Knutson,
Minnesota; Leonor Sullivan, Missouri; Edna Kelly, New York; Kathryn Gran-
ahan and Vera Buchanan, Pennsylvania; and Maude Elizabeth Kee, West
Virginia. All but the latter three appeared.

of flowers, from which dozens of pigeons were to be released. The pigeons flew straight to the electric fans and got caught. A friend wired me: "Come home, before there's human blood on the floor." There almost was later when the Southern delegates walked out.

There is a good reason, of course, for having a woman as national party Vice Chairman. There will always be women who want to honor someone from far away, preferably Washington. So when the national party Vice Chairman comes to town, she creates an occasion for women to put on their white gloves and give someone of their own sex the VIP treatment. At the hearings on the Democratic platform held around the country in 1960, I was the only woman among businessmen, Congressmen, Senators, Governors, and former officeholders. In every city we visited, the women insisted on entertaining *me*, because they were proud of my presence.

When the party is out of power, being Vice Chairman is even more important. You get this heady feeling of the power of women and of yourself as their spokesman, even though you know none of it will stand up in a polling booth. I never counted the chickens, peas, speeches, heartaches, clergymen, clichés, handshakes, hurts, or horrors. They filled my seven-year stretch with a sense of accomplishment. I liked the meetings on the hustings better than the green baize of Washington. Even now, I think of the muddle of the road with nostalgia.

The Muddle of the Road

WHEN DEMOCRATIC NATIONAL COMMITTEE CHAIRMAN STEVE MITCHELL provided me with a brand-new political career, office, and staff, he also gave me some advice: "Hit the road! Washington is one kind of politics, the rest of the country another. Get out among the people." Hit the road I did in all but four states.

Political meetings, as Steve Mitchell had warned me, were quite different from the orderly ceremonial events in Washington. They came in all sizes, shapes, and formations. The atmosphere was informal, the arrangements haphazard, and the enthusiasm uninhibited. Their sole reason for taking place was the expected presence of someone from headquarters, someone who knew who was in and what was out.

My curiosity matched my endurance so I went willingly, and even went back. With me went my aide and friend, Geraldine Sohle, a former Minneapolis newspaper reporter, who helped me cope with politics and press, transport, food, lodging, and insomnia. After we clocked the first ten thousand miles, we quit keeping track.

Someone once described me as a short-term cynic and a long-range optimist. On the road, I managed to reverse this verdict. I always expected serene skies; calm, cooperative coordinators; agreeable accommodations and undemanding hostesses. It was Gerry who prepared for the worst.

In between trips I would forget the tepid, tasteless breakfast coffee that offered a limp hand when I needed a strong arm, the lidless toilets, the sideless sinks that left no place for cosmetics, and the showers that did not run but spluttered.

We always requested adjoining rooms (not only comfortable for us but ideal for receiving at the same time two warring political factions) and got everything but. The grass-roots interpretation of my status demanded a suite, thereby isolating me from Gerry, who took to sleeping on a cot in my parlor.

In time we learned that nothing ever happened as planned. From the moment the greeting party walked toward us, brimming with hats and good will, we prayed we would not call the right woman by the wrong name. From past mistakes we learned that the one holding the orchid corsage was not necessarily the leader.

The local TV and press came next, barking the inevitable directions, "Smile and keep talking." Why, I wondered, had these men never discovered woman's natural supply of running hot-and-cold talk? The greeters, the ins and almost-ins of the party, would depart with the press and we would begin to receive the outs and way-outs. The outs were the recently deposed, and the way-outs had never made it and never would. When my restless gestures did not stem the tide of tales, I would begin to undress. The talk then usually shifted to my undergarments.

On my first trip south, in 1955, I traveled by train to North Carolina. For five hours en route, I was overbriefed by a knowledgeable native North Carolinian who left me confused and alarmed about the dangerous mistakes I might make amid the welter of factions. When three brown orchids were presented to me at a breakfast for ninety-one ladies, I memorized the donors' faces. All through the invocation, soloist, and compliments I concentrated on memorizing their names. Later, at a VIP luncheon at the country club, there were white orchids—given only to the Governor's and Senator's wives and to me to distinguish us from other VIPs wearing ordinary purple orchids. These donors, I decided, must be another faction.

When my morning hostesses came to take me to a tea, I changed back to the brown orchids. At the tea I met ladies from all parts of the state, but I observed that the Governor's and Senator's wives were still wearing the white orchids. Had I goofed? For the pre-dinner reception I donned the white orchids again and wore them confidently through dinner and into the post-dinner receiving line. Suddenly my brown orchid donors hove into view. As they progressed down the line, eyes averted from my flowers, I had an inspiration. When they reached me I whispered: "I'm saving your most exquisite corsage to take back to Washington." (Once, when traveling in the West for the party, I was unexpectedly handed an eighteen-pound salmon. All salmon, it occurred to me, must be Democrats, because every spring they swim upstream.)

Politics is mostly a listening game, but a party official is supposed to produce some kind of substantial help or advice. At headquarters we prepared a whole marketing list of "how to's," which our disciples pretended to accept as gospel but never bothered to read. Our manual on "Care and Treatment of Speakers" never seemed to stop the local chairman from overloading the platform with men and women who spouted gratuitous platitudes until the principal speaker of the evening stood up to face an audience that required a soul-saver to wake them up. The fault was not limited to women's meetings. President Truman once told me about a dinner at which he did not get on until midnight.

In between trips I would compare notes with Bertha Adkins, my counterpart on the Republican National Committee. Both of us, we discovered, faced the same enthusiastic audiences, the same hardships, and the same good-natured indifference to our painfully worked-out instructions.

After a year of traveling I decided some interstate gatherings would not only save fatigue and time but would provide some healthy intra-party exposure to new people and new ideas. The first such regional meeting took place in Milwaukee, Wisconsin, planned to the split second. As the seventeen head-table guests filed into the dining room on time, three hundred women delegates and quite a few men rose to applaud. Just then the dinner chairman, an ebullient, lovable female, Marguerite Benson, seized my hand. "Heavens, Katie," she gasped, " 'The Star-Spangled Banner!' " Since no one had rewritten the lyrics recently, I failed to grasp her panic. To my consternation she turned and fled, flinging words back over her shoulder, "You announce it, I've got to go play it!" She was a woman of astonishing versatility; having overseen every detail of the meeting—hotel, tickets, rooms, badges, programs, attendance—now, finally, huffing and puffing at the keyboard, she produced the only version of "The Star-Spangled Banner" in deliberate waltz time I was ever to hear.

My husband always chose my travel reading. He chose difficult fare in order to "change my thinking." He knew, if left alone, I would slip a mystery into my emergency bag along with a cardigan sweater, a hot water bottle, and sour lemon drops. En route from Minneapolis to Glasgow, Montana, by train, I read Alfred North Whitehead and mused over such passages as "The task of democracy is to relieve mass misery and yet preserve the freedom of the individual." I tried to reconcile such lofty thoughts as these with the plain fact that I was being sent there as a peace offering to make up for indiscretions committed by the last official visiting Democrat.

My visit to Glasgow had a lasting effect on my travels. I drank the local water and became so sick I was immobilized for eight hours. Thereafter, we ordered and drank club soda. This led to some misunderstanding too. Upon arriving in Las Vegas at 6:30 A.M. by train, we were escorted to a downtown hotel (the famous strip was in its infancy then) by a very proper matron. When I ordered ice and soda, I happened to glance at my hostess' face. Hastily, I explained that I could not drink water. "There's a bottle in your room," came her whispered reply. This kind and proper lady still thinks I nip before breakfast. My eating habits likewise underwent a metamorphosis; at the dinner in Glasgow, I was gently chided by one host, "If you're not going to eat that roll, the least you can do for the farmer is crumble it up." From then on I followed the hint.

Of course we went to Texas. En route I developed butterflies, the giant size, appropriate to the state's oversize grandeur, wealth, and factionalism. I took with me a veritable Baedeker of advice; "Be funny and be evasive" seemed to be the password in 1954.

It was summer and the weather predicted was "warm," pronounced "wawm." We had even heard there would be air-conditioned cars. We didn't have such things in Washington then.

At the first stop our escort—male—met us with an air-conditioned car loaded with freshly picked camellias. We got to talkin' about huntin' and he shared his favorite recipe for stag stew which began: "You take half a steer . . ."

In Houston I was introduced by a delightful elderly judge. As he read from his notes, I failed to recognize myself. Finally the enigma was solved: he was quoting from my *husband's* biography in Who's Who. At that time I had not yet made the VIP register.

The following year I discovered International Falls, Minnesota, the second coldest spot in the United States. Sixty Democratic leaders from seven other "cold states," Montana, North and South Dakota, Wisconsin, Michigan, Kansas, and Nebraska, met at a resort there over Labor Day weekend. The proprietor of the camp and his wife, with the help of a half dozen local girls, fed us mounds of pancakes for breakfast, mounds of spaghetti for lunch, mounds of franks and beans for supper, while the good Democrats from the seven states fed us mounds of talk in between.

My camp cabin contained a room with picture window, three cots, a cookstove, sink, icebox, two bedrooms, a bathroom floor littered with washrags, a permanent odor of brewed coffee, and all the noise eight incarcerated females could make.

My roommate kept hushing the other inmates: "Sh, Katie is tired." Then she would drop off to sleep and snore. The cold crept over my weariness. I wished I had not taken off my underwear. I reached for my coat, doubled my blanket, and whispered to my companion to cease her snoring. "Oh," she sighed, "I must be on my back," rolled over, and snored just as loudly on her side.

The days were warm and fine. We climbed slopes, waded in

sandy streams, and held conferences on the rocks while watching red squirrels drag oversized acorns into hiding. Nights, however, remained miserable. Overhearing the churchgoers talk of eight o'clock mass, I was inspired to suggest they all sleep together. This permitted me to swap my snoring roommate for a quieter model.

Real adventure awaited us on the return journey. Six of us, including Senator Hubert Humphrey, climbed aboard a twin-engined Beechcraft. We were no sooner aloft than the door flew open. Everyone tried but no one could close it. The smooth-talking pilot then sent back his seat companion, a Minnesota state official, with special instructions. But the door remained open. The pilot finally gave piloting instructions to the state official and went himself to the rear. Just as we heard the door slam shut, we shot straight up in the air like a rocket. The state official had moved the stick in the wrong direction. Everyone shrieked; the pilot scrambled back to the controls on his hands and knees. When we were righted, Hubert decided to take over as pilot. He toured us over the Iron Range, dipping our wings for a better view while all of us nervously urged him to return to his seat.

After you have been to California several times, you discover that it is really two states, North and South, with a Mason-Dixon line somewhere in the Tehachapis. Of the phenomena that seem to unify the state, the eat-your-salad-first habit is the most significant. Another is the common complaint that all the fertile land is being eaten up by developers, and a third is the universal voluntary exile of the inhabitants. They all seem to come from somewhere in the snow belt where they tired of wearing galoshes and shoveling themselves out of their doorways.

On my first trip in 1955 I saw nearly all of California. Even the introductions reflected regional tastes. At a San Francisco luncheon the former National Committeewoman and a long-time Ambassador's wife, Lucretia Grady, introduced me as "Madam Ambassador." No other title, she indicated, would have been suitable. Down south at a highway restaurant near Fontana, I was forcibly

restrained at the door until several hundred voices broke out in
"K-K-K-Katy, K-K-K-Katy" as a welcome.

At a political fashion show at a private home in Beverly Hills,
four hundred women showed up to occupy three hundred camp
chairs on the pool deck and a private parking lot. I got to speak
somewhere between the couturier display and the raffle of a mink
stole. Mickey (Mrs. Paul) Ziffren, the hostess, commented when
she ran out of toilet paper that the event would have been a
greater fund-raising success if she had just charged for use of the
facilities.

Back in Washington, I reported with some pride that I'd gotten
to know both political factions in Los Angeles. "Only two?" Chairman Paul Butler remarked. "That's not up to California standards."

In September of 1957, Paul and I made a swing around the
country, holding a series of regional workshops to try to find out
why we lost so disastrously in 1956. The sessions often began at
9 A.M. and lasted until midnight. I invariably sat between a wall
and an air conditioner, wondering if we were as technologically
advanced as we think. It was a grim trip, with the only moment
of levity provided by an old-time officeholder from Florida who
made his point about unkept promises: "I promise the voters of
my state one thing—I'll always show up on payday."

The meetings were best summed up by Senator Theodore Francis Green[1] of Rhode Island, then ninety. When he removed his
brand-new hearing aid it broke. He looked at it without regret
and said simply, "I've heard enough."

Four years earlier the Senator had sent for me when he first
heard of my appointment by Steve Mitchell. His old-fashioned
courtesy combined with fine-edge repartee was beguiling. When I
prepared to leave his office he said, "My dear, I have only one piece
of advice to give you: make them all chairmen."

I did my best to follow the venerable Senator's advice. At every
ceremonial turn I doled out titles. Every now and then the ladies
paid me back—they listened.

[1] Born 1867, died in April 1966. Served in the Senate, 1936–61.

One of the incongruities of politics is that, while failure is distressing, success can be infuriating. On the road it seemed that all unsuccessful gatherings were held in barnlike ballrooms at ground level and all successful ones were tucked away in the hotel roof garden, accessible only by one slow elevator. Typical of the latter was a women's luncheon in Indianapolis, where it seemed several thousand ladies had to be lifted to the Roof Garden Room five at a time. Lunch was late, the program was late, and the National Committeewoman made such a lengthy opening speech she forgot she had stood up to introduce me. When she recovered her wits and I finally reached the rostrum, there was a stir in the rear of the room. Adlai Stevenson, surrounded by his court, swirled into view. The ladies were snatching at him as he drifted across to the platform. When he reached it, he turned to me and whispered, "What am I supposed to do, Katie?" I replied with some asperity, "Say a few words."

Along with every quadrennial political hero there springs up a whole new breed of instant politicians known as the "Citizens for X." It became my cause, my cross, and my constant concern to try to blend this bonanza of brains into highly organized just-plain-practitioners of politics. It took a strident-voiced but endearing female regular from the river ward of St. Louis to help me realize that oil and water don't mix.

Anne Fuerst[2] had a way of speaking that even Professor Henry Higgins couldn't have altered. Middle-sized and medium gray, only her voice made her stand out in a crowd, for she was constantly attended by silent, suitably hatted, loyal minions.

Of a luncheon given in my honor in a converted skating rink, I wrote in my journal: "Anne's authority begins with hats and extends over plateaus of cut velvet, plumes, surtouts, bosoms, beads and pearls. She introduced each leader by name. It had overtones

[2] Anne Fuerst is one of Congresswoman Leonor Sullivan's principal Committeewomen. Mrs. Sullivan, leading advocate of consumer legislation in Congress, is Chairman of the Subcommittee on Consumer Affairs and Secretary of the Democratic Caucus, as well as a member of the Democratic Steering Committee. She is serving her ninth term.

of a roll call with lesser functionaries calling out, 'She's sick, she couldn't get here,' when someone failed to respond." I wondered if absence caused a black mark to be entered somewhere against the names.

From the skating rink I went to a gloom-turreted house guarded by stone lions to meet with the local egghead citizens' group. The dark wainscoting affected me like an indigestible dinner. The people were earnest and pleasant but I enjoyed getting back to Anne, who toured me through the city—the French cathedral, with its lemon-colored square stone façade and its golden look of neo-classic simplicity, and the massive German fairy-tale proportions of the Anheuser-Busch breweries, all carved gates, high windows, and courtyards where one could picture wicked ogres flinging profligate princes to their doom. All the while Anne filled me in on her adventures with the Citizens for Stevenson-Kefauver in 1956. She told of a highly successful party they had given. "That day," she related, "this Citizen creature comes up to me and asks, 'Where'd they come from, those eight thousand women blocking the streets?' My own people were asking the same question another way, 'Why did you do it?' My own I told, 'I'm a sucker for the Democratic Party.' All that the Citizen ladies were worrying about was where they'd put the candelabra and the tea-cups. Tea, I had to laugh. They're lucky if they get a cooky. Then this Citizen woman said, 'We've got to give them food and a proper tea, it says so on the ticket, or they'll all leave.' I told her, 'They're not going to leave, they're going to stay and hear the speakers.' But that volunteer type said, 'That is misleading them.' And then I just gave it to her straight. 'Honey,' I said, 'I got news for you. We've been misleading 'em for years.'"

At a banquet on January 12, 1958, at the Conrad Hilton in Chicago, another formidable woman Democratic leader held sway. Majestic, gray-haired, in sumptuous folds of blue, Mrs. Elizabeth Conkey (since deceased), then Democratic National Committee-woman for Illinois, embraced me upon arrival. Such a demonstration of affection promptly raised my status with the other head-table guests.

The dinner was organized down to the last white chrysanthemum corsage, shower of white balloons, and white chiffon-gowned dinner chairman. We were properly integrated with a large number of black ladies and a satisfactory representation of Jews. It was an overflow crowd of more than three thousand at $12.50 a ticket. I asked Mrs. Conkey who had produced this turnout. "Any committeewoman who can't dispose of ten tickets," she assured me, "doesn't last long."

We also were properly ecumenical. Following an invocation by a priest, a Protestant prayed for peace at mid-meal and we had a rabbi at benediction. The evening was a veritable blizzard of redemptive gestures.

Everything and everyone was prompt and orderly. The preliminary speakers were mercifully brief and there were not too many of them. Mrs. Conkey, who introduced me, paid me the ultimate tribute: "I have worked with many women chairmen but none who has understood women as Katie has. The women like her and, besides, she doesn't make the men mad."

I detected an abrupt, abrasive honesty in her voice that made her compliment seem all the more valuable. Deep in her seventies, Mrs. Conkey held unfashionable opinions. Privately, she made it clear to me that she was not enthusiastic about integration and "planned-whatever-it-is" (parenthood). Despite the immutability of her views, Elizabeth Conkey stood for what was best in the old school of ward politics. She cared. She believed passionately in helping others, in welfare programs and the Democratic Party. Her loyalty was unwavering and she understood and respected the command. She was proud of the support she had from men in the party organization as evidenced by the presence of Mayor Daley at the table.

"I told them I got tired of being a ladies' auxiliary," she remarked in recounting her struggle to win recognition for her women. For proof of her success she inclined her head toward the Mayor, who was rising to speak. "He will tell them," she announced. And he did. Brandishing his ungrammatical, Irish rhetorical sword, the Mayor delivered a lyrical polemic about women. He moved the audience to cheers and applause. "Women are wonderful and none more so than the women behind the men in public life. I want every man's woman in this room to rise for a bow." They did, too, amid a roar that sounded many a basso note for the man who recognized women.

They gave Mrs. Conkey a trophy that night. It was oversized, festooned with eagles, and sentimentally inscribed. She was forthright and unsentimental in her acceptance. "Whatever I've done, I have done because I like it," she said simply.

After dinner I had a drink with a young Chicago alderman and his pretty wife. "Some of the women are restive," he said. "They've waited so long for Mrs. Conkey to quit. But it would kill her if we took her off the County Committee, so we won't." It was quite a contrast to the Pennsylvania committeewoman who remarked as we made a tiring tour of her state, "No need to kill yourself, Katie, when they're through with you they will put you on the shelf." Mrs. Conkey was never shelved. Other big-city queens were clever, some were mean, and a few were even timid. None of them ever seemed to me as genuine as Elizabeth Conkey and Anne Fuerst.

Wherever the road led, we could always count on local infighting. The women had their own feuds. Once I sent four National Committeewomen from four Far Western states into a room by themselves to decide in which state they wanted a regional meeting to take place. Afternoon wore on to evening and no one emerged. Finally I asked a state Vice Chairman to go in and inquire what was going on. Flashing fire and brimstone, her committeewoman emerged: "I had it won until you sent that woman in." There was never any satisfactory way of settling such disputes. All we could do was leave a little good will and a lot of materials.

On the first anniversary of my tenure as Director of Women's

Activities, my staff presented me with a cartoon depicting four women witches torturing a fifth on the rack. Above it was pasted a quote from one of my speeches: "Politics would be a far sorrier and far different affair were it not for women."

Tea with Daisy

IN 1948, I WAS BUSILY ENGAGED IN DISENGAGING MYSELF FROM ALL the worthy organizations that cluttered my life. I refused an invitation to a meeting supporting the newly formed AAUN (American Association in support of the United Nations), only to have Michael Straight insist that I accompany him. Michael was then editor of the *New Republic*, where I had worked before the war. "You must meet Daisy Harriman," he informed me as we walked over to the Carlton Hotel. I did. I was struck by her piercing blue eyes—of a color one could describe as cerulean and still not do them justice. Besides, she was as noticeable as a lightship—exceptionally tall, her ramrod carriage graceful and imposing.

That afternoon, after the usual number of speakers, Daisy—Mrs. J. Borden Harriman—spoke briefly. She made no attempt to impress her restless audience; her voice was low and sometimes almost inaudible, she hesitated between ideas, she spoke as one might to a friend. Her very non-professionalism had its own appeal. I listened carefully. "She means it," I whispered to Michael. On our way home Michael, whose mother had been one of her very dear friends, told me about her.

Like her cousin Averell, Daisy Harriman had entered early into the turbulence of Democratic politics. Unlike him, Daisy was not rich. But her beginnings were equally enviable and auspicious. Daisy's growing up took place in a house at 615 Fifth Avenue in New York City. Her neighbor and later friend was J. P. Morgan. As a small child she hung over the banister to watch Presidents

(Arthur, Garfield, etc.), members of Congress and Parliament walk through the front door.

After the election of Woodrow Wilson in 1912, Daisy and her handsome husband "Bordie" moved to Washington from Mount Kisco, New York. His death in 1914 left her a fetching widow of forty-four.

"She's known best for her Sunday night suppers," Michael told me. "It's quite a thing to be asked. She's a people snatcher, her guests are always among the amusing new dragons in town. You must go."

Later I did go to many of Daisy's famous suppers. And my husband (whom she liked so well that she made him an executor of her will) used to say: "Another Sunday night affair, that means we'll be involved from beginning to end." He was correct: I helped make the guest list and sometimes actually did the inviting. Walter helped arrange the seating.

Before we got on these terms, I was invited to tea at Daisy's. There were to be many such occasions; for me it was the beginning of an extraordinary education and a mutual affection that on my part was composed equally of awe.

Sitting beside her, I would drink her sumptuously served tea. Daisy pretended to eat vigorously, but this was merely to prompt guests. At meals, her own plate remained untouched, but at tea she would butter her toast and spread her jam with great gusto. Tea was a meal she enjoyed.

To be a politician, Daisy-style, one had to be positive and wellborn. The fact that in her day "Democrats were chased in the streets of New York like stray dogs" had not deterred her. She learned early to look beyond human frailties and fasten her penetrating gaze on the larger view.

Among her other talents, she could count a rare ability to communicate the exhilaration and splendor of the political panorama. As a beginner, I was an eager listener. "My dear," she would say, quoting from her own book, *From Pinafores to Politics*, "I've had a box seat at the America of my times."

Then, with a little prodding, she would recall meeting Woodrow Wilson in Bermuda (before he became a candidate) and her immediate impression that here was a man of rare gifts. As she described him, the man of letters, of bookishness but great charm and an ability to verbalize the issues and the need for reforms, Daisy would subconsciously betray her own ambivalence in being an aristocrat with a social conscience.

Years later, Alice Roosevelt Longworth told me that had Wilson not defeated his opponent Champ Clark at the 1912 Democratic Convention, Daisy would undoubtedly have supported her father, President Theodore Roosevelt. (Mrs. Longworth explained that he stood for all these same reforms that in Wilson had so magnetized Daisy.)

In 110-degree heat in Baltimore, where the Democratic Convention was held in 1912, Daisy had been sent to William Jennings Bryan's suite to promise him he would be Secretary of State if he would swing his support from Champ Clark of Missouri to Wilson. The "boys," as the men around Bryan were called, were all sitting fanning themselves, their shirt sleeves rolled up. "Everywhere I looked," she would shade in the details, "there were dirty dishes." Bryan stopped fanning himself long enough to rise and greet her. He did come along and he was made Secretary of State.[1]

After Wilson's successful campaign and Daisy's participation as what we might now call "Women's Chairman," Wilson named her to the Federal Industrial Relations Commission and she began her climb up the political ladder.

One afternoon at tea we talked about how she looked in an early photograph, wasp-waisted, riding sidesaddle on a handsome mount. "I liked to ride that horse," she mused. "We would gallop to the top of the hill. He stood in gold up to my saddle." Missing the connection, I inquired whether she had meant goldenrod. "Certainly not," came the reply. "The golden light of the sunset."

[1] Secretary of State from 1913 to 1915. Ran for President 1896, 1900, and 1908.

I was often to hear her talk about the beauty of the sunset or the music in the movement of clouds. Her constant enthusiasms were remarkable, because by the time I knew her well, her own golden light had begun to fade. She had long since moved from her elegant Uplands estate on Foxhall Road to a house on P Street in Georgetown and then to a still smaller house on 26th Street, around the corner from us. But, with Daisy, lack of space could not diminish a grande-dame ambiance. The little house was intensely personal, warm, and crowded with beautiful objects, some in varying stages of disrepair. The furniture was mahogany and light woods, with brocaded seats on a variety of Chippendale chairs. All about, on fine Sheraton tables, rare porcelains crowded one another against old photograph albums and bronze busts of the famous. Bookcases, candelabra, sconces—I counted three pair between the entrance hall and the crowded combination living-dining room—the whole created a luxurious cluttered effect which Daisy carried off by disregarding what was lacking.

Sitting by a bright fire (Daisy never was without one in the cold months), she would delicately demolish her youthful association with coming-out parties and the coach and four she once drove up Fifth Avenue. Mrs. Whitelaw Reid, whose origins were simple but who ended up as wife of the United States Ambassador to the United Kingdom, arrived at Daisy's debut and announced to the hostess (Daisy's grandmother Jaffray): "I started out to go to the Vanderbilts, but I really wasn't dressed for it, so I came here instead."

Swiftly she would shift gears; we would be back in Wilson's White House, where Joseph Tumulty[2] stood guard over who should or should not enter the President's office. Imitating his ungrammatical brusque speech, she would describe the crowded waiting room and his stage-whispered questions that everyone could hear: "Who is that man with one glass in his eye?" Collapsing with suppressed laughter, Daisy would name the British General

2 Served with President Wilson from 1911 to 1921.

with the monocle. Later, we had progressed to the Al Smith[3] campaign of 1928; reporters once asked the beloved Governor of New York which besides his own states he would carry. Al Smith waved his hands and started a roll call of states that did not get him out of the mid-Atlantic area: "Massachusetts, Connecticut, Rhode Island, Pennsylvania, New Jersey." Mumbling, he pointed to the faithful McCooey (his aide). "Ask him, he's got a map."

The french windows of Daisy's all-purpose living room opened onto a deep garden. In summer we sipped our iced tea looking out at her roses. In their white ticking overcoats tied with neat bows (before there were zippers), the solemn chairs reminded me of my own childhood when our New York house was dutifully smothered in slipcovers and the chandeliers and lamps encased in cheesecloth. A large circular fan Arthur Krock had given her kept us cool. "I have often been angry at him, and he has been horrid to me"—Daisy liked the word "horrid" and used it like a dagger—"but still I'm fond of him." (Arthur once told me he found Daisy's Sunday suppers a great bore; you had to sit there and listen to other people talk.)

The Supreme Court was then in the news (as it has been pretty regularly), reminding Daisy that it was at her house that Dr. Cary Grayson (Wilson's doctor) and Norman Hapgood, editor of *Collier's* magazine, discussed the possibility of Brandeis[4] being appointed to the Court.

With a little encouragement, Daisy would talk of her appointment by President Roosevelt as Minister to Norway in 1937. "How foolish I was," she laughed. "When the State Department cabled me to locate the *City of Flint*, I sent back word I thought it was in Michigan." How was she to know there was a battleship by this name? But when the Germans invaded, she was the first diplomat to cable the news home. She organized a convoy of cars and left for the north. (She later wrote of her experiences in a book called *Mission to the North*). En route, her gallant aide stopped

[3] Governor of New York 1920 to 1928. Ran for President 1928.
[4] Served on Supreme Court from 1916 to 1939.

to go into town for the latest news and was shot dead. Dodging the bombs, they pressed on, his body across the "motor"—she never called it a car—their wheels sinking in the frozen snow until the chauffeur begged dogs and a sled.

At one of the teatimes I was told I might call her Daisy. Later other privileges were bestowed; she had a way of making her every wish seem an important part of my political education. The 1952 Democratic Convention was for me indelibly associated with Daisy. At her urging I had run for—and won—a spot as her Alternate Committeewoman, an office established during her service in Norway.[5] Daisy's comments, her commands, her personality related to everything—the balloons, the speeches, the corn, the courtesy, marching, sitting, riding, losing, finding, trying—in the circus that determined the standard-bearer.

Our journey began on the station platform at Wareham, Massachusetts (Daisy summered at Martha's Vineyard and we at Chatham on Cape Cod), where we entrained for Boston and Chicago. Chaperoning Daisy's eleven pieces of luggage, fending off greeters (a field in which I was to acquire great expertise), and choosing our reading material in the midst of clinging heat and clanging confusions took all my attention. Suddenly Daisy exclaimed, "Wouldn't it be too lovely if Averell gets the nomination—then we'd have everything!" As I cast my glance over our combined possessions, it seemed to me we already did.

By the time we reached Albany we had had two eyeglass hunts, both successful, family trees interspersed with Averell's chances, anticipated the car which was to be at Daisy's disposal (National Committeemen and -women are always given a car and driver), skimmed over earlier conventions, and survived a slight skirmish over my incompetence at Canasta—a lack I found bearable but which Daisy wanted to remedy (on our journey home eight days later, I *was* taught canasta). The inevitable graham crackers, a staple of Daisy's meager diet, had been sampled and found satis-

---

[5] Mrs. Harriman served as Democratic National Committeewoman from 1924 until she resigned in 1956.

fying; I was unaware that at later, less convenient moments I would be charged with replenishing the diminishing supply. Sometime in midweek I found myself demanding graham crackers at bars, delicatessens, and carry-outs only to return with oatmeal cookies as a substitute and have Daisy say sweetly, "My dear, they won't do."

In ever so many ways Daisy reminded me of my mother; like all ladies of more lineage than means, they invent small economies which they then offset with planned extravagances in order to meet the standards society exacts. Daisy carried her own hatbox in order to save twenty-five cents, only to turn around and buy an expensive talked-about novel she would not have time to read. Her hat, a practical tan straw, she pointed out, had seven different-colored ribbons that transformed it into seven different hats. (There were five more in the suitcase.) My mother had just such a summer hat.

"Come in, tell me what to wear," was to prove a daily convention ritual. She enjoyed the process of adorning herself. Over the years, I have memories of her in a certain blue that matched her eyes. She wore it in varying textures and thicknesses, even used it for the satin facing on her leopard robe. Superb and impeccable, she would not hesitate to don the castoff clothing of her richer friends if it suited her. And she dearly loved to brag about her bargains—"My dear, that dress cost practically nothing." She had old favorites, too, a brocade jacket she wore over black chiffon, a violet-sprinkled silk, and always the inevitable hats—she was never seen in public without one. On her birthday, July 21, we surprised her with a District of Columbia breakfast. (Daisy hated early morning engagements but nine-thirty proved to be the only free time we could find.) When a news story appeared with an earlier photograph of her in a fur-trimmed hat, she looked at it for a long while: "My dear, I always remember all my hats, but I can't place that one."

"Never mind," she went on, "a lady is never well dressed without one." I would wear one for dinner, I offered, if she would take care of it in her box at the convention hall. She agreed. I spent that evening balancing the hat on my lap, since wearing a hat would have interfered with the vision of delegates seated behind me and Daisy claimed the box was too crowded.

Everyone who was anyone stayed at the Hotel Blackstone. The lobby was never roomy enough for all the bystanders trying to make believe this was their hotel. Daisy's entrances and exits were always regal. She would greet someone warmly and then turn to me, asking, "Who in the world was that?" But VIPs always knew her and she them; somehow they never forgot one another.

To her great distress, it was discovered that the car had to be shared with National Committeeman Melvin Hildreth, who had brought his wife. Hildreth, in turn, had been having room problems; fortunately, however, he had just encountered his old friend, the circus fixer, a man who goes out ahead of the tent and "fixes" the complaining neighbors with the wad he carries about with him. Hildreth had long been a circus fan; the fixer found him a room. Sharing the car, however, was another matter. One night, when Hildreth and wife had vanished, car and all, I stood outside the stockyard with Daisy and no conveyance of any kind in sight. She suggested I stand in the street and flag down the first passing limousine. To my delight, a large black car stopped; riding in front with the chauffeur was an old friend of Daisy's, Judge Toohey of Milwaukee, Wisconsin. The latter was so captivated by her presence, we were invited not only to ride but to dine. Passengers in black limousines, I decided, would always turn out to be admirers of Daisy's.

She could be very demanding. She would pretend that my other duties (meeting with my delegation, attending endless caucuses, and serving on the Platform Committee) were of less importance than I gave them. One evening, escorting her in the hotel elevator, I announced a promise to meet a friend downstairs.

"Whatever for?" came the peremptory challenge. "You talked to him at lunch." Recalling her overpowering presence at that time,

I took refuge in a silent nod. After I had said good night and watched her turn away, I decided Daisy's back was as commanding as anyone else's full face.

The next morning I knew the moment I walked into her room that I was forgiven. Placing hands on hips, she produced a masterful imitation of Perle Mesta[6] imitating Ethel Merman imitating Perle in *Call Me Madam*—a sophisticated bit of mimicry which had taken place at Perle's party the evening before. No indeed, she had not attended (surely I would have seen her)—she wouldn't dream of going to "that creature's party." I had heard about her disdain of Perle before, but I regretted having no one to share Daisy's performance with.

The very last crisis of the convention bore no relation to the emergence of Adlai ("this little man with the crisp, cutting but cultured voice," I wrote in my journal), the fire on the convention floor, or the civil rights battle. As we sorted out possessions in the steaming Pullman, Daisy missed the graham crackers. With horror, I recalled putting down her precious parcel at Western Union while I drafted a telegram to explain my absence from the post-convention meeting of the Democratic National Committee. (Having to choose between two obligations, my vote as Alternate Committeewoman or escorting Daisy, I chose Daisy.) The train was to leave in minutes. Racing after the departing porter, I pressed a dollar bill in his hand and implored his help. The crackers were saved—and so was I.

The intimacy between us grew. We were friends, neighbors, Democrats, mothers, historians, and in need of one another. At first it was I who had need of her, then the need, with the death of Daisy's only daughter, became a mutual one. I was proud of our association and our few shared triumphs. Together, along with Emily Douglas (wife of the then Senator Paul Douglas[7]), we

[6] Appointed by President Truman as Minister to Luxembourg in 1949; served until April 3, 1953.

[7] Senator Paul Douglas served in the United States Senate from 1948 to 1967.

accomplished a change in the bylaws of the Women's National Democratic Club, which Daisy had helped to found. We won the fight for integration, against delaying tactics. Daisy was straightforward on this issue: "Segregation isn't Christian."[8]

I kept her scrapbook for her, and worried with her over articles she wanted to write. She liked to talk of suitors but not to write about them. General Pershing inevitably came on scene; in World War I, Daisy had organized a motor corps for the Red Cross, for which she had even designed uniforms. (They were becoming to tall women but looked awkward on others.) She saw a good deal of the handsome, popular Pershing overseas. Once he had thanked her for refusing an affair with him. "Then we would never have had this great friendship," he told her.

Senator Tom Walsh of Montana, famed for uncovering the Teapot Dome scandals,[9] had also courted her, hoping if he got to be Vice President on the John Davis ticket in 1924 she would marry him. Daisy had rejected him because, although he had character and brains, he lacked polish and, more important to her, had no sense of humor.

She recalled his opposition to Al Smith, whom Daisy favored. He was all right, Walsh had stated, "but he spits. He must have spit sixteen times when I was with him."

"Which do you think is worse," Daisy had retorted, "blowing your nose without a handkerchief, or spitting?" Walsh opted for the first. Daisy shot back: "That's what you do!"

He phoned her daily to advise on going up to the Senate. One day, when another Senator's mother who was refused entrance to the already crowded Senate family gallery objected loudly to Daisy's presence down front, the doorkeeper replied, "Oh, her, she's got a Senator hankerin' after her." Indeed, he was right.

On our last evening together in Chicago, she had recalled a

---

[8] Women's National Democratic Club integrated in 1956. Gladys (Mrs. Todd) Duncan became the first black member.

[9] Senator Walsh was named as prosecutor of the Investigating Committee in 1923.

clumsy delegate who, many conventions ago, made advances to her and, when she resisted, stormed: "What are you in politics for? The only reason women go into politics is to meet men." That same evening, she spoke of an unhappy wife, a close friend, who worried over her husband's infidelities. "If only we could realize when young what we learn in maturity, that infidelity is really very unimportant."

As she talked, the flush of youth and memory made her blue eyes flash. Her food remained uneaten. Like the listener in *The Arabian Nights*, I never tired of hearing it all; her breakthrough for women's suffrage, her decision in 1902 to found the Colony Club in New York (women at the turn of the century could not stay alone overnight in a hotel, so why not a women's club?), her convention sagas, her problems with wives who were jealous of her (neither the second Mrs. Wilson nor Eleanor Roosevelt ever invited her to their social events; they accepted formal calls but otherwise it was the Presidents who had her to luncheon or tea). She was an expert storyteller. Her manner of delivery was just as understated as her public speaking voice, but you knew it was all true and it came to life for you.

As a neighbor, her advice extended beyond politics to redecorating my house. Once I assembled samples of new draperies for our living room for her perusal. She cautioned me not to call them "drapes"—vulgar word—they were curtains. "And not any of those drab colors for this long cold room." She was correct, the room lacked not only warmth but central planning. As for bibelots, she had too many, but I had too few.

When Walter suggested that brighter colors for "curtains" would drown out our paintings, she laughed. "Nothing could drown out those paintings." And, pointing to a Miro: "What, will you tell me, is that?"

"A man and his image."

But why a man that looked like a nightmare? "I go as far as the Picasso Blue Period," she stated imperiously, "and no further."

Eventually, it was Daisy herself who insisted we remove two crystal chandeliers; they obstructed the paintings.

Daisy's famous Sunday night suppers adhered to a strict formula: an equal number of Democrats and Republicans (she did not believe in "partisanship," which she pronounced with the accent on the third syllable) at the dinner table, one or two well-known journalists, and a few old friends.

On the selected Sunday, Daisy would arrive at our house for lunch to plot and arrange the seating with Walter. Usually I could count on a Saturday call, asking for new names to replace the dropouts. There was always a shortage of interesting unattached men, and Daisy liked an even number. Early on I began keeping lists of bachelors or members of Congress whose wives were out of town. Daisy's old friend, Senator Theodore Francis Green, had long since been decorated with one of Daisy's quips: "He keeps his dinner jacket by his bed, prepared for the phone to ring, so he can rush into action like a fireman sliding down a pole."

Daisy was practical about the three tables which crowded her all-purpose room downstairs. Her chairs were a mixture of solid and fragile. "No," she would sometimes counter our seating suggestions, "he's too fat for that chair."

Arriving guests stood awkwardly around tables and chairs, minus cocktails (Daisy never served any), until the last had come and we squeezed into our places. Decanters of scotch and bourbon always stood on each of the tables, with magnificent Meissen tureens in the center. There was much to-do about ice. Suddenly, dinner would be served on lovely china by two venerable butlers and a young girl apprentice.

Conversation purred over "Soup Delightful"—a shellfish and cream concoction for which Daisy would never relinquish the recipe—and subsequent equally delectable courses. She liked substantial food and would, on occasion, invoke Bordie's long-ago derision of others' fare: "Never take me there again. I like to chew my own food, and everything was a mousse."

After large coffees arrived, still at the table, Daisy would rap
and prompt her guests: "Do push your chair back, make yourself
comfortable, feel free to move about." As if we could have moved!
Twenty-odd people with nary an inch to spare sat politely in place.

I can recall a dinner at which the historian Claude Bowers,[10]
recently returned as Ambassador to Chile, reviewed the threat of
Communism in South America. And Senator Henry (Scoop) Jackson of Washington, then unmarried, bemoaned the "too many
committees" on the Hill. At still an earlier date, Daisy and her
guests decided General Eisenhower could have been elected on
either ticket.

Like an orchestra conductor, Daisy would urge one guest to
speak out while restraining another. She skillfully encouraged
Scotty Reston, Mark Childs, William White, and other such columnists to ask penetrating questions, but would not hesitate to
ask Mrs. Robert Low Bacon (an old friend and prominent Republican hostess) to listen and stop talking to her neighbor. When
the subject was the lack of linguistic skill on the part of some ambassadorial appointee, she would remember that "Bryan bragged
he traveled around the world on English."

Justice Hugo Black, who sat beside me on one occasion, told me
that before the tree of liberalism could be renewed in the South
a few candidates must water it with their blood. He had so advised
a Congressman running for Senator. "He tried to straddle. He
got beaten as he should have."

In 1960, one Sunday supper produced a galaxy of Senators:
John Sherman Cooper of Kentucky, Eugene McCarthy of Minnesota, and Paul Douglas of Illinois, and their unusually sophisticated wives. The gathering that evening was in honor of
Ambassador Frances Willis, a distinguished career diplomat just
back from Ceylon. (I recall producing three men for that occasion,
in response to a Saturday noon call.)

At Daisy's request, Miss Willis gave us a factual, statistic-laden

[10] Ambassador to Spain, 1933–39. Ambassador to Chile, 1939. Died 1958.

account of her post. The Senators debated the competition among the armed services, who was to blame for the missile lag, Pentagon waste, and lack of support among the public (that amorphous mass) for the additional taxes required to meet the cost of our defense. We refought the "bring the boys back home syndrome" which led to disarmament after World War I and Korea. Later there was general agreement that we were fortunate that Roosevelt took us to the left (New Deal measures were considered leftish) during his first administration, thereby avoiding revolution in the thirties.

Before we left, Daisy delighted us with a recollection of an encounter with Joseph Tumulty in what he called "Aspery" Park (his summer home). She had driven down on a hot day to talk to him about a threatened railroad strike. Their entire conversation took place in and around her car. She was never invited into the house, although she would have dearly loved a glass of lemonade— even water. Years later he confessed that his wife was "jealous, just jealous," and forbade him to offer any hospitality.

These suppers taught me that there was a civilized, informative way to entertain, one at which everyone could be spared the tedium of an endless evening of tête-à-têtes, first with strangers at one's right and left, and later over coffee with women batting tiresome subjects (children, schools, illnesses, diets) across the room like balls over a ping-pong net.

Daisy taught me many things; among them, to savor the wonders about us and, more important, to overlook the hurts and slights. She despised a prominent Ambassador who had once paid homage to her and later turned away. "Perhaps he thought I was no longer useful," she sighed, "but he need not have been rude about it." Then she repeated her favorite maxim: "My dear, one must simply rise above it."

Going off with Daisy was always full of surprises; after a dreary political dinner, where the speakers had been too prolific and had used too many clichés, Daisy praised them all, but remarked: "Did you see that woman sitting in front of us with the Tammany face and the low-cut dress?"

Once when I was visiting Daisy at Martha's Vineyard she swam past me, calling back, "Beware of Charles Evans Hughes' whiskers [the seaweed]!"

In the 1950s she became a dedicated supporter of home rule for the District of Columbia. In a letter to the New York *Times* in 1955, she called for a "Boston Tea Party" for the disenfranchised citizens of the nation's capital. Erect and elegant at eighty-four, she led a parade through the city of Washington to protest "taxation without representation."

As she aged, she became gaunt-looking. When her pangs or pains bothered her, she recalled humorously what Bordie used to say when she complained of feeling ill: "Poor Daisy, such a good Christian Scientist (which she was), but she still has all the aches and none of the pleasures. She sounds like I do after a hangover."

Following a 1962 Christmas dinner with her close friends the Robert Woods Blisses,[11] she remarked ruefully, "We were all so old and decrepit. They talked about their ailments. Later Bob (Bliss) read a parody on 'The Night before Christmas' with everyone's name in it. If it had been good it would have been sad, but it was so awful it was sweet."

She spoke often of the hereafter. "Wherever it is," she said, "I want to be with Bordie and Ethel, my loved ones."

Bordie, according to Daisy, had been "naughty," an innocent adjective which might have meant a number of things, and Ethel, her only child, had been talented and demanding. I had met Ethel only once, and reported to Walter that she was a pale copy of Daisy. But Daisy adored them both. That's what love, for Daisy, was—looking past another's shortcomings.

Two friends who had long loved Daisy, Ethel and George Garrett (he was Ambassador to Ireland under President Eisenhower),

[11] Appointed Ambassador to Argentina February 17, 1927. Gave Dumbarton Oaks to Harvard University in 1940.

invited twenty-two of us to celebrate her ninetieth birthday in June of 1960 (a month before the actual date).

The Garrett home, like its chatelaine, is self-effacingly elegant: French furniture, the right pictures, brocaded sofas, and Aubusson carpets in which, if one is not careful, a heel can catch in the fine threads; all of it reeks of cultivated good taste—without a brand name. The rooms smelled of perfumed summer, from pale pink peonies and white lilies on the piano to quantities of summer bouquets on the tables in large black urns.

The garden was cool, set in stone and greenery. From the open doors to the terrace, the lighted glass globes on the tables, the indirect lights on statues and trees created a lovely summer stage set. Even the newly opened magnolia blossoms seemed especially timed for the occasion. Among the guests, besides Daisy, were the New York *Times's* Scotty Reston (and his wife Sally), the (then) Senator and Mrs. Leverett Saltonstall, the Robert Woods Blisses, Judge and Mrs. Homer Ferguson, Joseph Alsop (the columnist), Mrs. Dean Acheson (the former Secretary of State was away), Alice Roosevelt Longworth, Justice Felix Frankfurter, and a few others.

After the many toasts, Justice Frankfurter rose to describe Daisy as "a woman with no expertise for the many posts she held right from the beginning. All she had was common sense and an ability to get along with everyone and a charm none could resist." Then, looking about the room, he added, "It would be difficult to find a common denominator among those gathered here." There was none—except Daisy's friendship.

At ninety-two she astonished us all by acquiring a ten-week-old poodle to replace a boxer that had died, and proceeding to housebreak him.

During these final years, fewer friends took time to visit. The exception was Mrs. Robert Woods Bliss, mistress of Dumbarton Oaks, whom John Walker, then Director of the National Gallery of Art, once called the Byzantine Empress of Washington. (Her collection of Byzantine art is preserved in a jewellike museum adjoining Dumbarton Oaks.) It was Mildred Bliss who originated and instigated Daisy's Citation of Merit for Distinguished Service, the very first such award presented by the President.

Daisy and Mildred Bliss had been friends since they were in Paris during World War I. "I have always considered Daisy one of the really great women," Mildred Bliss once said. (Mrs. Bliss, herself an unusually gifted person, was both modest and generous as well.) She warned that Daisy must never know who plotted the idea for the citation.

The ceremony took place at 6:30 P.M. on April 13, 1963. Guests were escorted through the Diplomatic Lobby of the White House on up to the Blue Room. From the windows, where we had been standing in uneasy clumps, admiring the lilacs and narcissus in bloom, we could turn to see Daisy, surrounded by relatives, looking as tall as ever. She wore a dark blue suit with a light blue brocade blouse, and the inevitable hat.

Her grandson Boy (Daisy all over again—tall, with those blue eyes and the strange, almost hooked nose that looked so well in their kind of face), Boy's wife (Mrs. Charles Russell), and Daisy's granddaughter Phyllis (Mrs. Oliver Marcy), along with six of her many great-grandchildren, aged ten and up, surrounded her, all of them looking at ease, pleased, and handsome. After the ceremony, which was brief, the smaller boys scurried to President Kennedy for autographs and went sliding off on the East Room's highly polished parquet floors.

Averell and Marie Harriman and other cousins (Mrs. Ray Atherton and Mrs. Louis Gunther), Mrs. Robert Woods Bliss—very elegant in white-dotted black crepe—with her cane, Ambassador and Mrs. Angier Biddle Duke (Chief of Protocol), Assistant Secretary for European Affairs and Mrs. William R. Tyler (he is now Director of Dumbarton Oaks), Ambassador and Mrs. Paul Koht of Norway, former Ambassador to Ireland and Mrs. George Garrett, General and Mrs. Alfred Gruenther, Mr. Mangor (First Secretary of the Norwegian Embassy), and Mrs. Kennedy's mother and stepfather, Mr. and Mrs. Hugh D. Auchincloss, were among those present. Tish Baldridge, Mrs. Kennedy's social secretary, managed to settle us into two semicircles, in the center of which stood the President and Mrs. Harriman.

The President, his tan set off by a dark blue suit, spoke simply. "We honor this great lady. This is the first time a citation of this nature has been given." Then, holding up the rather large and impressive framed citation, he added: "Mrs. Kennedy designed the citation herself" (she was away at the time of the presentation).

CITATION

Florence Jaffray Hurst Harriman

TO ACCOMPANY THE AWARD OF
THE PRESIDENTIAL MEDAL OF FREEDOM

By direction of the President of the United States, under the provisions of Executive Order 10085 of February 22, 1963, the Presidential Medal of Freedom, First Degree for an especially meritorious contribution to the interest of the United States is awarded to:

Florence Jaffray Hurst Harriman

Florence Jaffray Hurst Harriman served with distinction under President Woodrow Wilson on the Federal Industrial Relations Commission from 1913 to 1916. During the first World War Mrs. Harriman rendered outstanding service to her country as Chairman of the Committee on Women in Industry of the Council of National Defense. She further demonstrated her qualities of leadership in France as Officer in Charge of 500 drivers for the Red Cross Women's Motor Corps. In 1937 Mrs. Harriman was appointed by President Franklin Delano Roosevelt as American Minister to Norway. When Norway was invaded in the spring of 1940, she led her Legation staff to Stockholm and eventually to London. In London she served as United States Minister to the Norwegian Government-in-Exile. In this position, operating under trying circumstances, she served with distinction. Mrs. Harriman's initiative and dedication to the service of her country over a long period has been given with spirit, imagination, energy and skill in keeping with the highest traditions of this Republic.

They shook hands and Daisy introduced her family. Then the press and photographers advanced, there were handshakes, more photographs and, of course, champagne (with champagne glasses full of chilled ginger ale for the children). It was as Daisy liked it —serene, gracious, and gay.

Its origin remained a mystery. One afternoon, looking at the scrapbook I had had specially engraved for the White House photographs, Daisy asked: "*Why*, after all these years?"

I answered: "Because so many, including the President and Mrs. Kennedy, wanted to recognize your achievements and express their affection for you."

She paid me little heed. She began guessing: "I wonder if it was Jim Farley [former Chairman of the Democratic National Committee, whom she had known well] or perhaps Bill Bullitt?"[12]

I kept the secret.

Daisy died at the age of ninety-seven on September 1, 1967. Services were held in the Washington Cathedral.[13] Former Secretary of State Dean Acheson, who had known Daisy since his own boyhood (she had been a friend of his father's), gave the tribute. "From her earliest youth Daisy Harriman reached out to life with the joyous embrace of great vitality. This extra gift of the life force itself is, perhaps, the greatest that God gives to his sons and daughters. It is given not as a reward for virtue, but in a discriminating and mysterious way to a remote ancestor here and there and passed down. Daisy Harriman had it. . . . Her great energy,

[12] Ambassador to the Soviet Union, 1933–36; Ambassador to France, 1936–41.

[13] Mrs. Harriman was buried in Woodlawn Cemetery in the Bronx, New York.

her enormous courage, and her assurance of her own pre-
eminence brought her magnanimity. Rarest of the rugged, old-
fashioned virtues, one sees it all too seldom now in our Capital
City; and yet more than anything else it sweetens life around
those who possess it."

I was fortunate; Daisy had sweetened mine.

The Joe Smith Express

"CAN'T SEE YOU FOR WITCHES," I CALLED OUT TO ADLAI ACROSS THE table. Our hostess explained that the paper witches burning in dry ice were there to exorcise devils. We were in Santa Fe, New Mexico (August 1956), and these scorched symbols were part of the local mythology. Of course, they were female.

Sante Fe was hot and dry. The parade cars were all open. The sun scorched. I declared myself a sunburned, daytime witch.

On the speakers' platform, I ran for the shade, stealing a VIP place beside Speaker Sam Rayburn. "You're getting to be a pro," he said, "making a beeline for the shade." Later on in the program, when I had to run back to center stage to be introduced, he chided me gently, "Don't run like that, child, you'll break a shank."

We were on the road—and anything could happen. I spent a good part of the afternoon getting a birthday cake baked for Majority Leader Lyndon B. Johnson, and the evening celebration trying to find food for Mr. Sam, who kept asking, "Lord, Katie, when do we eat? All I've had is whiskey and I've about hit my level." When supper was served about eleven and the candlelighted cake wheeled in, both Lyndon Johnson and Mr. Sam had gone.

After the 1956 convention, Clayton Fritchey, Adlai's press man, called to deliver the official invitation to "travel with the Governor" as the "ins" called Adlai. Subsequently, three other pros called to tell me it was their idea. I hadn't been this much in demand since dating days. On August 26, a muggy humid morning, we emplaned from Chicago at 7:30 A.M. Eventually we got used to break-of-day departures. Dick Rowan, the ever unruffled young man who handled the baggage and ran the mimeograph machine, headed his orders of the day "The Morning Call." Slid under our hotel doors, the instructions invariably read: "Baggage out by six." After that first shock, nothing mattered.

The staff sat in the back of the Joe Smith Express, as Adlai's plane was called.[1] Sometimes my seat mate was Chicago lawyer Hy Raskin,[2] but most of the journey was spent with Barry Bingham,[3] Co-Chairman of Volunteers for Stevenson-Kefauver. Roger Tubby,[4] John Bartlow Martin,[5] several indefatigable young secretaries, and a score of others alternately crowded the aisles on their way back to the lounge in the rear. Picture taking, conferences, and elbow bending all took place on this semicircular seat, sometimes all three at once.

On my first trip forward, I discovered a bed, reserved, of course, for Adlai. Bill Blair[6] urged me to take possession. Adlai and Senator Estes Kefauver were in their customary seats plotting strategy. For two happy hours, that first morning out of Chicago, I spread out with blanket and Evelyn Waugh's *Men at Arms*. When Adlai did come up to talk with his son, who sat opposite, he quipped, "Katie, I can't decide whether to put you out or ask you to move over."

Santa Fe remains remarkable for how well one sleeps at an altitude of seven thousand feet, Albuquerque for the expression on the local newsman's face when John Fell Stevenson (Adlai's young-

[1] Joe Smith's name came into national prominence at the 1956 Republican Convention in San Francisco. A Nebraska delegate, bored with the proceedings, nominated plain old Joe Smith for Vice President. Joe Smith himself turned out not to exist, and his name was expunged from the official Republican Convention records.

[2] Raskin, tyro with nine lives, survived right through the John F. Kennedy, Lyndon B. Johnson, and Hubert Humphrey campaigns.

[3] Popular editor and publisher and owner of the Louisville *Courier-Journal*.

[4] Tubby later became Ambassador to the European office of the United Nations at Geneva.

[5] Well-known writer and official biographer of Stevenson.

[6] William McCormick Blair, Jr., a partner in Stevenson's law firm, Ambassador to Denmark and the Philippines, now General Director, John F. Kennedy Center for the Performing Arts.

est son, then twenty), inquired where he might obtain a copy of _Death Comes for the Archbishop_ by Willa Cather. A bystander came rushing up. "We have that book. Please give us his address so we can send it to him."

As the calvacade for the airport lined up, Adlai asked me to ride with him. "I'm tired of politicians, Katie," he said, summoning me. Seeing my look of consternation, he added, _"Elected_ politicians or candidates for office." As usual, we waited interminably for Estes, who could keep everyone fuming while he took care of his adieus. Earl Mazo, then with the _Herald Tribune,_ produced a wisecrack that stuck: "Adlai is always one half hour ahead of Estes and two hundred handshakes behind." In time Adlai turned the truism into a witty remark: "I've been shaking hands against Estes for so many months (the long winter and spring of bitterly contested primaries) that shaking hands with him is a lot easier."

By the time we had heard about cattle, water, veterans, farmers, small business problems, we had changed climates and totaled up many miles. Reboarding the plane was always a twice-daily scramble: Helen Rank, the capable stewardess who had traveled with AES in 1952, would call out to the thirsty press corps, "Wait, wait till I get my track shoes on."

Clayton handled the plane mike, giving us schedules, and the press the release time of the next speech. Adlai, meanwhile, would be rewriting this very release (speech), and Estes would be asleep with mask on his eyes and slippers on his feet. The two wire service photographers, Tom Shafer, UPI, and Charlie Knoblock, AP, would have started their perpetual card game. The latter pair were later replaced (when the press acquired their own plane) by two representatives of labor who slapped down cards in identical rhythms. I would have borrowed someone's typewriter to prepare the next stop's remarks. The _Life_ photographer, Howard Sochurek, whose giraffe-high measurements made him and his three cameras even more conspicuous, would stalk the aisles, snapping us all, until Adlai directed Clayton to bench him. On landing, Clayton announced over the mike: "The Governor wants Barry Bingham and Katie Louchheim to get off with him." David Bonn, then president of Young Democrats, followed us. We trade-named ourselves: Women, children (Young Democrats), and volunteers.

Ours had been a precampaign regional tryout. James Finnegan's[7] plan went with the act; charts were unveiled at each stop. Finnegan, the man who loved *not* to speak, would then point to a twenty-seven-state area where we needed to change only 480,000 votes in order to win. Matthew McCloskey, the Santa Claus-faced party Treasurer, who dearly loved his Pat and Mike jokes, told them with increased virtuosity at each stop. Eventually Finnegan would turn toward me and mutter, "Katie will tell you in a few words what we plan for the women." He used the same phrase at each stop and invariably looked at his watch. I suspected him of counting my words and minutes.

Later on the campaign became one continuous tug-of-war between the pros and the eggheads. When I had an idea, some political pearl I dredged up, I would first run it through whispered conference with George Ball, Willard Wirtz, Newton Minow, and, of course, Bill Blair, who often had the final say. The structure of Adlai's entourage reminded one of a court: one sought out the courtiers in order to gain the ear of the king.

Bill could always get Adlai's attention. He served as strategist and as the first line of defense when Adlai's exuberant advisers tended to overwhelm him. He managed to combine the offices of appointment secretary, confidant, and political weather vane. Fortunately for Adlai, Bill was blessed with an even disposition and an abundant sense of humor.

Hy Raskin and Jim Finnegan represented the pros, and very ably. Finnegan, Adlai's chosen campaign chairman in 1956 (because of his phenomenal success in winning elections in Pennsylvania), looked and talked the part. In these doomed weeks of the campaign, when the vapors of impending defeat enveloped us, the pros were calling for a showdown. Finnegan, who could have

[7] Adlai's campaign chairman.

passed the egghead test, attributed Adlai's recurring problems to a case of mistaken identity: the pros ended up thinking they were eggheads and the eggheads became convinced they had become pros.

But all of us suffered, pros, pols, no matter which. We met, made plans, disbanded. We sought vainly for encouragement from one another, called long distance, "How goes it with you?"

Talking to Mrs. Eleanor Roosevelt revealed more problems; she spoke harshly of Carmine de Sapio (then Democratic National Committeeman and official Tammany boss). Apparently the swing around New York City made by Adlai, Mayor Wagner, Governor Harriman, herself, and Senator Lehman had run into strategic microphones that did not work. "No one can convince me," she enunciated with contained wrath, "that Carmine did not deliberately foul us up."

Issues, quite naturally, were a constant problem, in contrast to the variables such as factions, frowning skies, delays, and TV disasters.

Riding to the airport one morning, I listened while Adlai and Estes talked about the past day's imponderables; had the National Committeeman of Minnesota, Gerry Heaney, been correct in saying that the Republicans had convinced the public that the Democrats were the war party? "If so," inquired Adlai, "what are we going to do about it?" "Talk about what we've done for peace," Estes drawled in his peculiarly mellifluous flat voice. "The Marshall Plan, Aid to Greece and Turkey, Point Four . . ." Taking up the historic review, Adlai went back to the League of Nations, giving us a breathless, convincing exposition. Suddenly he paused. "We might as well say the Republicans were responsible for the Spanish American War, the Civil War—" He had made us laugh; ours was a kind of private, lost laughter one could not really rejoice in.

On sunnier occasions, I could really rejoice because Adlai would make use of some phrase or idea of mine. Often my opportunity to get his attention took the form of a ride in his car. One noon I had been talking to Barry Bingham while Adlai studied his text. "The Republicans are penny-wise and people-foolish," I said, quoting myself. Adlai looked up. "Who said that?" he inquired. I had, at the last stop. "Well, my dear," he said, giving me one of those endearing smiles, *"you've* said it for the last time."

In October Adlai had been booed by students at Yale (a revealing 1956 curtain raiser for what was to come), fogged out in West Virginia, and brooded over by all his well-wishers. John Oakes, head of the editorial page of the New York *Times,* talked with me about the paper's concern over AES's fiscal policy. After four meetings and many telephone calls, my husband and others drafted a TV text tackling hard money, inflation, the cost of carrying the public debt, etc. Joe Fowler (later President Johnson's Secretary of the Treasury) raised the funds, but the Suez crisis killed this plan.

But what worried Adlai intimates more was his divorce. "That is still our biggest drawback," remarked Bill Wirtz, close friend and Adlai's partner, later to become Secretary of Labor. "The Divorce" pointed up the woman problem, which, by virtue of its sex, fell within my jurisdiction. "More women," came the cry, "must ride in the plane!" The experts held that the presence of women in numbers would make up for the absence of a wife and negate the subject of divorce.

Among the permanent fixtures aboard were Adlai's older sister, Mrs. Ernest Ives,[8] the Co-Chairman of the Volunteers for Stevenson-Kefauver, Mrs. Edison Dick, and the first woman ever to serve as Ambassador, Mrs. Eugenie Anderson.[9]

Jane Dick, whom Clayton Fritchey once described as couth, looked just that; she had a pristine prettiness that outshone her custom-made clothes. Her white gloves, her hat, her correct speech

[8] She pronounced Adlai differently, as if it were Ad-e-lay.

[9] At the recommendation of Mrs. India Edwards, then Vice Chairman of the Democratic National Committee, President Truman appointed Mrs. Eugenie Anderson Ambassador to Denmark in 1949. Appointed Minister to Bulgaria in 1962 by President Kennedy. Appointed to the Trusteeship Council of the UN by President Johnson, 1965.

bespoke advantages one did not have to make for oneself, they were included when she was put together. A prominent rich Republican (Stevensoncrat), she laid claim to a large share of Adlai by virtue of seniority (she had campaigned for him as Governor) and mutual social backgrounds in which their friendship gardens grew.

Eugenie Anderson, a humorless, serious Minnesotan, was given the title of Foreign Policy Adviser to Stevenson. The title was intended to nudge Eugenie ahead of Jane Dick but it changed little. Buffie Ives continued to make the papers and take the roses at each stop.

In politics one learns daily that the brighter they are, the more people differ. Every one of our triumvirate of intelligent women was dedicated to the cause of Adlai and to the man himself. What they lost sight of was that it mattered not which one of them held sway or by what right they did so. In the end Eugenie and Jane became inseparable. They co-authored scripts and speeches that Adlai never used. But then this happened to all of Adlai's exceptional experts, men like Ken Galbraith, John Hersey, Arthur Schlesinger, and others.

In late September, Finnegan summoned Jane Dick and me to a meeting. "We are not doing very well with the women," he announced. Hy Raskin, seated opposite, gave me a silent thank-you nod for not laughing out loud at the understatement of the 1956 campaign. Some of us had been aware of these female withdrawal symptoms for weeks, except that we would have included husbands among the disappointed. Finnegan's remedy included cost-of-living fliers and organizing listening parties to a special TV morning matinee directed by Adlai to the ladies.

Reams have been written about the general campaign pandemonium, but to describe the confusion attending this particular program would take a book. No satisfactory locale could be found to fit into Adlai's schedule; when Boston was settled on, Mrs. Roosevelt could not rearrange her plans to be there. The fliers did not suit one of our vital target areas, California, and so the local organization produced their own, only to destroy millions of them because of a small but serious typo.

In the end, we hoped that the fliers developed their own invisible airborne units and helped local candidates. Bill Blair saved the telecast by suggesting and securing Mrs. Rose Kennedy. All three of his sons, whom Adlai insisted on having with him, and Adlai III's pregnant wife Nancy were to complete the group.

After the TV show I wondered whether anyone had ever discussed the whole idea with Adlai. He behaved as if the news had been broken to him that fatal morning. Probably Adlai's most unpopular stand (adopted into law in 1963) was on the banning of the H bomb. A *Newsweek* friend informed me that on this issue the voters stood four to one against him.

Expensive minutes went ticking by as we watched in stupefied fascination while Adlai gave the H-bomb issue a long bow. Mrs. Kennedy did her best, pouring out questions and coffee. But it was a college lecture by Professor Stevenson we got that morning. Adlai never mentioned the listening women, not to thank them or to bid them carry on. I know how they felt—I took all their brokenhearted calls.

But that night, in a typical Adlai reversal, he rang the rafters in Faneuil Hall; the audience went wild and stood cheering.

Like everyone else's, most of my policy ideas got sidetracked. But every once in a while we scored on political participation. We sent hats owned by Mrs. Truman and other VIPs flying across the country to be auctioned off at 165 hat parties.[10] The take was over fifty-five thousand dollars. Though the proceeds were supposed to be split fifty-fifty with headquarters, the moneymaking local groups with their stories of no funds were so heartbreaking, we let them keep the total. Subconsciously we knew the money couldn't do us much good, but it might help elect a Congressman.

[10] Mrs. Clifford Davis, wife of the thirteen-term Congressman from Memphis, Tennessee, ran the hat program. Operation Crossroads, was run by Mrs. Hale Boggs, wife of the House of Representatives Whip. Mrs. Oscar Chapman, wife of the then former Secretary of the Interior, ran the speakers' bureau.

My most effective idea was Operation Crossroads. It sent out fleets of decorated station wagons carrying loud speakers, fliers, and attractive housewives. The drivers were male recruits from the Young Democrats, among whom was Allard Lowenstein, later elected to the 91st Congress from New York.

Our great ordeal occurred five days before election; up till then the feminists promoting the Equal Rights Amendment had been put off. Every candidate for public office was and still is subject to their persistent lobbying. They had to be received. Eleven strong, they waited for Adlai in a Bellevue-Stratford parlor in Philadelphia; the hour was late, he had just delivered a major speech at the University of Pennsylvania at which student booing had again distracted the audience and disrupted the dearly bought TV time. Escorting him down the hall, I felt much like a jailor and said so. Referring to a long day's harassment, he snapped at me: "I've had about all I can take." These were the only sharp words he ever addressed to me.

My worst fears were soon realized. One persistent pleader sat not only beside him but practically upon him. Crossing her hands on her breast in martyr fashion, she bombarded him with long impassioned pleas and large pieces of paper with the signatures of prominent public figures. When Adlai finally broke in to relate his experiences as Governor, referring to the many organizations opposed to this legislation, Alice Paul, their statuesque spokesman, announced that the opposition had crumbled away. Opposition, apparently, these fourteen years later, is still crumbling. In the end it took a combined force of Mrs. Ives, Eugenie Anderson, and TV newsman John Daly physically to pry the Governor loose.

Even the elements those last days were against us. The garment district parade on Seventh Avenue, New York, was rained out. A great show of fabulous woman power at the Hotel Astor sat through Adlai's text in stunned silence; he said nothing about the Suez crisis which had broken that day. The teeming schedule took us to Erasmus High School in Brooklyn, where the audience in the well of the auditorium seemed dreadfully young. From the principal we learned that she had been told of Adlai's appearance only *that* morning and could not dismiss her classes.

In these troubled last days we gathered in twos and threes at the Biltmore Hotel headquarters; someone was always en route, we hoped with a message of cheer. I remembered Finnegan's charts, the wild applause, the reporters' refreshing edict that Americans don't split their tickets. Perhaps we could count on Senate and gubernatorial races—perhaps. Other less favorable omens came to mind: Tom Finletter's[11] caustic comment about "too many prima donnas" and Hy Raskin saying to Finnegan that last week: "We have an idea, try to sell it to Adlai—and Estes is the one who uses it."

Every campaign for the presidency has its final hoopla at Madison Square Garden. To some of us, the huge arena looked strangely empty in spots; Anna Rosenberg (former Assistant Secretary of Defense)[12] kept up a voodoo chant: "Let the crowd in." But no one came.

Explanations were offered by our New York managers: the TV cameras needed the space. Meanwhile, a friend showed me two-column newspaper ads listing the speakers and the time but *not* the place. Eleanor Roosevelt was right; New York pros did their best to sabotage Adlai.

That night I got the kind of lumps you can't swallow when Adlai stepped forward to introduce his three sons. If only, I said to myself, over and over, if only he had a wife. Not just for then but for the years ahead.

[11] Secretary of the Air Force, 1950–53; U. S. Ambassador to NATO, 1961.
[12] Mrs. Rosenberg was appointed to her post by President Harry Truman in December 1950 and served throughout his term.

Adlai's Parish

IN A POEM BY W. H. AUDEN, WRITTEN ON THE DEATH OF W. B. YEATS,
he catalogues all the human perils Yeats survived. Among these
Auden mentions "the parish of rich women." Yeats and Stevenson
were almost contemporaries, and certainly, in the Auden sense,
they had a common talent.

Of course, not all of them were rich, these hundreds and thousands of women who adored Adlai from near or from far. One day
in 1955 some of the press women gathered outside my office, waiting for Adlai. Liz Carpenter, then co-partner of the Carpenter
News Service, spoke of the effect he had on her: "Something comes
over me and I feel weak all over." Betty Beale, whose sharp pencil
records Washington's changing social panorama, remarked impatiently: "Where is he? Where is he staying? Why can't I ever have
him to myself?" A waiting aide added: "My wife is forever after
me: Can't I get to hold his hat or his coat?"

That same day I had a call from an exceedingly pretty neighbor,
one of the many shareholders in Adlai's corporate destiny: "For
heaven's sake, Katie, take those pencils and pads away from him!"
At noon Maxine Cheshire, the Washington *Post* columnist with
the gimlet eye, inquired about Adlai's gold watch and chain. Had
I noticed he seemed interwoven with it? How he fiddled with it?
What did it mean to him?[1]

Could one rob him of the pencils, watch chains, the doodling

---

[1] The gold watch and chain belonged to Governor Stevenson's grandfather.
He fiddled, as Maxine described it, with anything at hand.

space needed on great yellow-lined pads? Did they hide uncertainties? Wherever he went, there were always women: that very morning one had called to say she had a letter of his grandfather Stevenson's, Vice President under Grover Cleveland, and wanted to see him. When Adlai appeared, I told him of the call and added, "She did not sound like a crackpot." "She most certainly is not a crackpot," he replied. "She's very pretty, I'll see her." Bill Blair, standing by, grinned. "The Governor met her yesterday," he explained. One could envision them all, but still, Adlai seemed enormously alone.

Once he spoke to me of the house in Libertyville he loved so well: "It's very cold in winter; one needs either weather stripping or a wife."

He was transparent to those of us who cared for him, a man too many women longed for. Perhaps, came the nagging doubt, he liked it this way; their numbers gave him immunity from the one he might have loved. I wanted then to believe this "one" might still be found.

The nearer one came to the top, the more one recognized how formidable were those ladies who kept Adlai company over late suppers, cared for him over short weekends, answered his summons despite other plans. They kept watch over him, each in her own style. Some were objective, some were not. A few were selfless. The gracious grande dame of the selfless was Mrs. John Paul Welling of Chicago. Adlai came and went for many a season in Harriet Welling's Chippendale-lined brownstone on fashionable North Astor Street. His room was always ready, he had a house key. Adlai had long appreciated Harriet Welling's objectivity and her wisdom, served piping hot with his breakfast. She was quite content to talk about the "Guv's room," purring gently that no one else might ever occupy its premises. If you made your home in Lake Forest, as Adlai did, or lingered in Springfield when Governor, you needed a room reserved for you in Chicago. Harriet's good deeds (be they community, cultural, or political) were all accomplished in almost whispered anonymity.

Another selfless, long-term hostess and old friend was Washington-based Laura Magnuson, whose late husband was the great bone surgeon, Dr. Paul Magnuson. Laura had been in "Ad's" bridal party. They had been members of the same exclusive clubs, surviving to embrace the milling masses of politics. When Laura agreed to become a Stevenson delegate from the District of Columbia to the 1952 convention, some remarked amiably that she was the first elected representative of the nation's capital to ride around in a chauffeur-driven Bentley!

Other heroines of the selfless brigade were his devoted secretaries. They too adored him; although Carol Evans told me in 1960 (after almost twenty years) that she could not face another campaign. Soon afterward she resigned and moved away. Fortunately, Carol is now helping Professor Walter Johnson on the definitive collection of the Stevenson papers. At the UN there was Roxanne Eberlee,[2] who through the long strenuous nights and days of Adlai's tenure radiated serenity and devotion. And all the others who pampered and protected, hovered and helped.

Adlai's sister Buffie had his turn of phrase; she spoke of the line-a-day notebooks of her childhood "where you squeezed your soul into three lines a day." Grown-up Buffie was still squeezing her soul—pouring out her energies—into electing Adlai. When she let his name roll over her tongue it had a wonderfully splendid sound, like a fountain's splashing. She wore small hats and jade hatpins and scarves and her gestures were sudden and roomwide. Adlai once described her as "playing marchesa" at the extravagant villa in Florence which she and her husband Ernest rented every summer. Adlai was right. I had visited there; she played marchesa well, but then she walked on stage in this suitable role wherever she was.

There were aunts, too—shadowy, faded old ladies taken out of their frames in the first weeks of Adlai's 1952 campaign. Somewhat reluctantly they bore the anguish of public exposure, not so

2 Roxanne Eberlee worked with John Bartlow Martin, Adlai's official biographer.

much because of pride in their nephew as to prove him the exceptional grandson of his illustrious grandfather.[3] Adlai's gallery of
admirers extended on and on, through famous names like Barbara Ward (Lady Jackson, writer, economist, and formidable
speaker), Ruth Field (Mrs. Marshall Field), the late Alicia
Patterson (owner and publisher of *Newsday*), Mrs. Eugene Meyer
(whose name is synonymous with improved public education),
Mrs. Albert Lasker (art collector, beautifier of her native New
York and Washington), and the most renowned of all, the First
Lady of the World, as she was called, Eleanor Roosevelt.

Men frequently remark to me that Adlai seemed to be dominated by women. From what I observed, the Adlai admirers
counseled and advised, badgered perhaps, but dominated—never.
He had a curious, marvelously sleight-of-hand manner of absorbing
and dismissing them all at once. Certainly he could not have done
without them: was it true, I once asked him, that he had spoken
of Nancy "X" (since remarried) as number nine in the list of
favorites? He chuckled, and admitted he had. There were others,
beautiful, exquisitely turned out, and free, who got tired of waiting and married someone else.

Ever since that night in 1956 at Madison Square Garden, I had
not been able to erase the image of him as a lonely man. For four
years I had been trying to find the courage to tell him how I felt.
Ours was a friendship, I reasoned, that transcended the political
situation that first brought us together.

In the late spring of 1960, I found myself alone with Adlai in
his office in Chicago. I cannot remember how I led into the subject. Perhaps I just jumped in: "What I would wish for you is a
wife." He did not seem at all startled. He had, he confessed, given
the subject much thought. "After the campaigns, the frantic traveling, the continuous demands on one, I thought I would settle
down and try once again to live a family life. But things never do
quiet down. I wouldn't make much of a husband. I wouldn't even
be around much; I'd never be home."

[3] Adlai E. Stevenson, Vice President from March 1893 to March 1897.

I'm afraid I interrupted. "At our age," I said, "it isn't necessary to be much of anything."

He swiveled his chair, so that he was looking right at me. "I suppose you are right," he began. "At sixty, one no longer has to act as one used to." Suddenly his mood changed. "Have the women"—that foreign body I represented—"have they been talking about my not having a wife?"

Quite the contrary, I assured him. They liked him just as he was. Some of them, I jested, might tear me limb from limb if they knew I had suggested his marrying. We found ourselves joking, albeit sedately, about who "they" were. "You'd better send me a list," he warned me. I would, I promised, in the order of their importance. And then once again he became his serious, responsible, aloof self. "I suppose if by any chance I were to be nominated and elected, I would be bound to be lonely, very lonely."

The subject of marriage was never mentioned again, neither at this meeting nor at any other time. In later years he became a party-goer, a kind of grudging social butterfly—in Washington of the "in" set, in New York of the UN set, and world-wide, of the VIP set. But I never ceased to hope.

In the crucial summer of 1960, Agnes Meyer and Mrs. Eleanor Roosevelt, abetted by Mary Lasker, were laying plans for Adlai.

When the history of that convention is written, much of the credit must be given to these women who refused to give him up and, in turn, refused to let him relinquish his right to the nomination. I remember a pre-convention party given by Agnes Meyer, a lawn party at a posh estate in Pasadena for the privileged few. Adlai was late, as he often was, but like many of his seemingly political actions, his tardiness was accidental. He had not staged the entrance.

He seemed to come right out of the clouds. Everyone gasped happily, as if he had been released from some danger, some murderous threat to their hopes. I shook his hand. "Think of it," he reported breathlessly, "five thousand people waiting at the airport in that sun for three hours." One could hear him inhaling the adulation of the crowd.

Standing aside, I watched the faces of his sponsors. Mrs. Roosevelt wore a contented look. Mary Lasker had a sweet manner that belied her iron will. The expression of Mrs. Meyer was one of bemused accomplishment. She had said to me earlier that spring, "If Adlai does not make it, I'm for Jack—I can help him. My stand against aid for parochial schools is well known, so I can talk about Catholic prejudice and put it in its place."

The Adlai elite were all present: names like Barry and Mary Bingham, Gay[4] and Tom Finletter,[5] Willard Wirtz, Bill Blair, Senator and Mrs. Mike Monroney,[6] Tom Finney and John Sharon,[7] Jane Dick, Marietta Tree, Harriet Welling, Lucretia Grady,[8] Nan McEvoy,[9] Joe Clark[10] and Genevieve Blatt,[11] Phil and Kay Graham, daughter and son-in-law of the hostess, and all their cohorts. Kenneth Galbraith and Arthur Schlesinger, however, had already pledged themselves to Kennedy.[12]

Talking with Gay Finletter, I found myself defending Jack Kennedy. Daisy Harriman suddenly challenged me: "You are for him. You always have been. Don't you realize we only get an Adlai Stevenson once every fifty years?"

[4] Writer, daughter of Walter Damrosch, the conductor. Deceased December 1969.

[5] Finletter was Secretary of the Air Force, 1950–53, U. S. Ambassador to NATO, 1961.

[6] Senator Monroney of Oklahoma was the only elected official to campaign openly for Stevenson.

[7] Tom Finney coordinated the Draft Stevenson movement and John Sharon helped search out delegates; both are young Washington lawyers.

[8] Mrs. Lucretia Grady, grande dame of California delegates.

[9] Of the San Francisco *Chronicle*.

[10] Senator from Pennsylvania.

[11] Political leader of Pennsylvania.

[12] Mrs. Roosevelt, angered by a letter from Schlesinger and Galbraith defining their support of Kennedy, made a rousing speech at a California caucus held by Governor Brown that same evening. A prepared release announcing that California would support Kennedy had to be destroyed when, after Mrs. Roosevelt's speech, the vote for Stevenson defeated the Kennedy delegates by two.

Was Daisy's accusation a fair one? I was concerned lest Adlai be
hurt by permitting his name to be put in nomination for the third
time. Over the years I had become convinced that he never ceased
to care for public life, that he wanted more than anything else, as
do all men who have put their hats in the ring, to become President. But he had no appetite for the political machinations that
might take him to the White House. One could not help retaining
an enduring admiration and affection for this man—wanting to
calm him, to restore what had been rubbed so thin by being in the
public eye. One wanted to tell him that he had given so much,
there would now be a kind of nobility in giving way to someone
else, and there were too many holes in his political shoes.

During the winter of 1959–60, everyone's doubts took different
forms. Adlai had some of his own.

He wrote me:

> Do you—very frankly—think I can with dignity and propriety de-
> cline to come to the dinner (Democratic National Committee
> fund raiser) in January? It is almost more than I can face what
> with the burden of work and getting off on a long journey to
> South America. I would welcome candid counsel.
>
> Yours,
> Adlai

The way to overcome his reluctance, I knew from experience,
was to agree that his excuses were valid and his presence was not
really essential. True, some of his admirers might stay away, the
receipts might dwindle, I told him by telephone. I named names:
"these and those" might absent themselves. "Do you really think
so?" He sounded genuinely surprised. His naïveté was always very
close to the surface and convincing. He had thought of coming but
not speaking at all. We debated this proposal; he might take over
former President Truman's role as master of ceremonies. He gave
what stage directions call a short laugh. "Or I could come and
give the benediction."

Each time he seemed inclined to reconsider, I tried driving

through his doubts with pro-attendance arguments: "If you really want to remove yourself from consideration—" I began. He interrupted: "If I kept out of politics, out of the limelight, and let events take their course—" He repeated this political fable in different forms: "I just thought if I were as obscure as possible . . . You know, I've become a political fatalist. If it happens [his nomination], then it will have to be endured." Had he thought, I inquired, of pointing to someone else, coming out for another candidate? He pretended not to hear me and described yet another subterfuge. "I could plead ill health, say my health just could not stand it."

Once I had hung up, I asked myself, "What did he mean by a political fatalist?" The only conclusion I could draw was that he would let himself be drafted. He came to the dinner.

I learned later that Adlai had upbraided Bill Blair for taking rooms in Los Angeles. "I am not even going to the convention," Adlai had protested. Bill had paid him no heed and gone right ahead with his plans.

When Adlai next came to Washington I went to see him. Bill, who was on hand to greet me, told me he believed Jack Kennedy could beat Nixon.[13] He did not think the "Governor" (as he called Adlai) could, and he added, "I'm not sure he should run for a third time."

"What does Adlai think?" I asked. Bill wasn't sure.

"Does he want to run?" I persisted. Bill doubted that he did.

When I walked in, I handed Adlai a copy of Agnes Meyer's speech given the previous week at the Woman's National Democratic Club. We agreed that it was a superior document and he insisted I tell her he thought so.

"She's inordinately vain, but then aren't we all?" he said, precisely as he meant it, humanly and with humor. It pleased him, this world in which a few could admit to being inordinately vain.

[13] In December of 1959, Bill Blair prophesied that the ticket would be Kennedy-Johnson.

He chuckled: I recognized that possessive laughter as an indication of his fondness for Agnes Meyer.

Every now and then I reminded Adlai of my gratitude: how much I had relished the opportunity he had afforded me.

"I must say you seem to enjoy it," he said, making a half turn on his chair and looking at me approvingly. "Although for the life of me, I can't see how you do it. It takes so much patience, so much fortitude . . ."

He twirled the watch chain. How were finances? How was the debt?

I gave him what information I could: the campaign debt was about half paid off.

"What I really want to talk to you about," I began again, "are the issues. How can we win this next election?"

Immediately he struck an attitude; he revolved on me with a small speech.

"One: we must tell, convey in simple words, exactly how we come out of this session of Congress, despite this nest of snakes from Wayne Morse to Harry Byrd. Two: we must remind the people that all the virtuous things President Eisenhower and Vice President Nixon are doing and saying have been said by us before them."

He gave as an example the speech that he had written for President Eisenhower in 1957, on centralization of our economic efforts with our Allies. The President did not use it then, but now it appeared in the State of the Union message. As for Nixon, "We must give constant attention to the fact that character, in a President, is most important. The presidency has nothing to do with efficiency."

He concluded with a brilliant summation of our institutions: "They can survive only as long as they command respect."

The "parish" of his feminine admirers kept growing. And he continued to delight and manage them. As I walked out into the sunshine after that visit, I tallied up my unanswered questions.

Was Adlai really a political animal, or just a gifted citizen, a writer, orator, thinker but not a rough infighter?

Did he really want to run? Would he be lofty, as he had been before? How could he win?

Some weeks later I ran through my doubts with George Ball. "Don't you know what Adlai's waiting for?" He stared me down. "He's waiting to be raped."

In early June of 1960, I had been a member of a traveling platform committee. We were on the road to learn from citizens' groups how they felt about the issues. At breakfast with Senator Joe Clark in St. Louis, we talked of Adlai. I was on my way to Chicago to visit with him.

"Ask him," Joe said, "if he'll come out and admit he'll accept a draft. Ask him if he'll give people like Mike Monroney, George Ball, Mrs. Roosevelt, Agnes Meyer, and me something to go on."

It was a lovely warm blowy day in Chicago when I went to Adlai's office to talk about these matters. I sat facing him, the strong hot sun between us. Out the window I could see a vague blue, and knew it was forty-three stories down, and there were boats.

Adlai had on a gray suit, striped shirt, pale blue tie which matched his eyes . . . looking, as always, fit, clean, exuding a kind of unobtrusive masculinity. The magic of him enveloped me.

"What are you going to do?" I put the question.

"What I've been doing," came the quick reply. He would not come out for anyone, nor would he be part of any "Stop Kennedy" movement.

What was it Joe Clark had suggested? I repeated: "You must come out and say you would accept a draft."

Yes, he had been pressured by Senator Humphrey and former Senator Bill Benton to do just that. They wanted to start a "Draft Adlai" movement.

"They can," he nodded, "provided I am not connected or involved."

What would he tell the press? "Naturally I will accept. I'm draftable."

I spoke of the convention floor. How could he handle the maneuvering? Would he have any pledged delegates? I tried to point out the practical realities. How would they manage his nomination?

He kept saying, "I don't know."

Then he leaned back and sought a phrase: "I'm like the French general who said, *'J'y suis et j'y reste.'* I don't want to do anything: I can't say this often enough. The most important thing is to beat the Republicans."

He would, of course, support Jack Kennedy or Stuart Symington[14] or Lyndon Johnson, though he worried over Stuart's preoccupation with weapons and defense.

I reported that Mayor Robert Wagner had told the press in St. Louis that New York county leaders were ready to come out for Jack. Adlai looked astonished.

"What kind of President do you think Jack would make?" I inquired.

He replied, "I have only one reservation: no one can be in that office and lack humility."

He did not know any of the people around Jack, except his brother Bob, "and I want no part of him."

I mentioned Ted Sorensen favorably but Adlai was not listening. "Jack would undoubtedly throw himself into the job. He has lots of ambition but no training."

Then he asked, "Has he vote-getting ability?"

"Very much so."

"If Jack were to be nominated and elected I would not want to be beholden to him. If I were to serve in his Administration, I would want to do so because my strength was such that Jack would recognize me because of my position."

If he saw the convention turning into a shambles, he would

[14] Senator Symington has since turned dove.

step in and act—but he never spelled out what he meant by this.

We were edging away from the subject, rambling on about the convention, about who would do what, when Bill Wirtz, his partner, came in. I teased Bill later about being a bouncer. But I knew I had more than stayed out my time. That was the trouble with Adlai, it was always difficult to leave him.

Afterward it occurred to me that Adlai's consent to his own nomination might also have been motivated by a desire to impress Jack Kennedy with his political strength. Perhaps he wanted to show the TV audience, as well, the latent power he possessed. The tumult he caused certainly did not go unnoticed.

Senator Monroney of Oklahoma master-minded the Stevenson supporters' convention strategy. Mike Monroney's and Adlai Stevenson's friendship was long-standing and completely free from any political motivation. Some years later Mike was to say to me, "I'm a champion of lost causes. Adlai never had a chance against Ike. He had to make this try—this was his real chance to be President."

In another post-mortem session I asked Senator Eugene McCarthy (who nominated him) whether Adlai could have beaten Nixon. "Yes, but he would have had to make up his mind to announce the winner before the convention and carry on an active campaign for delegates." Of the earlier attempts Adlai had made, Senator McCarthy believed he "came at the wrong time; the country was in the grip of anti-Communism, suspicion, and an unresolved war they disliked [1952]." Besides, "no one can run against a national hero."

Both Senators agreed that Stevenson could not have disappointed the young people who came clear across the country to see him nominated. Later, Senator McCarthy observed that they had resembled his own 1968 supporters: "They slept in sleeping bags in a dreadful barnlike structure that wasn't nearly big enough. I can remember how Adlai felt when he had to tell the kids to go home."

Senator Monroney spoke of Adlai's attempts to withdraw. "We held his feet to the fire. At one point he was ready to capitulate and nominate JFK. He couldn't understand why we would not let him." Part of Senator Monroney's strategy was based on his conviction that there would be a second ballot; that neither Kennedy, Johnson, nor Symington would make it on the first round. By talking this way, he prompted the intensive first-ballot push the Kennedy supporters made.

The Treasurer of the Democratic National Committee, Matthew McCloskey, gave me a stirring postconvention account of a 3:00 A.M. call he and Governor Dave Lawrence (a long-time Stevenson man and undisputed leader of the Pennsylvania delegation) paid on Adlai. Both men tried, successfully they thought, to persuade Adlai that he must withdraw, call off his backers, and nominate Jack Kennedy. (The Pennsylvania and Illinois delegations had both declared for Kennedy on Monday, July 11, the first day of the convention.) They told Adlai he was the most popular man in the Democratic Party, if not in the whole country, but that he could only hurt himself by letting his name be placed in nomination. Besides, they warned, he would get only a handful of delegates. He agreed. But in the morning his most obdurate backers reversed him.

Any convention is as full of tensions as it is delegates, signs, noise, and confusion. Los Angeles in 1960 was no exception. The supporters of Majority Leader Lyndon B. Johnson and Senator Stuart Symington knew that, though they had been deferentially treated, they were not Paul Butler's favorites. He was an out-and-out Kennedy man.

Adlai's intentions (for he had not announced) were much discussed. He remained in seclusion in his bungalow at the Beverly Hills Hotel.

It took a long time for rumors, busses, cabs, and convoys to reach the Los Angeles stadium. My telephone, however, in that steaming preconvention week, brought me all the news I needed to know. Libby Smith,[15] California National Committeewoman and a strong Kennedy supporter, had forewarned me. She would have no trouble getting the men among Adlai's supporters to switch to Kennedy, but the women, she sighed, might never come unstuck.

The night the convention opened, when any VIP made an unexpected entrance or exit, the hall went berserk. I shall never forget Mrs. Eleanor Roosevelt's entrance during the keynote speech of Governor LeRoy Collins. When quiet had been restored, Governor Collins quickly concluded his remarks. Sitting down beside me, he muttered in desolate tones, "I worked on that speech for *six months*." The TV audience, I reassured him, had probably paid less attention to the drama and more to his words. I hoped I was right.

Tuesday night Adlai made his entrance in the middle of a speech by Chester Bowles (former Governor of Connecticut). I heard Bowles gasp; there was a rush of air down his gullet very much like the last breath a man takes before drowning.

The hordes struggling to bring Adlai to the platform resembled a gallows-bound procession. I saw forests of walkie-talkie antennas and beneath them an unswerving coagulation of human beings. The real struggle took place at the foot of the platform, where uniformed security police formed a cordon and refused, inch by inch, and human by human, to let anyone pass.

Behind me, radio and network representatives began screaming at me: "Which is Daley?" As an escort for Adlai, Daley was extremely visible, but not yet a familiar face. Finally Adlai emerged.

When he reached the platform and moved to speak, no one had to tell the crowd to be still. His single eloquent comment sums up so much of Adlai—his wit, his endearing ability to laugh at himself: "I now know who this convention will nominate. It will be the last survivor."

During a break I searched backstage for Senator McCarthy. I

[15] Mrs. Elizabeth Smith Gatov, a gifted politician, was appointed U. S. Treasurer by President Kennedy.

found him surrounded by Stevenson supporters in what was unhappily known as the "ready room." Did he have a text? I asked him. I know it was a foolish question; Gene McCarthy preferred to give his superb speeches from notes. He had typed the speech, he told me, while waiting in the Stevenson headquarters trailer. The press had insisted on a text, but he actually spoke from notes. Afterward, we compared his words with typed copies given the press corps; they were nearly identical.

The words that most moved the convention audience were: "Do not turn away from this man. Do not reject this man. Do not reject this man who, his enemies said, spoke above the heads of the people, but they said it only because they did not want the people to listen. He spoke to the people. He moved their minds and stirred their hearts, and this was what was objected to. Do not leave this prophet without honor in his own party. Do not reject this man."

Senator Herbert Lehman of New York seconded Adlai's nomination.[16] Senator Monroney, meanwhile, had signaled me. He wanted a ruling on whether a non-delegate could nominate, namely, Mrs. Roosevelt. The parliamentarian certified that she could.

After all the nominations had been made and all the votes tabulated, the count for Adlai was 79½.[17] Kennedy's total was 809, Johnson's 409, and Symington's 86. I have a vivid recollection of Joe Alsop standing on the desk and shouting; "Katie, Katie, what are we waiting for?" Tallying the obvious Kennedy victory did seem superfluous, but the rules required it. James Reston wrote: "In 1952 he [Adlai] did not want to be drafted and was. In 1960 he wanted to be drafted and was not."

From there on we were done, candidate-wise. There remained but the televised night of acceptance speeches. I had come with

[16] Other seconders were Lieutenant Governor Glenn Anderson of California and Lieutenant Governor Wilson Wyatt of Kentucky.

[17] These were mainly from the following states: California (31½), Colorado (5½), Hawaii (3½), Nevada (6½), Montana (2½), Washington (6½), and West Virginia (3).

Congresswoman Edith Green of Portland, Oregon, and lost her in
the attendant confusion. Leaving, I found myself in a small tor-
nado behind Adlai. A very perspiring and red-faced young man
appeared from nowhere. He was in shirt sleeves, carrying a flag
which he kept trying to hand to Adlai, murmuring, "Governor,
here it is. This is the flag—" A push sent him flying backward.
Bill and Mike Monroney formed a safety belt to keep me from
going down on my knees. We advanced, we retreated. All through
this extraordinary disorder Adlai remained serene and confident.
We surged forward or fell back to the shouts of "Governor, Governor, take my hand," or "Adlai, Adlai, let me take your hand, let
me tell you, touch you—"

By the time we reached a large black limousine in which sat a
cool, calm Mary Lasker, I was terrified. Someone pushed me into
the waiting limousine. Bill Wirtz followed me. As soon as the
door had shut on us—Adlai and Mary and I on the back seat,
Bill Wirtz and Mike on the jump seats—the crowd began rocking
the car. Adlai calmly ordered the windows opened and began shaking hands. He was very much in command; he jested, he laughed,
and the crowd responded. These were adoring people, they had
no intention of harming him. Their behavior, however, reminded
me of wild animals playing with their victim before they devour it.

We finally got away. Who was the boy with the flag? Adlai inquired. He may have been part of a fife and drum corps that
paraded while we were waiting for the TV time to roll on: they
appeared just as he got up to speak.

A great many well-intentioned, gifted, and persuasive people
had held fast to Adlai. Back in Washington, Scotty Reston asked
me, "What will happen to those intellectual liberals and those
intelligent women who were persuaded Adlai was the only answer?" "They will go to dinner with you and talk about their
cause," I replied. And added, astonished at my unabashed cynicism, "This was one of their objectives all along."

He Was Always Vulnerable

HARRY MCPHERSON, THEN SPECIAL COUNSEL TO PRESIDENT JOHNSON, turned to me: "You must have known Adlai well."

"No one knew Adlai well," I replied.

We were cruising on the *Honey Fitz*. I rose and left the breeze in the bow and walked back to the depopulated stern. Why did we always add and substract Adlai as if he were a column of figures? Because nobody in public life really knows anyone else well and we were constantly working out new sums to prove our theories about him correct.

Because he captivated us, because he was so generously human, because he was always vulnerable, as I tried to say in the poem I wrote:

IN MEMORY OF A.E.S.

He was always vulnerable.
So incandescently human,
seduced by reason and delight,
awed by history's harsh commands
to be keeper of our conscience,
he made temples of his prose
where the discomforted might hope.
He held humility as high
as most hold pride: he could not hide
his hurt, his doubts, his loneliness,

and yet he leaves a legacy
of larger loneliness for all
who waited in the heat-brimmed noon
or on cold corners for his voice,
the quick smile in surprised blue eyes.
Gathered into his grand design
were all their little dread days doom,
his heart was bigger than his time.

Perhaps because of his heritage he worshiped history and its dignity and pomp. He held high the duty to serve. Even our constant criticisms—like his failings, often petty—recognized that fate had not been kind. First, the Smiling General, then the young God whom some thought Apollo, others Zeus, stood in his path. Then there was President Johnson, from whom Adlai tended to isolate himself. They respected each other but spoke a different political language.

He was always too thin-skinned. I recall the time he and I walked through O'Hare Airport when a man stood in our path. "How are you, Governor?" He held out a hand which Adlai reluctantly shook. "And how's Alger Hiss?" the man asked, snarling. Adlai's expression as we walked away was horrified. He suffered as if the man had struck him.

"How did you learn to get along with people?" he once asked, as if this were a rare talent. We were in Chicago in 1956 for a pre-convention meeting of the Executive Committee. At cocktail time I felt a pull on my arm. "Katie," Adlai startled me, "come with me to Harriet Welling's, then we'll have dinner." I murmured excuses: my plane was due to leave in an hour. Later, a word from Hy Raskin encouraged me to reconsider. It was too late for the Wellings. Adlai suggested we go straight to Libertyville.

A friend at the party noted our exit. "This looks bad," he quipped. "It's worse than you think!" Adlai returned, hurrying me out the door.

As we climbed into a taxi, the lid flew off my hatbox. I was relieved that the graham crackers did not fall out.

First, Adlai and I went to the wrong parking lot. Then he produced the wrong keys for the car door. He was never well organized.

En route at last, he pointed out Chicago landmarks. "That one," he said as we passed a gray stone building of the late nineties, "that one belongs to my wife. What anguish she causes." He made what was for him a grimace; his face disappeared behind a frightening mask.

We moved safely from the unreality of the past to the demands of the political present. Was foreign policy an issue? They told him people didn't really care about that. They were correct. Wasn't the issue big business and leadership responsibility? he wanted to know. "To tell the truth," I told him, "the battle is three quarters the candidate. His personality." "Really?" He sounded hurt. In 1956 "charisma" had not yet entered the political vocabulary but I sensed its power.

We wound on and off highways toward Libertyville; the countryside emerged in sweet smells and splashing colors. "What about Truman?" Adlai offered. He had never seemed to get on the right foot with the man from Independence. "Ex-Presidents require constant attention," I replied. "But I give him that," Adlai protested. (Friends of Adlai would rehash the reasons for Truman's dislike. Why did Truman feel such disdain? The answer was simple: they were completely incompatible. Adlai lacked the vibrant cockiness that Harry Truman exuded. And Truman had little patience with Adlai's semantically resolved decisions.)

As we turned into the gravel drive of this home he loved, the stillness of a hot July evening mingled with the stillness of fields and trees and space, and refreshed one. The white clapboard house fitted the landscape, giving forth a peaceful attuned air.

It turned out to be larger than it looked. A comfortable living room, Adlai's study, and a sizable dining room were surrounded on the south by a long screened porch, a very white, cool place, looking out on the tennis court and some large elms that interrupted the slope on its way to the Des Plaines River. Sheep kept the grass cropped. If we walked to the river, Adlai informed me, we might just see a large blue heron rising on its wide wings and taking off fast. Instead, we settled for a tour of the house.

The living room held a piano, a sofa, and lots of comfortable chairs, and the right number of tables with inconspicuous lamps on them. All of it looked very lived-in, even to the casual clutter of magazines and probably unread books. The study featured bookcases along one whole wall, a big desk, and an air of brownness, not gloomy, just browsy. In the dining room there were two large windows facing west; our timing was perfect—we caught the full splash of sunset in the glossy wood on the refectory table, on the blue and white dishes displayed in open shelves.

Down in a basement rumpus room Adlai kept all his trophies and gifts from round the world. Mrs. Welling had told me of his habit of giving away these gifts, in turn, at Christmas. One year, however, he brought her a lovely scarf from Benares which inspired her to include in her thanks a compliment for his shopping assistant. To her dismay she found she had offended him: he had picked out the scarf himself.

That evening, sitting on the lawn, we talked above the music of crickets. He asked what I thought of his taking a flying trip to the Soviet Union, stopping in Poland, perhaps in West Germany, to find out what people were thinking. I was not enthusiastic. I thought it far better for him to stay home and talk to farmers, labor unions, veterans' groups, small business, etc. We agreed the farm vote was unpredictable. He wondered if I was preparing to counter the growing Republicanism in the burgeoning suburbs, and if the unions would succeed in involving members' wives in political action.

We moved our chairs across the lawn to view the moon and our subject from politics to historic symbols. He had already shown me his remarkable Lincoln memorabilia. Now he described the dozens of Indian heads that were found on his seventy-two acres. One could take a canoe, he told me, and, starting from the Des

Plaines River that edged the property, paddle right down to the Gulf of Mexico.

Suddenly he said solemnly, "Why, I ask myself, am I doing this?" Every now and then the fraud and the hypocrisy became so apparent—"telling people what they want to hear." I answered that a certain amount of fraud was to be found in everything one did. Adlai sighed, "I'm afraid I'm not as cynical as you."

I remembered his telling me en route to Libertyville that he had lost the couple he had for eighteen years and now the current couple were leaving. "The man drinks. It's a wonder there was anything to eat in the house," he ended, and then let out a laughing sigh: "Some days I think I'll marry the next woman I meet."

The next morning I heard the calls he made to employment bureaus and the long-distance arrangements he completed for a trip for one of his sons. There was a sense of sadness, of having left him adrift, like a boat off its mooring. How much easier *not* to be a front runner. Poor AES and poor U.S.A.! His eloquence had almost isolated him. He had been hurt in his eagerness. He was never, however, either solitary or sad—nor would he have wanted anyone to be gloomy about him. His ready wit held us all enthralled; we waited at close attention lest we miss a quip, an impromptu riposte we might repeat.

This happened to me one morning as we landed at Washington at 3:00 A.M. Adlai paused to give my daughter Judy a welcoming kiss. "Look at your mother," he said, "still on her feet. We'll make a politician of her yet."

We were forever having Washington meetings which Adlai felt obliged to attend. Once, on a lunch break, I carted him off to our house for an impromptu meal. When I apologized for the staple political menu (chicken was the feature), he assured me, "But that's why I went into politics, because I love chicken!"

His political barbs, no matter what, stayed sunny. At a Women's National Press Club dinner in 1962 he was asked about Romney. "He's a fine eighteenth-century painter," came the fast rejoinder. "What about Romney as presidential timber?" the questioner persisted. "I'd have thought they would want at least a nineteenth-century man," Adlai replied. Speaking of the United Nations, his present career base, faults and all, he compared it to Eve hesitating when Adam proposed. "What's the trouble," Adam inquired, "is there someone else?"

In 1960 I wangled a seat to hear him on a panel before hundreds of editors, along with Hugh Gaitskell, leader of the British Labour Party and Mike (Lester) Pearson, head of the Canadian Liberal Party. Both were then out of power. Mike and I had worked together during the war, and I knew Hugh Gaitskell. The real reason for going, however, was Adlai. He did not disappoint me. He explained to the audience that his plane had been delayed at the airport by ceremonies welcoming President de Gaulle. "It's a curious thing," he commented, "how often some national hero seems to be in my way!"

Defeat became Adlai, a paradox only he could make plausible. In the sixties he could still refresh himself with the elixir of public acclaim. Why had I ever thought he needed anyone, least of all a wife? If he had married again, he would have had to pay attention to someone else.

He was idolized everywhere, even abroad. One summer morning in Rome I was standing in front of the Excelsior waiting for Walter—looking, I am certain, like all other American tourists. "What are you staring at, Katie?" called a man who sounded like—and was—Adlai. Immediately, a strange American rushed out of the lobby. "It is, it is!" he shouted back to wives, cousins, and aunts.

Finally, after Walter and I had disengaged Adlai from the group, the three of us set out for an art gallery. Every step or two a woman would espalier herself around Adlai. Italians gawked and shook hands, but Americans—tourists, Fulbright students—totally submerged him. He was jubilant. "I'll bet they aren't even contributors," Walter commented acidly. "What are you going to do about all these people who want only you as President?" I teased him (it was 1959). "Run for office *here!*" he exclaimed.

At the end of day I wrote home: "My meeting with Adlai . . .

leaves me convinced the reluctant dragon is about to get a pedicure, the better to drag his talons."

In July of 1962 I ran a seminar for hundreds of summer internees at the request of the White House. The meetings took place in Constitution Hall. Just coincidentally, it was the hottest day of the summer and the hall was not then air-conditioned. Flocks of young people who had flung off their coats and loosened their ties hung from the balconies. Seats even had to be provided on the stage.

At 9:30 A.M. I met Adlai at the airport. He looked, I told him, like a Princeton undergraduate. A soft turned-down leghorn shaded his bright blue striped tie and brighter blue eyes. He asked all the necessary questions about the audience. As usual, he paid no attention to the answers.

When I introduced him, he walked on to a standing chant of cheers. "Makes me think I ought to make my acceptance speech," he said, giving the young a chance to roar all over again.

We told Adlai to take thirty minutes. After fifty-five minutes I stood beside him murmuring through the continuous outbreaks of applause: "You can see what time it is by that big clock opposite. You're the one with the schedule."

He answered a few questions, then hurried out, followed by the usual retinue. Adlai wanted to see the DAR Illinois Room,[1] and his grandmother's and great-aunt's portraits. We raced through corridors and by portraits on the double. As he stepped into the waiting limousine, up came Mary McGrory.[2] "Get in, dear," he invited, and she did. It was all as if time stood still and we were about to take off in his plane for the next stop and the next campaign speech.

The last time I ever saw Adlai was at a dance at the Carlton Hotel, given by columnists Joe Kraft and Tom Wicker and their wives, in May of 1965.

The whole point of such a celebrity-jammed party is to make each guest wonder whether he has seen or has been seen by every

---

[1] Daughters of the American Revolution.
[2] Mary McGrory, syndicated columnist.

other guest. So, you meet, greet, part. These conditions suited Adlai perfectly.

I had a hard time getting Adlai to sit down, but he finally did —at our table. He kept wishing for drinks, or excuses to escape, and we furnished the former. Finally settling down, he talked about the last ten days—when he had been defending the U.S. role in the Dominican Republic. He found our position unpleasant, distasteful: we should not have gone in without consulting the OAS. "After all, if you make international agreements, or if you subscribe to international codes, you should abide by them."

Adlai was never stuffy no matter how many worshipers crowded round his table. Unlike some public figures, he did not have a public and a private manner. Nor was he ever rank-conscious. When Arthur Goldberg stepped off the Supreme Court to replace Adlai, he insisted on a full-dress ambassadorial suite with his name in large letters over the door. Adlai never thought about status or the perquisites due him. He worked in a small office hidden behind the more impressive quarters of others.

I did not go to the funeral services, but I did attend the UN memorial gathering. The words were worthy but the master word spinner was no longer with us. Sitting there in the anonymous hall so typical of our stress on magnificent meeting places, I thought of Adlai's quite special quality; the very rooms he spoke in would seem to be listening—every object, light, dark, round, flat, sharp, or soft, became aware. But perhaps he would have forgiven us these earnest proclamations; they had the very remoteness he had when he talked about himself. He always made it sound as if it were someone else.

On the way out, a friend not remotely connected with that disreputable profession known as politics, stopped me: "We needed Adlai's voice. He should have been with us another twenty years." I knew what she meant; he was the keeper of the public conscience at a time when people were ready to relax, forgive the McCarthyites, and forget the war. They wanted moderation and the General with the marvelous smile—not someone who forced them to discuss the need for an atomic test ban treaty, the elimination of the draft, or precautionary measures on the Israeli-Arab border that might have averted Suez and the subsequent forays.

He would never have become an elder soothsayer. He might even have remained happy with a slight touch of Olympus in the background. The constant stream of famous callers at Libertyville would have continued. But with his sudden fall onto an English pavement, he did have an end suitable for a hero, an unforgettable topple that school children will have no trouble remembering.

Political success demands a ruthlessness I do not believe Adlai could or would have wanted to acquire. He was too cerebral, too independent. I find myself listing the minuses in whispers. And contradicting them at once with a plus. This was the man the Illinois bosses (in 1948) chose as their gubernatorial candidate because they (mistakenly) believed they could control him. (They had exiled Paul Douglas to the Senate because they knew they couldn't handle *him*). But Adlai fooled them; he turned out to be a passionate reformer, a man no one could control. In 1952 he shocked us all when he refused to receive Congressman Tad Walter of Pennsylvania on his campaign train because he was the co-author of the McCarran-Walter Act. That particular display of righteousness cost him dear in terms of votes. In 1956 no one could stop Adlai from taking unpopular stands on issues he felt strongly about, such as the draft and disarmament.

What about his famous inability to make up his mind? His terrible need to confer, I venture a guess, might have disappeared with the access of power the White House affords. Had he felt the need to confer, he would have had access to the talented men he had acquired, or sequestered.[3]

The odds, in the sixties, as we lived to see, would have been

[3] Many of Adlai's entourage went on to become able tough-minded public servants: his law partners Willard Wirtz (Secretary of Labor) and Newton Minow (Chairman, Federal Communications Commission); men like George Ball (Under Secretary of State), William McCormick Blair, Jr. (Ambassador to Denmark, the Philippines), Carl McGowan (Judge, U. S. Court of Appeals), J. Edward Day (Postmaster General), etc.

against him: superhuman hostilities, racial conflict, the terrible problems of power, Vietnam, disaffected youth, plus the advent of the image makers (Adlai on television batted a smash, a flop in almost predictable succession). He would have semanticized over the problems, and his effect upon a Congress he never really understood would have shackled his words and thwarted his solutions.

As Secretary of State for President Kennedy, he would have been sure, certain, confident of the diplomatic skills he possessed, skills which were wasted at the UN. But his stubborn unwillingness to read the political facts of life correctly (and to outargue his devoted mentors at the 1960 convention) swindled him out of that superbly suitable post.

His decision to let himself be nominated was an act of pure political hara-kiri. Of the tense Monday-Tuesday first-ballot struggle in Los Angeles, a Kennedy intimate had said to me, "At that time Adlai could have had anything he wanted—Secretary of State, anything—if he had come out for Jack."

In the 1960 Kennedy campaign we were both speaking at the Hotel Bellevue Stratford in Philadelphia on different floors and to different audiences. I found Adlai behind stage rewriting as passionately as if it were his campaign and he were the candidate fighting for the White House. It was painful, this recollection of him bending over papers with pencil in hand, oblivious to the audience waiting for his glance, his autograph, his handshake across the banquet cloth. With time racing past, the typists would stand by like runners, clutching the white sheets as they came fluttering off his desk, and running them to the machines. Thus it would always be. But the finished version would be vastly superior to the various drafts and his delivery almost prophetic, the cadences falling over the audience, exhilarating them with the hurled virtuosity of his oratory.

Professor Walter Johnson, one of the earliest Stevenson men, came regularly to the nation's capital to attend various meetings. We talked frequently of Adlai. Did I have any letters to give him? Professor Johnson had been appointed official editor of Adlai's papers. I promised to look through my files but found very little of more than routine interest. When I reported this lack, he spoke to me of those female friends of Adlai's who would not give up their letters. He pleaded with them, but to no avail; he assured them they could remove any personal comments or references of private concern. One lovely creature showed him a whole suitcase full of letters and then changed her mind. Another would not even see him. And so it went; these were the women who owned a share of Adlai's destiny.

Speaking of one of the many serious contenders for Adlai's attention, a friend of his remarked: "She's happier now that Adlai is dead. She doesn't have to share him with anyone."

No defeated candidate ever held his following for as long as Adlai did. No matter what, they never wavered, male or female, rich, middle class, or poor.

All the touters of his felicitous phrases, who built him up and in turn tried him and found him guilty—they too never lost their susceptibility. "You can't be a virgin twice," they said in 1956, and in the next breath sent up speech lines they had liked, jokes they wanted retold.

In the end, one must rate him a happy man. He could admire himself in history's glass: he had fulfilled a great need for honesty and eloquence; wasn't that enough?

Leonard and Adele Scofield,
parents of baby Kathleen,
aged two.

Katie Louchheim, Public Affairs Officer, UNRRA (United Nations Relief and Rehabilitation Administration), touring Displaced Persons Camps, U.S. Zone, Germany (1945).

Daisy (Mrs. J. Borden) Harriman, Democratic National Committeewoman of the District of Columbia, and her alternate, Katie Louchheim, at the 1952 Democratic Convention, Chicago.

Mrs. Franklin D. Roosevelt, speaker at Democratic women's Conference, with the Vice Chairman, Mrs. Louchheim (1958).

Author arrives in Portland, Oregon (October 1954), to campaign for Mrs. Edith Green, then a first-time candidate for the Third Congressional District, now a veteran of eight terms in the Congress.

(Above) With Vice Presidential candidate Estes Kefauver and Presidential candidate Adlai Stevenson in August 1956. (At right) Displaying a hatful of dollar bills to candidate Stevenson, Kansas City (1956). (Below) Getting the problem to the listener, aboard the Joe Smith Express, the Stevenson plane (1956).

Senator Stuart Symington of Missouri and the author enjoying a quip of President Truman's at a fund-raising dinner for the Democratic National Committee in Washington, D.C. (January 1960).

Flanked by Senators Humphrey and Kennedy at the Women's National Press Club dinner for the Congress in January 1960.

Mrs. G. Mennen Williams, wife of the Governor of Michigan, and Senate wives Mrs. Stuart Symington, Mrs. Hubert Humphrey and Mrs. Lyndon Johnson (wife of the Majority Leader) had "Coffee with Katie" at the Democratic National Convention in July 1960.

Being introduced by keynoter Senator Frank Church of Idaho to the 1960 Democratic National Convention.

As Deputy Assistant Secretary of State, I held a weekly staff meeting.

The Federal Woman's Award winners of 1963 called on President Kennedy: l. to r., Author; Bessie Margolin, Associate Solicitor, Department of Labor; Dr. Eleanor L. Makel, Supervisory Medical Officer, Department of Health, Education and Welfare; Verna C. Mohagen, Director of Personnel, Soil Conservation, Department of Agriculture; the President; Mrs. Blanche Noyes, Air Marking Specialist, Federal Aviation Agency; Miss Eleanor C. Pressly, Head, Vehicles Section, National Aeronautics and Space Administration; and Mrs. Katharine Mather, Chief, Petrography Section, U.S. Army Engineer Waterways Experiment Station (Jackson, Miss.), Department of the Army.

Secretary of State Dean Rusk (at right, above) and Deputy Under Secretary William J. Crockett helped to launch the Office of Community Advisory Services, a program that brought Foreign Service officers on leave in closer touch with their communities. Vice President Hubert Humphrey came to the Department to meet with Junior Foreign Service officers (center), here he greets Alex Davit, Course Coordinator. Senator Gale McGee of Wyoming (below) addressed summer interns.

The President and His Boss

"DEAR MADAM," RAN THE LETTER, "I LISTENED TO YOUR EMPTY-headed remarks last evening—and couldn't help but realize what an apt pupil you are of Harry Truman. My advice . . . is to go back to your home, husband and children."

The year was 1958. I was then Vice Chairman of the Democratic National Committee and I had been on the radio. I promptly mailed the letter to former President Truman.

His reply came a week later:

> Dear Katie:
> You have arrived; from now on these "nut" or "crank letters," as you may call them, may be embarrassing to you, but it only means that you are in a class with the rest of us who are trying to do something about things which are of important interest to everyone.
>
> Sincerely yours, etc.

I had caught my first glimpse of President Harry S Truman on a bright, sunny day in July 1945. Along with other gawkers, I stood at the top of a huge staircase at SHAEF (Supreme Headquarters, Allied Expeditionary Forces) in Frankfurt, Germany, watching President Truman and General Eisenhower ascend a long flight of marble steps. The President and the General were on their way to the Potsdam Conference. "What a charismatic presence," I remember thinking, "this gleaming General and the tough-minded indomitable President!"

I knew I would be seeing the General's photograph often; he had an unforgettable smile and an unmistakably American look. In a quite different way, so did Mr. Truman.

The first time I got into conversation with the Trumans was at a reception at Blair House. They had kindly invited the officers of the Women's National Press Club to tea the day after the annual Congressional dinner at which we spoofed the politicians of both parties. (For many years I had enjoyed writing some of the satiric skits we put on.) We talked of timing, of laughs, and President Truman commented, "Spoofing is good for [deflating] the ego."

Both the former President and Mrs. Truman have a granite goodness that makes them believable and formidable. I never saw either of them take on airs, and yet their innate dignity left one well aware that respect would always be tendered them. Mine soon became tinged with affection.

In July of 1955, I followed President Truman on the program at a Democratic dinner in Portland, Oregon. We had spent the day as the guests of Mayor Fred Peterson at the annual Portland Rose Festival. Mrs. Truman, acting on my advice, wore a dark suit. The Mayor's wife, who knew her climate better, wore white. The sun wore its fiercest, brightest rays. By that evening President Truman had turned red, which caused him to ask the Oregonians to let their sun turn a man blue instead so he'd look better on television. He began by remarking to Senator Wayne Morse, who had recently changed his party affiliation from Republican to Democrat: "I liked him when he was a Republican." He waxed lyrical about the Far West: "I love these states, Oregon, Idaho, Montana, Utah, Wyoming; the best of America—for after all, everyone in them comes from Missouri." He was at his Harry-give-'em-hell best.

Then I went on. I could feel the crowd, my first such sensation. Harry had warmed them up so well that they were ahead of me on the laughs.

At the request of Congresswoman Edith Green (elected to

Congress in 1954) we stayed at the Hotel Roosevelt, then the only
hotel in Portland that employed union help. The Secret Service
put me in a room opposite the Trumans because they did not
want strangers that close. The room was small and the hotel was
not air-conditioned, but the company coming and going more
than compensated for the discomfort. Down in the modest lobby
sat the lone telephone operator.

Before the banquet I heard her arguing and stopped to listen;
seeing me, she exploded: "How did I know that was really Margaret Truman? I wasn't going to take a chance, I just wouldn't
put her through."

At seven the following morning, I found Mr. Truman in the
coffee shop. He had already taken his famous early morning con-
stitutional. As I greeted him, an elderly female at the next table
suddenly rose: "It is you, isn't it—how are you, Mr. President?"
"Pretty good for an old codger."

Because Mrs. Truman (the "Boss," as Mr. Truman fondly calls
her) doesn't like to fly, they usually travel by train. Most of the
head table turned up that afternoon at the railroad station
to bid them good-by. Walking along, Mildred Morse remarked:
"I love the Democrats, they always have fun. All those years with
the Republicans, really, they are dreary."

After various encounters with the Trumans, the President let
me know we were friends by kidding me in public. One such occasion took place at a dinner at the Chase Hotel in St. Louis on
November 23, 1957, in honor of Senator Stuart Symington. The
paeans of praise for Stuart saturated us with clichés. Though I cut
my text, I added my own share to the platitudes. "The difference
between a statesman and a politician is—the politician thinks
about the next election but the statesman (our Senator Symington) thinks about the next generation."

When Truman rose to speak he looked down the table at me
and remarked, "Katie, don't you ever say that again. Don't you
know everyone at this table is a politician? It's an honorable profession, but a statesman is nothing but a dead politician."

Every politician in that jam-packed ballroom howled and hooted. "Because it's you, Katie," Mr. Truman concluded, "I forgive you."

At a regional meeting I held in Kansas City in 1955, I had, of course, invited both the former President and Mrs. Truman to attend. Mr. Truman was to speak at the final luncheon, arriving from another engagement, and Mrs. Truman at her insistence drove herself in from Independence. When the escorting party arrived in the lobby, five minutes ahead of time, there sat Mrs. Truman, "aheader."

In the middle of Congresswoman Coya Knutson's[1] speech, my assistant, Gerry Sohle, signaled from the door that Mr. Truman had arrived. I had two choices: to hurry Coya or interrupt her. I chose the latter. As he entered, Mrs. Truman whispered, "You should have kept him waiting till she was done." After the applause subsided, Coya went calmly on with her speech and Mr. Truman laughed at her jokes.

After luncheon I escorted Mrs. Truman to the parking lot. One of the things she liked best about private life, she told me, was "getting into my own car and driving off." An attendant rushed to open the door for her. I watched her drive away with a flourish, full of admiration for this "independent" lady from Independence. The girl in the cashier's cage detained me, talking about Mrs. Truman, Margaret's marriage—and, of course, their President. After all, she felt part of the family.

In October 1957, I accepted an invitation, long since tendered, to visit the Truman library in Independence. The day was fair and warm, one of those perfect fall days that still smells of summer. Before entering the building I walked all around the long, low, white structure. Sitting on top of a slight rise, surrounded by wire fencing and new shoots of green grass, it suited the landscape like a glove.

Rose Conway, an extraordinary, self-effacing woman who had

[1] Elected to the Eighty-fourth and Eighty-fifth Congresses: 1955 to 1959.

served the President as secretary and general amanuensis for years, greeted me with smiles and coffee. The President's presence startled me. He slid into a chair and opened with an account of his last visitors, the Future Farmers of America. "They forget I'm just an ordinary citizen," he began, as if he really were one.

As I listened to him, I realized that here was a man who had an affirmative view of life, a man who exuded an enormous enjoyment of the role history had cast him in. His singular charm was neither polished nor smooth but avid, intent, political in its best sense.

He spoke of former Governor Faubus of Arkansas: "a good liberal," he remarked, "in the days when he belonged to my regiment. He certainly didn't consult any of his old friends, not me, nor McMath."[2] Had he been President at the time of the desegregation crisis in Little Rock[3] he would have federalized the National Guard right off and avoided all that havoc. He peppered the political landscape with his puckish comments. The economy, he ruled, was bad. "Read Baruch." He paused. "An arrogant, opinionated man—but he knows one should never let government bonds go down."

He found fault with the Congress: "Right after they elected Eisenhower, they turned right around and made him a lame duck with that twenty-second Amendment" (limiting the President to two terms).

When I mentioned having seen him at SHAEF in July 1945, he reminisced about the Potsdam Conference. General Patton arrived wearing stars on his helmet, his shoulders, his belt buckle, and his tunic sleeve. Later, Truman sent him a new Presidential seal he had designed with the stars of the forty-eight states, remarking that only the President could wear that many stars. He remembered how some of the military had stood there astonished when he said there would be no revenge on Germany, no reprisals. "One

[2] Former Governor of Arkansas. Elected in 1948 for a two-year term and re-elected in 1950.
[3] August 30—September 1, 1957.

day they even questioned my asking a Catholic bishop to conduct
a service. I reminded them I was the Commander in Chief."

Later I roamed over the library with him; we looked at the
trophies, the jeweled swords, the attention-getting gifts (ranging
from a chair made from bottle caps to one of solid silver). He
stopped in front of a sword to tell me how he had teased "Bess,"
offering her one of the diamonds if she would only trip up Senator Bricker.[4]

In parting, he slipped me a library commemorative coin and an
adage: "Never forget a favor and never bear a grudge." He had
borne only two grudges, he said, a former Governor of Missouri
and the then Vice President Richard Nixon: "Both consigned
me to hell, but I just wouldn't go." A mischievous look accompanied both the gift and the adage; but even Harry Truman can
forgive and forget. I thought of his adage and his comments when
twelve years later, in 1969, I saw the photograph of President Nixon
with him, playing the famous library piano with Mr. Truman looking on.

When Mrs. Truman came for me she remarked that where the
library stands there used to be a public park. On the ride to the
house, she said, "I tried to teach Margaret to play tennis in this
park but I gave up." Margaret was "unathletic." Since my younger
daughter was too, I understood.

Up West Truman Drive, past rows of homes looking just like
those in other towns of this size, we approached a large white
house, impressive in its appendages of turrets and carved wooden
friezes, its two great panels of ruby, green, violet, and amber col-
ored glass climbing down the front in two parallel bars of light.
The house had an air of stability, of certainty, of triumphing and
presiding over an era that held ample space and conforming proportions to be all-important. Was the house, I inquired, what we
call American Gothic? "Heavens, no." Mrs. Truman gave one of
those earthy chuckles. "Just plain old Victorian. It was built in

[4] Ohio, 1946–58.

1893." How the house, too, I thought, must laugh at the crowded present we have shrunk into.

The neighbors in back of the yard are now separated by a fence the security guards installed. The long lawn covered with falling leaves reminded Mrs. Truman that she wished mightily for a gardener. We walked past the porch they added on, a cozy white affair with comfortable furniture and a ceiling fan, and snug under it, a woodshed neatly piled with logs. "It gets hot here, most summer evenings that's where we sit."

We came through the back door into the house. A sense of order struck me, dark wainscoting and oil portraits of Truman. We settled in the living room, full of flowers, comfortable chairs, and polished mahogany. We talked of the blessings and drolleries of grandchildren. "Are you a card-carrying member of the grandmother league?" Mrs. Truman asked as she pulled out a wallet full of photographs. We even compared notes on self-willed daughters.

"Now I'm going to show you where we really live," she announced. We walked through a formal room where a covey of inscribed portraits in their silver frames on a grand piano occupied center stage, on into a smaller room lined with books. The President's chair, a large red leather affair, faced a card table piled with papers, inkwell, and other reading matter. Opposite stood a radio-record-player combination and two cozy chintz chairs. While Mrs. Truman went to get ready to take me to luncheon, like Goldilocks, I tried all the chairs and found them perfect.

Back in town, in the Kansas City Club where we lunched, a red-haired waitress hovered over us, busily chatting on about how pleased she was to see her "First Lady." A whole tableful of lunching ladies came to pay their respects. Beguiled, I watched Mrs. Truman take all this attention with a natural warmth, a warmth that was never strained because it was so genuine.

We enjoyed a long leisurely lunch. I admired the width and space between the tables which helped to make one feel unharried. How different from the close quarters at most Eastern restaurants. No one jostled past one.

When our families and their curiously dominant personalities crisscrossed our conversation, I realized how much I could learn from Mrs. Truman. Knowing that her husband and daughter would do as they pleased, she provided the balance wheel, the sensible unheeded advice, the amused response, and the laughing regret. It was she who had made her family the indivisible force it had become.

We talked of politics, too; she was sorry that the Trumans were never asked to help in the campaign of '52 (Governor Stevenson's first try). She remarked how much she had been for his candidacy in 1956. Her comments were not "personal" in the usual sense. She was talking with candor, as she always did.

They had recently traveled to the dedication ceremonies of the Rayburn library. "We went by train in the President's private car." For a moment I thought she was talking about President Eisenhower; she corrected me laughingly, she meant the President of the Missouri-Kansas-Texas Railroad Company, whose private car was put at their disposal. All sorts of kinfolk attended the Bonham ceremonies and, of course, celebrities and Texans by the planeload.

After coffee, I asked if I might smoke. She nodded and added that, to make me feel comfortable, she would join me (although she never smoked) but, if she did, she'd shock all her neighbors in Independence. "I might even find that they'd put all my possessions out on the street by the time I got back home." We laughed at her jest, but it told worlds about living in a small town.

She had a way of talking that suited her; her tone of voice expressed her self-assurance, and yet she never talked down to one. She had a way of walking, I noticed as we left, deliberate, not slow, but paced and yet leisurely. She even had a purposeful way of pulling on her gloves that was in tune with her definite personality.

Another luncheon I particularly recall took place in 1961 when

Mrs. Helm and I were guests of Mrs. Truman at the Mayflower Hotel in Washington. Edith Helm had been social secretary to the Trumans and prior to that to Mrs. Roosevelt. She was an Admiral's daughter and an Admiral's widow, with a keen twentieth-century wit and a late nineties look.

The headwaiter conducted us to a wall table at which Mrs. Truman insisted on sitting with her back to the room. When I suggested changing places, she told me she was tired of being stared at and did not want to stare back.

The Trumans had come to Washington for a dinner in their honor given the night before by President and Mrs. Kennedy. "Was the dinner fun?" I inquired. "Not really," Mrs. Truman replied in her candid manner. "It was beautifully done and I enjoyed it. But it was never fun. I kept wondering all evening why it wasn't." And then she went on to comment that it was so good of the President to have done this, especially "after all those things Harry said about Jack." But, of course, he had gone on and campaigned for him "just as he said he would."

"You know, I had forgotten how charming the President could be. My, but he is delightful. So is she, but she drops a curtain in front of you. No one will ever get to know her."

Mrs. Truman and Mrs. Helm enjoyed their reminiscences. Hadn't Nehru, the Prime Minister of India, been a difficult guest? and what about the time a practical joker introduced a stranger into a Blair House lunch? The poor woman kept saying, "I thought it was peculiar being asked on the telephone and at the last minute."

Over the coffee Mrs. Helm produced a compliment for Mrs. Truman: "A friend of mine remarked that you were the most completely satisfactory First Lady she had known." Mrs. Truman gave one of those harrumphs that ended in a throaty laugh. I couldn't resist adding my own comment: "People sense you have a special quality, you are always at ease, you make no effort; they know you are a happy wife and mother and that feeling communicates itself to others and they are reassured. Being reassured makes it so much easier—one can go on from there and understand why one likes someone." For a moment Mrs. Truman seemed surprised and then, looking straight at me, she said: "You know, I never thought of that." I was tempted to say, "That's just the point." Later, she remarked, "Margaret has always given me joy. I have always delighted in her." It reminded me of one of Truman's comments. "Being a grandfather," he said, "is the most fun I've ever had with a non-controversial matter."

In the late fifties and early sixties the Trumans often came to Washington. Once when calling on him at the Mayflower, I found the former Secretary of State, Dean Acheson, and a man from B. Altman, showing them the finished drawings for the library décor. We studied the plans room by room, viewing what was to be the rose garden. Mr. Truman suddenly turned to his former Secretary of State. "Mrs. Truman and I are to be buried right here in this garden. We have selected our tomb, and you, Dean, are to see that our will is carried out." Mr. Acheson replied, "Well, Mr. President, it is not exactly the task I should have selected but I am afraid you will haunt me if I don't carry out your wishes."

When Mrs. Truman did not accompany him, he would talk about her. "They came and offered her a lot of money to do a book but she told them two hams in the family are enough."

He never lost his attraction for the press; they would follow him around town like bloodhounds. In 1959 the two favorite questions were: had he come to get rid of Paul Butler (then Chairman of the Democratic National Committee) or to stop Kennedy (who was then on his way to capturing the 1960 Democratic nomination for President)? At a political candidates' dinner in New York that winter, he took pot shots at "hothouse liberals," keeping us all guessing whom he meant—Mrs. Roosevelt, Herbert Lehman, or others? Word had gotten round that he was to use the phrase and everyone tried to stop him, but stopping Harry Truman was something no one had ever succeeded in doing. As if accepting the challenge, Mrs. Roosevelt, in her dinner remarks, replied that she made no such distinction, all liberals were acceptable to her.

On several occasions the Trumans came to our house; I will never forget the Sunday luncheon when the roast beef was so undercooked (the cook got excited and misjudged her timing) that none of us could eat it. Because everyone had seen them arrive, we had neighbors anxiously awaiting a handshake. In between entertaining us and greeting one and all, Mr. Truman played the piano, discussed Chopin with me, and proved to my husband that he knew facts and figures on such recondite matters as industrial expansion and the pressures on gold in the international market.

When Edith Helm died in 1962 the Trumans came on for her funeral at the Washington Cathedral. Afterward, they invited me to luncheon. Mr. Truman told me of an exchange of correspondence he had had with Edith regarding the dedication ceremonies for his library. He had written to her begging her to come and help him; ex-Presidents and other notables had accepted invitations to attend and he was unsure of his protocol. In her reply she had begged to be excused; she was too old, she wrote, it would be too hot in July and, besides, all those years in the White House when she had advised him on such matters he had never paid any attention.

Mr. Truman was on his way that afternoon to attend similar ceremonies at Abilene, Kansas, where President Eisenhower's library was to be dedicated. Several times during luncheon, Mrs. Truman would remind him: "Harry, be sure and send that suit out tonight at the hotel to be pressed." Each time he would look at me and say, "You see, Katie, I'm still being bossed."

The day of President Kennedy's funeral, I decided to brave the crowds and call on Mr. Truman at Blair House. As always, Mr. Truman was well supplied with visitors; Margaret had taken charge, and one at a time was the order of the day. When I complimented him on his spryness, he quipped, "I tell them all I'm physically fit, mentally unbalanced, and financially unsound." Of course we talked politics, an escape topic that seemed safe. Apropos of some difficult pending bill, he commented: "You can't advise the Senate. I know, I was once a Senator." Those of us who knew him well knew he relished being Senator and had always wished he might return to that body. We spoke of Senator Dirksen (the Minority Leader in the Senate) and how much we liked him. "He knows politics and has his own style" was Harry Truman's accolade. "He's not afraid of showing off, or taking advantage. You've got to admire him."

When it was time to go, Mr. Truman tried another quip: "You know, Katie, I'm going to ride today in the funeral procession because President Eisenhower is too old to walk." Later, friends of Mr. Truman's told me that after he'd been to the White House to call on Jackie he wept so they had to put him to bed for a rest. But he and the other ex-President did ride in the procession.

Harry Truman has not stopped time any more than anyone else, but he has made history and lived life as if every part of it were exhilarating. As for Mrs. Truman, when I get too homesick for that delightful chuckle, that unexpectedly hearty laugh, I call her up. Invariably we talk of children, grandchildren, and even of our mothers. I once confessed that after her death I sometimes held imaginary conversations with my mother, and Mrs. Truman replied that although she'd been on in years when her mother died, she too held such conversations.

Had they been too strict, our mothers? Mrs. Truman had wanted to be a pediatrician, but Mrs. Truman never got past her mother's firm *no*. I was glad Bess Truman's mother had been so intransigent, or we might never have known her as First Lady.

An Extraordinary
Human Event

ELEANOR ROOSEVELT'S FUNERAL ON NOVEMBER 10, 1962, WAS AN
event. You might describe it as a historic event or you might
just characterize it as a human event of unusual dimensions.

Everyone knew what to do: the telegrams had gone out telling
us where to be at what time. Some of us were bidden to the
church, some just to the interment service in the Rose Garden.
But the crowds that lined the approach to Hyde Park, up to the
church doors, had not been invited. "They must have come from
all over," our driver remarked, "not that many folks in our town."

The service, the people, the gray and alternately sun-swept sky,
the autumn brilliance of the countryside, all bordered on the extraordinary, as if they followed some hidden command.

The Reverend Mr. Gordon L. Kidd said, "Today we seem to be
such a practical people—strongly utilitarian, that is—that we do
only the things that we feel sure will bring in some return; and we
have our doubts at times whether prayers for those who are gone,
pay." Gently he reminded us that although "we pride ourselves on
being a land of self-made men, yet who is among us who does not
owe much to those who have gone before?"

Eleanor Roosevelt became a legend in her lifetime. Wherever
you went you heard her name, whether mention of her came about
through her actual presence, or merely through her deeds or her
words, or both, for they were inseparable. With her death she be-

came one of the legendary subjects in the earthly lexicon of the beloved.

On the plane to Hyde Park, I talked with Ed and Janet Murrow (he was then Director of USIA) about Mrs. Roosevelt's lack of vanity. Perhaps that made it easier for her, we decided, to express the selfless interest she poured out on all and sundry.

I had never known Mrs. Roosevelt as a friend—the way I had other First Ladies. By the time I met her it was too late to try to penetrate her inner circle. And besides, in 1940, I was too timid. I had seen her in the thirties, but never to talk to, just to shake hands with in receiving lines. In those days all the senior officers of each government agency (my husband belonged to this classification in the SEC) were invited to formal evening receptions at the White House. She was very imposing, a family jewel on her simple black dress, her half-smile, her gracious handshake. She looked directly at you, even though, despite a military aide's introduction, she had no idea who you were. She managed to overcome her naturally aristocratic bearing and still retain her good manners.

The obituaries had included many photographs: as a bride, small-waisted and tall, her height accentuated by long full skirts and full puffed sleeves; in her first inaugural gown, a photograph like so many others that showed her to be indifferent to her appearance. The dress hardly suited, but it was the correct length, and even the most critical must have pronounced it appropriate for the occasion. Certainly no hairdresser or stylist had been summoned. One felt certain the picture had been taken as quickly as possible; if they insisted, she seemed to be saying, then she would pose.

In 1950, I served as publicity chairman for UN Day. Mrs. Roosevelt, as head of the American Association for (the support of) the United Nations, chaired the meetings. She invariably wore a governessy kind of watch-pin, a gold and diamond fleur-de-lis, from which hung a round gold watch. It undoubtedly had some sentimental attachment for her. As for the rest of her costume, she could not have told you what she had on. Nothing matched—hats, shoes, or pocketbooks; what would be another woman's carefully chosen accessories were, for her, just items that must be anonymous and comfortable.

After my appointment in 1953 to the Democratic National Committee, I saw her quite frequently. But somehow I always retained the feeling that it was an imposition to ask for her undivided attention. She came to speak at all the meetings I asked her to, her words were always wise, her delivery (she never used a manuscript) held one's attention, and what she said was adroitly targeted to the objective. In response to my request, she would devote one of her widely read columns to our programs calling for greater political participation. Soon after my appointment, she invited me to luncheon at her New York apartment. To my great disappointment, I shared her with cousins and other projects. But I understood; she was just too busy to see any of us separately. On those occasions when she spoke for the Democratic Committee, I seemed forever to be pursuing her through hotel kitchens, her escape route from the handshake seekers and the "just one word" assailants. She had an almost languid way of loping up steep stairs. I soon discovered even this pace was deceptive. I never caught up with her. I was always ten steps behind.

She liked to talk about the early days when she and Congresswoman Caroline O'Day[1] and Molly Dewson, the first Director of Women's Activities for the Democratic National Committee, crisscrossed upstate New York in FDR's campaigns for Governor in 1928. Mrs. Roosevelt and her companions were ardent feminists. One day Mrs. R. visited a state committeeman to urge him to accept women as party workers and officeholders. His wife, trying to protect her husband from this unwelcome invader, told Mrs. R. he was out. "Then I'll wait," she replied, and calmly sat down on the front porch and took up her knitting. Eventually the committeeman surrendered; he not only appeared, he granted her requests.

[1] New York, 1935–43.

The very last time I saw Mrs. Roosevelt was at a meeting of the Commission on the Status of Women. Esther Peterson, Executive Vice Chairman of the Commission, had asked me to testify on a recent trip to Japan. Mrs. R. questioned me closely about the practice of "extended families," where the mother-in-law not only lived with the young couple but dominated the household.

How appalled she had been, she told us, to find wives so subjected to a mother-in-law's discipline and favors. She wanted to know if this unhappy condition had been remedied. In the cities, I told her, traditions had yielded to change as Japanese women emerged and took up modern ways. But about rural areas I could not give her the encouraging reply she wanted. As we talked, her own experience with an overwhelming mother-in-law came to mind. President Roosevelt's mother had never yielded her scepter —hadn't her multifaceted handsome son been given her that she might govern while he ruled? Eleanor Roosevelt must have realized what had gone through my mind, for she remarked: "*But* the lot of Japanese women struck me as infinitely more difficult. There was no way they could rebel or resist."

As the group went to lunch, Mrs. Roosevelt escaped once again. She had gone to another room to dictate in order to answer some of her ever increasing mail. She never had a free moment without calls on her time. I had wanted to pay my respects, but decided it would be wrong to intrude. Somehow she left one feeling that there were already many too many intrusions upon her days.

When the news of her death came, I thought of how often I had heard her called the First Lady of the World. Once, in introducing her, I had referred to her as the "conscience of America." When she rose she remarked, "I wished I had been the imagination of America." Both of these she had been. She was the first First Lady to go to the trouble spots, the human trouble spots, and the first to insist on practical answers to haunting questions. When we needed her, and all of us needed her in so many ways, she was always there. Her interest in others had a dispassionate quality that inured her to the vagaries of human beings. She had learned long ago that she could not live with people on their terms, so she made her own. She was always in a great hurry to help, she had no time for studying the implications.

The funeral with all of its trappings was a worldly one. It had to be. The hierarchical distinctions had to be made and the past had to be recast in its proper ceremonial pomp.

We were a curious set of characters; strangers might have mistaken us for movie extras, summoned and costumed for the occasion. The weather added its own supernatural note. The sun broke through just as we left for the church, hovering just long enough to get us there. The skies darkened, the big black cars emptied, we hung back, not wanting to push or shove. All of a sudden we were dark-looking people, dark reflections in the pools of water from the morning rain.

Ushers moved us forward, giving us instructions one knew in this crowded interior to be irrevocable. I could see Agnes Meyer, ahead of me, hesitate. She did not want to leave the arm of her son-in-law, Philip Graham, as she turned reluctantly into a pew where there was no room for him.

Mrs. Murrow, beside me, whispered that Marian Anderson should have been urged to come in, even though her wire only invited her to the service in the rose garden. We regretted her absence; Mrs. Roosevelt would surely have wanted her to be there.

The family walked in, heads up, self-conscious, trying not to acknowledge the stares and turned heads. We, in turn, tried not to look. How they had aged, Anna Halsted (the President's daughter) and those sons of Eleanor and Franklin—they were once so young, handsome, and rambunctious. The grandchildren, almost running, hand in hand, their quick steps hurrying them along, followed their parents.

As the service ended, church bells sounded out over the music, ringing sweet and pure in the open country air. I can remember the doors opening, the organ fading, and the bells carrying us on. There must have been four hundred people at the graveside, standing so close they were one group, with waves of varying head

levels. I stood beside Ambassador Angier Biddle Duke, the
Chief of Protocol. Ahead of me I could see the tall Chief Justice,
Earl Warren, and Mrs. Warren in one of those fussy hats she always wore, this one of rippling green velvet. Beside me stood
Frances Perkins (Secretary of Labor from 1933 to 1945), smaller,
shriveled almost, in one of her ever unchanging tricorn hats. Jim
Farley,[2] who broke with President Roosevelt over the third term
in 1940, stood out because of his height. Henry Morgenthau,[3]
close friend to both the President and Mrs. Roosevelt, had earlier
worn his hat pulled way down over his face as if he wished to remain unrecognized. Basil O'Connor, Chairman of the National
Foundation for Infantile Paralysis and FDR's boon companion,
even former Vice President Henry Wallace could be seen in the
closely woven tapestry of the famous.

As I stood there, watching the Reverend Mr. Kidd, the pag-
eantry of the crucifer, and his following clergymen walk slowly
toward us, I noticed that the darkening afternoon highlighted the
color of the sprawling wine-red barn behind the rose garden. Was
it the presence of persons of great import—two ex-Presidents, an
ex-Vice President, the Governor and the Mayor of New York, a
former Governor of New York, a corporal's guard of New Dealers
—stiff, stern, subdued, walking out of the church together, that
made the colors and the ceremonies and the people seem painted,
almost, onto the canvas of the ritual? The shapeless barn sprouted,
enormous gray turrets without function or meaning. Behind it
stood a huge maple, turned fiery red, its color fighting the wine
red of the barn for supremacy.

By the simple long white headstone stood an array of floral
tributes. Some were awkward and ugly, but all were bright and
purposeful, splashed against the soft green of the garden. We recited the Lord's Prayer in trailing unison. James, the tallest and
eldest son, stood beside the coffin with its simple evergreen boughs.

[2] Chairman of the Democratic National Committee 1932–40; Postmaster
General 1933–40.
[3] Secretary of the Treasury, 1934–45.

Behind the wreaths and the tributes, the press crowded forward, topped by the scaffolding for the TV cameras.

After a short eulogy the service ended and the group opened like a fan. I managed to shake hands with Mrs. Truman. "Harry" —she turned to the former President—"it's Katie. I was just saying I hoped I'd see you." I found ex-Governor and Mrs. Herbert Lehman. She turned suddenly to her husband and told him to put his hat on, warning him that if he didn't he'd catch cold. But Herbert had no intention of putting on his hat. He wanted to stay bareheaded and cold. He looked smaller and older. My war years working with him in UNRRA and all of the bureaucratic and legislative battles we fought came flooding back to me. We touched on the "old days" and I told him how good it was to be working in a new field—in the State Department. "You always enjoy what you do," he said with that firm kindness that does not patronize. I was not to see him again. He died in January 1965.

In the midst of the graveside eulogy I'd begun thinking of FDR. I found myself recalling his funeral, the slow heartbreaking pace at which the cortege wound its way up Pennsylvania Avenue. Now he was lying peacefully in his rose garden at Hyde Park. I remembered his indelible mannerisms, his corporate reality, the way he threw his head back when he laughed, how he twisted that cigarette holder, leaned on his son James's arm. Perhaps by now he was truly free of us and wanted us in turn to let him go.

I wondered what they would say to one another, these two such extraordinarily different human beings, who had opened so many doors for others. Would he ask her about all those homely things we ask after a long separation? Would she take up her knitting and tell him? Or is there nothing we take with us, as the Scriptures tell us, but our new self, innocent of the world and its discordant hours and fragmented days?

Power, Pomp, and Tears

ON FRIDAY, NOVEMBER 22, 1963, I WAS HAVING LUNCHEON IN THE executive dining room in the Department of State with two old friends. We were talking about the Bobby Baker case—then an unhappy Washington affair—when a secretary came hurrying in with a piece of paper torn from the news ticker. As the message passed around the room from table to table man after man rose and left. I exclaimed: "Something must have happened to the Secretary's plane." The Cabinet and the Secretary of State were en route to Tokyo to return the visit of the Japanese Cabinet to the United States.

Not waiting to read the message, my group followed the rest of the forty-odd public servants out of the room, almost running to the elevator. "The President has been shot," someone whispered. The phrase echoed down the corridors, repeated again and again by new voices. The man across from my office had a radio and had set up calls to Senator Ralph Yarborough's office in Texas. My husband arrived with his own portable radio.

Jim Grant, an AID Director, came rushing in with a new piece of raveled yellow paper—"cut down" was the verb used. We rushed across the hall, as if there were something that hurrying could change. Just then Senator Yarborough's office called back (the Senator had been part of the Dallas motorcade): "The wounds were serious." We stopped short of saying the dread word "fatal." Then a woman in a red dress walked in and announced, "He is dead." I had no idea who she was. It didn't matter.

There was nothing we could do; we were like inanimate lumps sitting in chairs or on window sills, looking out and seeing nothing. Finally we were all told to go home. Polly Shackleton[1] and I walked home to Georgetown. In a daze, mostly in silence, we stepped on and off familiar curbs without feeling them. Walter had gone ahead and I carried his radio; it was heavy, but I barely noticed. People we passed held radios to their ears or stood still, weeping.

Saturday morning it poured. Midmorning we were called by the Department of State to say that we might go to the White House where President Kennedy's body lay in state in the East Room. When we walked through the black-draped main entrance on Pennsylvania Avenue men in uniform clicked their heels. A serviceman stepped forward to escort us.

The East Room was empty—so it seemed—stark and bare. Walter and I stood in the doorway clutching one another; we could not bear to go on, we could not speak. The black-draped chandelier, the long, silent, empty room, the four servicemen of the honor guard who seemed not to be breathing, the candles on the catafalque, the flag, the overpowering sensation that a live, vibrant man was locked up forever in that casket and no earthly power could release him was almost too much to bear. To hear a man sob is appalling; as we neared the bier Walter's anguish broke into waves of gulping sound.

They routed us out of the East Room down the stairs into the south (diplomatic) entrance. We spoke with friends. I ran after Larry O'Brien, who was walking away at a rapid pace—just to shake his hand. As we waited for our cars, we spoke of the terribly trivial circumstances under which the news reached us, insignificant details that satisfied our need to converse: Assistant Secretaries of State Edward Martin,[2] Harlan Cleveland and their wives, Am-

[1] Polly Shackleton served as my successor as District of Columbia Democratic National Committeewoman and later as a valuable member of the City Council of the nation's capital.

[2] Edward Martin, Assistant Secretary of State for Inter-American Affairs, Harlan Cleveland, Assistant Secretary for International Organizations.

bassador William Attwood[3] all of us were afraid to be alone with our thoughts.

Once we were home, I suggested we walk over to see Marie and Averell Harriman, who live close by. We had this strange sensation of wanting to do something, this feeling of must—must do, must go, must talk.

On Sunday morning my good friends Donna and Senator Lee Metcalf, from Montana, saw to it that I might stand with them in the rotunda of the Capitol where the body was to lie in state. All through the streets leading up to the Capitol steps there were people standing behind barriers, miles of them, stretching in all directions, skeins of humanity winding their way into the Capitol plaza.

We were ushered into reserved places behind a circular velvet rope. We faced the entrance. Behind us were grouped the cameramen, the cameras, and the TV tripods. A special upper tier for TV had been constructed on top of the black-draped wooden scaffolding. One thought of execution squads, of jurors astride tripods, of a modern incarnation of the final day of judgment.

It was painful to see the strained faces: Ken Galbraith, Ambassador to India, so tall he towered above the White House staffers, the Congressional leaders, silhouetted in the doorway, standing in stiff twos and threes. One could feel the anguish, it began to have depth and texture, it settled on us like a mantle, we were to take it everywhere with us. We needed this cloak to hide our real emotions, for we could not always be seen weeping.

The sound of muffled drums, then music, came floating up the steps and through the open door. Another element beside the human one, an advance guard, a disembodied herald announced the arrival of the procession.

Four servicemen bore the coffin without grace. They bent and stepped, bent and stepped until they had climbed the steep stairs to the rotunda and reached the doorway. There was an awkward-

[3] Managing Editor of *Look* magazine, on leave of absence and recently Ambassador to Guinea.

ness in their movement, as perhaps there should have been, for who could bear a slain President lightly?

The honor guard, three white men and one black, followed. They advanced in a peculiar pattern: they raised one foot, checked it alongside the other, and then set it down, all four in perfect unison. They were followed by sailors carrying the President's flag.

When Jackie came through the doorway, hidden under a black veil and holding the two children by the hand, an unexpressed sigh swept through us. We held still, riveted by her dignity and her sorrow. I thought about her grief, about her wish to have this elaborate ceremonial funeral so that the whole country might participate, and so that none of us might forget.

The voices of the Senate Majority Leader, Mike Mansfield, of Speaker John McCormack, and of Chief Justice Warren were carried away by the rotunda echo. The quiet positioning of a wreath by President Johnson ended the formalities with understated solemnity.

When Jackie knelt beside the coffin with her children, I kept thinking, "This is a private farewell, we should not be here." But if one were to weigh the purpose of this action, the choice of setting, the high-echelon speakers, the privileged observers, one might very well conclude that a President's widow had no right to private grief.

Jackie Kennedy, forever photogenic, mysterious, reserved, will always be the first "pinup" inhabitant of the White House. For some unaccountable reason, neither her husband nor her mother understood her enormous vote-getting appeal; they saw only those enigmatic qualities that made her "different-looking." Her mother once asked her, "Can't you look more like Pat Nixon?"

When I first called to make suggestions for the 1960 campaign, Jack Kennedy replied that his wife probably wouldn't do very much. "She doesn't really like politics," he said, and besides she was expecting a baby in November. Others told me how shy, how unsympathetic to the political urgencies she was.

I found her neither shy nor disdainful of the political facts of life. But the legend persisted. Doris Fleeson, the syndicated columnist, a cynical critic and observer, called after a supper with the then Senator and Mrs. Kennedy to say, "Why, she's no older than our daughters, Katie. There she sat, poor thing, caught in this maw of ambition, propelled into the role of wife to a hard-bitten ruthless man, this inexperienced girl brought up without preparation for the fate awaiting her—rich, shielded, unarmed."

How could sophisticated women like Doris be so mistaken? No one who knew Jackie could ever describe her as "unarmed." She knew precisely what direction to take without ever consulting anyone; she had an appealing personality that she used to its best advantage (in and of itself an armature of steel) and an alarmingly discerning sense of personal priorities.

Molly Van Rensselaer Thayer, proponent, biographer, and friend, would defend her. "Those harpies—Doris and May Craig [then reigning female journalists, of which there have never been too many]—they criticize her static face, they're jealous. They envy her because she's rich, beautiful, and happy."

I was never quite certain that Molly was altogether correct. Jackie was certainly both rich and beautiful, but I wondered if the course chosen by her husband did not, in her eyes, threaten her happiness. Certainly those who knew her were bewitched by her. But even her mother was to say, "Jackie is so talented, but she will always be unpredictable."

During the 1960 campaign I went to talk with Mrs. Auchincloss about using her residence, Merrywood, for a fund-raising affair. She showed me a drawing Jackie had made for the President-elect's birthday some years back. Two poems, one of the seventeenth century and the other, an original poem Jackie had written in seventeenth-century style, were surrounded by drawings of familiar scenes in their life together. There was nothing about it that was amateurish. Mrs. Auchincloss was quite correct. Jackie had an enormous talent.

My daughter Mary, who was Jackie's age, was amused when she heard that Jackie's mother had described her as unpredictable.

"But, Mother," Mary replied, "you can't say that about me. I am predictable. I will always react negatively."

Those close to Jackie might have described her as always reacting negatively. Certainly she had great charm; she always looked exquisite, carried herself with dignity, and managed to turn many political figures, including the Vice President, into devoted admirers. At a fund-raising event in the winter of 1959–60, I watched Lyndon Johnson bend his tall self to reach a communicating level, fetch her a chair, light her cigarette, hover over her.

She never cared for the practical side of politics, or for those who carried purely political titles. Her kind of politics took the form of elitism, arranging informal suppers for bright New Frontiersmen, or creating small dinner dances to which everyone in Washington coveted invitations—occasions when she would pick and choose among prominent officials, even at the Cabinet level, inviting some, omitting others.

On one of the rare occasions when Jackie appeared during the preconvention campaign, she introduced Jack Kennedy at the Woman's Conference on the day her husband won the West Virginia primary. "Caroline's first words were 'aeroplane' and 'West Virginia,'" she began. It didn't matter what else she said, the audience had been completely captivated.

She was to transform the White House from an over-lived-in, cluttered, haphazard official residence into a historic facsimile of what it might have been at its very quintessential best.

The fund-raising event at Mrs. Auchincloss' focused on a coast-to-coast network show. Jackie had filmed her part in her Georgetown drawing room. The Presidential candidate himself was to come on live from California. The large living room barely accommodated the more than two hundred eager women who had paid fifty dollars to be present (some gave as much as a thousand). Standees crowded the doorway. Afterward an elegant tea was served in the dining room.

Concerned lest she fatigue herself in her last weeks of pregnancy, I urged Jackie to leave when she wanted. She thanked me and in dulcet tones let me know she would leave when she pleased—but not now.

At the wedding of Ambassador Angier Biddle Duke to the lovely Robin Chandler on May 12, 1962, both the President and Vice President came with their wives. Jackie stayed on after President Kennedy left. About fifty guests stood around in Senator Claiborne Pell's (Rhode Island) pleasant Georgetown garden. Eventually I found myself talking with Jackie. She admired the Indian pin I was wearing. Her jewelry, a gold rope bracelet with diamonds and a ring of diamonds and emeralds, was conspicuously handsome. She looked very young, almost fragile, when one stood close beside her.

She wanted to hear about my travels; I described the Chiefs of Mission meetings instituted by Under Secretary Bowles to promote exchange of ideas and a closer look at New Frontier procedural and policy changes. In Baguio (Philippines) everyone had talked about the film in which she served as narrator and historic guide in the newly renovated White House. At each meeting, people wanted to know how they could get a print.

Jackie's voice always surprised me; what she said often contrasted with its quality. She asked me, "Aren't you pleased to have this fun job instead of that dreary, dull politics?" We agreed that I had fallen into a most desirable spot—thanks to the President. Although the years in politics were exhausting and exasperating, I had never found them dreary or dull.

Jackie had a way of drawing people out. Danny Kaye, at a White House dinner, once thanked her for making entertainers feel ten feet tall. The phrase caught on; some months later I received a letter from a remote African post; an appreciative wife wrote that I had made wives feel ten feet tall. At a swinging dinner party given by Ethel and Bob Kennedy, I had a chance to tell Danny

Kaye how his phrase had circled the globe. "Talk about a star, and you're sure to be quoted." We then told one another how enchanting this young woman was, and how well she understood this art of making people feel taller.

That evening Danny proved what a star he was—and how he could entertain in an informal setting. Seating Bob McNamara (Secretary of Defense), Stewart Udall (Secretary of Interior), and his host (the Attorney General) around a table, he launched a mock Cabinet meeting. Gesturing in his own fantasy fashion, he asked tortuous, absurd questions of his victims. When they crumbled with laughter, he twitted them for their ineptitudes.

As the stream of women leaders from abroad grew, I soon found that I had a fair-sized problem: all of them wanted to meet Mrs. Kennedy; some had brought gifts for her. I realized that the answer must always be no; one exception would make it mandatory for her to see them all. In exceptional cases, I would call on Mrs. Johnson, who was always more than generous in her response. Most of the time, the women had to settle for me and a photographer. My office began to look like a museum.

Angier Biddle Duke always proved to be a warm and sympathetic ally when we were faced with extraordinary situations. One time it was the visit of the Japanese Cabinet; they were to bring their wives, none of whom had ever left Japan before. I had met them all at a luncheon given for me by our Ambassador's wife, Mrs. Reischauer, when I visited Tokyo. The wives had then told me they *must* meet Mrs. Kennedy. Knowing the sensitivity of the Japanese, and the fact that our United States Cabinet wives had been received by the Emperor's daughter when they visited Japan, Angier and I put all our political muscle into trying to persuade Mrs. Kennedy to receive them. But the answer was no. In the end, the President did the honors, delighting the ladies, of course.

At intervals I tried to enlist Mrs. Kennedy's help through Tish Baldridge, her social secretary. I drew up lists of women whose creative skills were well known, prominent women in the professions, business, academia and, hopefully, a few political leaders (of both parties) whom she might entertain at luncheon. Tish would explain that such gatherings had no appeal for Mrs. Kennedy.

In the summer months, naturally, Mrs. Kennedy would take the children to Hyannisport, and the President would weekend with them. I can remember occasions when the President's mother or sisters took Jackie's place as hostess; at a luncheon for the President of Ecuador,[4] Mrs. Rose Kennedy, looking half her age, managed to make everyone feel honored by her presence. At another time,[5] Mrs. Auchincloss stood in for Jackie at a White House reception in honor of the seventy-fifth anniversary meeting of the prestigious International Council of Women.

Everyone respected Jackie's determination to preserve a private place, a refuge where her husband and her children could still feel they belonged to one another and not to the probing press or to the repetitive formalities of public life. The only trouble was that most everyone wanted to be the person for whom she made an exception.

Perhaps the President's wife should already have experienced a lifetime of public service, as had Mrs. Johnson, Eleanor Roosevelt, Bess Truman, and Mamie Eisenhower (who had certainly been part of a regimented orderly society that made its continuous demands on her for appearances, strained ceremonials, and formal interchange). Could it be that an older, more seasoned wife could more easily find her niche as First Lady?

I have never believed in generalizations, yardsticks of age or experience. Jackie at any age, I believe, would still have chosen her "yeas and nays." What she liked she did extremely well. What she didn't like she tolerated only when she had to.

Who can forget the President's comment at the dinner with De Gaulle: "I am the man who accompanied Jacqueline Kennedy to

[4] President Arosemena, July 23, 1962.
[5] Tour of the White House, June 24, 1963.

Paris"? Jackie had made her presence more desirable by insisting on her right to choose.

As for politics, I once heard Mrs. Longworth say she thought Jackie was just beginning to enjoy the idea of campaigning when the President was murdered before her eyes.

"At that breakfast in Fort Worth she looked radiant on TV—as if the world were suddenly encased in bunting and motorcades and early morning applause."

How tragically true, we agreed.

For two weeks after the funeral the press badgered Mrs. Johnson, wanting to know when Mrs. Kennedy would move out of the White House. The new First Lady finally made a statement: "I would to God I could serve Mrs. Kennedy's comfort. I can at least serve her convenience."

Lady Bird felt deeply for this young woman as did President Johnson; their hearts were full of compassion for her. They were to make many attempts to lure her back to Washington.

Mrs. Johnson immediately set about completing the Jacqueline Kennedy garden designed for Jackie by her friend Mrs. Paul McIlon. She urged Mrs. Kennedy to attend the formal dedication on April 22, 1965. But Jackie never came, not on this occasion or on others. Returning to the house of so much pomp and so many tears would be too painful, her regrets seemed to say.

In October of 1968, when Jacqueline Kennedy married Aristotle Onassis, my husband and I were in Paris. I was attending a UNESCO conference. The French reaction astonished us. How dare she desert her French public? they asked in different tones and in varying phrases. Jackie, they seemed to say, belonged to those thousands of Frenchmen who adored her, to their recollections of her glamorous visit to Paris, and to the old Hans Christian Andersen legend (the sorcerer casts a spell, turns the beautiful princess into a swan to keep her from returning to mortal ways).

A good many average Joes—Rotarians, farmers, postmasters in one-horse towns, subway riders in oversize cities, Elks on parade— might have expressed the same sentiments as the French. A lot of other Americans, however, might have agreed that it was high time she began a new life. I was one of those.

Jackie will always be a romantic figure—just as she and President Kennedy and their picture-book children were in the White House days. I wish it had been true that Camelot existed somewhere for them. I am afraid it was just a catchy melody with sentimental words, a favorite, perhaps, because the still youthful Kennedys needed to believe another life awaited them.

A good friend once described Jackie as both pragmatic and romantic. Jack Kennedy shared her pragmatism but not her romantic flair. He had given up the luxury of liking and disliking when he started up the political ladder. His imagination worked well in practical channels, be it with Lutheran ministers or steel moguls. He was an expert absorber, as I was to discover for myself.

One day in January 1960, I was invited to lunch with Senator Kennedy in his office. Word had been going round Washington that political leaders were extended such privileges so the Senator might assess their potential helpfulness in his imminent try for the Presidency. I was then Vice Chairman of the Democratic National Committee, a political summit for non-officeholding women.

There was hot food on a steam table, two folding chairs and a card table had been set up. He introduced me to the surroundings by displaying his collection of lithographs and pointing out a ticket to Andrew Johnson's impeachment.

Over chops, peas, milk, and a chocolate and whipped cream concoction that neither of us touched, we pursued our mutual subjects of interest. He was always gallant; he carried off the interview as if I were about to deliver the combined electoral votes of New York, California, and Pennsylvania.

We talked about the issue of religion in the campaign, about the upcoming primaries in Wisconsin, Indiana, and West Virginia, his political rivals, and about whether I could help. The percentage of real anti-Catholic prejudice nationwide amounted to only about eight or nine per cent, he told me. The top churchmen were not for him, he said, "which should be proof that the Church as such does not enter in. I'm not Al Smith," he said, but added that he had a strong appeal for the lace-curtain Irish. I ventured the opinion that a good airing of the pros and cons of electing a Catholic President was long overdue and might help get out a vote. I had been brought up, I confessed, to mistrust the Catholic Church, but had long since rejected this prejudice, along with many others.

Kennedy was certain he could get the plurality vote in Wisconsin but he and Senator Hubert Humphrey might split the delegates. He would hold the eastern part, Hubert the western, and the campaigning would be done down the middle. He was thinking of entering Indiana and West Virginia. Why didn't Senator Stuart Symington take him on in Indiana, the birthplace of the Klan and the most anti-Catholic state? (Senator Symington had not yet announced his Presidential candidacy, but would do so in March 1960.)

As we wound our way through current issues and political personalities, our points of agreement mounted and my comments grew bolder. Chairman Paul Butler had already begun attacking Nixon for his earlier campaign tactics in his fight against Helen Gahagan Douglas, whom he defeated in 1950. We agreed this was beating a dead horse and might embarrass us. Would he tell the Chairman so, I asked? "I wouldn't dream of trying to persuade Paul Butler to desist from doing something," he said with, for him, unmistakable sarcasm.

I suggested he speak more slowly in his public appearances. He told me that he hated reading speeches. "That's why I read them so fast. I'm getting better. I do them mostly without a text."

I tried another tack. "Wouldn't you make the audience feel nearer to you, perhaps warmer toward you, if you singled out one person, looked at him occasionally and smiled?" One got this impression, I added, of his being aloof.

He interrupted me. "It's part of being young, this being aloof, they go together." He then went on to prove that "they" liked him that way. Who was I to contradict? (But he did learn to speak more slowly and to manage his smiles and quips with great flair and "they" did like it that way. John F. Kennedy had broken through the old-style oratory to create a successful new breed of non-orators.)

He never let me feel that he had other business waiting, or that I was not getting his full attention. It was difficult to picture him as sensitive, as someone one could wound. Only later did I learn that he felt unsure of me. He had asked a friend: "Do you think Katie really dislikes me?" Ted Sorensen, Special Counsel to the President, repeated a conversation he had with President Kennedy in the spring of 1963. They had been talking about how few women they had appointed when the President remarked that if only there "were more Katie Louchheims" he could solve his problems.

I took the compliment with more than a grain of salt . . . the President had confidence in me because he knew me. Most men in public life are suspicious of women, and Jack Kennedy had already appointed all the women who had worked with him in the 1960 campaign.

While we were talking and sipping our milk, the phone rang; it was Congressman Wayne Hays, of Ohio, wanting Jackie to be interviewed by one of his home-state papers. "I'll see, Jackie has to do an awful lot of that—I'll see," Kennedy kept saying. He was just beginning to realize what a political asset his wife was; his staff had told me they received literally hundreds of such requests.

Before I left, we talked of his choice, if nominated, for Chairman of the Democratic National Committee. Neil Staebler of Michigan, a new-style political leader who believed in intensive citizen training, participation, workshops, and meetings, and John Bailey, the long-time successful pro of Connecticut, were the front runners.

"What about them?" he asked.

Staebler, I began, was a thoughtful intellectual who wanted everyone to be informed, articulate and, like himself, to devote full-time to politics. Bailey, I felt, understood that there were traditions and differences among the fifty states that defied instruction from the National Committee and its Chairman. Staebler was a product of the era of G. Mennen Williams[6]—who believed that every state could have its "Michigan-type team." Bailey knew better.

Jack Kennedy listened, as he had to all my replies, with courteous attention; he had, I was to discover, a positive genius for absorbing and sorting out advice. Bailey would be my choice, I said, if only he wouldn't persist in posing as a tough cigar-smoking old pro. It gave us such a poor image on TV, and it was a pity to hide his Harvard education under that disguise.

Jack looked at me and laughed. "Don't you like cigars?" he asked as he removed one from his mouth.

When I got up to leave, he reminded me he had wanted to talk about women in the party, but we'd gotten onto more absorbing topics. He let me exit laughing. I walked down the Senate corridor thinking about his offhand manner that hid a certain shyness, and how he never let another person's mannerisms or predilections intrude on his listening apparatus. He never tried too hard; he was neither too friendly nor too remote. If you were going to take up his time, he was going to get the best out of you. He practiced being himself and did it well.

(That same winter, Congressman Hale Boggs came by to talk about his chances of becoming Chairman of the upcoming Democratic National Convention. Hale was the choice of many of his discerning friends, among whom I included myself.

Chairman Butler pointed out that, since Kennedy might be at the head of the ticket, we ought not to have a Catholic convention chairman. Hale, who had nominated Paul Butler as Chairman, and helped him to victory in a close-fought battle, took exception to this point of view. His capable wife, Lindy, was acting as fund-raising dinner co-chairman at Butler's request. Butler's in-

[6] Williams was elected Governor of Michigan five times.

gratitude and prejudice caused Hale to exclaim, "Tell him he better go get himself a Baptist co-chairman.")

When the campaign went into high gear, I saw frequent evidence of careful advance planning and well-selected objectives. Rarely was there any overscheduling or unnecessary delay. But then I had never seen anything like the organizing genius of the Kennedys, whether they were setting up teas for the Senator's mother or sisters, or a rally for twenty thousand. They had always had their own organization—outside of the state machinery.

I first saw Jack Kennedy at the 1952 convention. Martha Rountree staged a television show called *Keep Posted* with unknowns asking questions of VIPs, who stood in for their candidates. We unknowns were seated in rows simulating a studio audience. I cannot remember what questions we asked, but I do recall that next to me sat the unknown Senator John F. Kennedy.

By the time of the 1956 Democratic National Convention everyone knew very well who Senator John F. Kennedy was. Looking back—a habit I find alternately helpful and painful—I can detect the first unmistakable evidence of Chairman Butler's preference for John Kennedy as the 1960 candidate. After Governor Frank Clement of Tennessee had finished his flowery keynote address, we were shown a film called *The Pursuit of Happiness*. CBS found the documentary of Democratic achievements dull and cut away to interview VIPs. Butler, duly exercised at this slight (the film had been produced and paid for by the Democratic National Committee), chastised CBS from the rostrum. The audience, happy to respond, loudly booed the CBS network. But the more historic feature of the event was the fact that the film had been narrated by Senator John F. Kennedy.

Kennedy came out of the Democratic Convention as a good loser in the fight against Kefauver for the second spot on the ticket, thereby avoiding the image-bruising effect of a national defeat. During the next four years I had occasion to call on him for help. Couldn't we find new leadership among the women in his state? Old-timers held a strange hold over younger activists, and Kennedy was cautious in his optimism. "Don't count on it," he said. I knew he was locked in a battle to take over the top state committee jobs and told him I was willing to bet on him. He gave me a brief smile. He smiled more broadly when he came up to me at a public gathering soon thereafter. "We did it," he said, not unaware of his success.

Before he moved into 1600 Pennsylvania Avenue, Jack Kennedy had taken off like a rocket; he was everyone's favorite topic of conversation and a few privileged persons' private property—shared on special occasions with newsmen, hostesses, and a few perceptive women's page reporters. Once Jack Kennedy became President, the privileged few became fewer and their company in turn a privilege in itself. We were lucky: Bill Walton, the successful artist and a Kennedy intimate, happened to be a friend and neighbor. Bill came at the top of anyone's list of the President's (and Jackie's) favorites. He had put his expertise as a reporter (war correspondent for *Life*) at JFK's disposal beginning with the West Virginia primary. We were on Bill's dog-walk route, which made us enviable and put us in the third strata of the fortunate: Relatives, Privileged Few, and Friends of the Privileged Few.

Bill and Charles Bartlett, a columnist, a knowledgeable contented man (he and his wife, Martha, had introduced the President to Jackie), often turned up at quiet dinners with the President. At one such, the President had talked of people, their worth and their relation to the issues. Kennedy had recently asked Dean Acheson to prepare a paper on Berlin, a subject that was heating up. The President had often called upon him for advice, and bestowed on him what in Washington "parlor parlance" are called Presidential attentions.

Acheson, a former Secretary of State, a dashing figure in or out of office, with a high IQ and a low tolerance for other people's judgment, had just criticized Kennedy before members of the Foreign Service. Wasn't he annoyed? Kennedy's dinner guests inquired.

"I know what he said and what he thinks, and I find the latter more valuable," Kennedy had replied. It mattered not whether he was "loyal," the President pointed out. He valued Acheson for his ideas and his brilliant expertise.

Leaving the White House at the reasonable hour of eleven, Bill found he was revved up like a top. Though he can take prizes for his cool, Bill admitted he had had a hard time getting to sleep. Later he ran into Charlie, who also had lain awake until the wee hours. Both agreed that the President undoubtedly went right off to sleep. As Presidents must, he had aired his problems with friends and thus forgotten about them.

When Indira Gandhi visited the United States with her father, Prime Minister Nehru, in November 1961 the Department of State arranged a special program for her. Mrs. Lyndon Johnson gave a lunch at The Elms, their house on Fifty-second Street. Thirty women stood in the drawing room (formerly Perle Mesta's) looking one another over; the President's sisters, Judge Sarah Hughes of Texas, and wives of the capital's most prominent columnists, Mrs. Lippmann and Mrs. Reston, were included.

Several of us were chosen to say a "few words." In my allotted three minutes I catalogued some of our virtues—patience, persistence, and imagination—the only way round seemingly insuperable problems, and summarized by saying: "We can bake a cake without eggs and we can change a world without a title." (This last was a pretty good description of my situation in the Department of State at that time. I held no rank in a rank-conscious bureaucracy.)

That night at the Indian Embassy the President stopped me in the receiving line to say, "I hear you made a very good speech this noon." My husband remarked, "That should hold you for a while." It did. A President's kind words are often more lasting than other more visible gifts. In Kennedy's case, the compliment put me in fighting mood when his amateur critics stopped by. Why didn't the President show more emotion? Why didn't he really let himself go when Gagarin, the Soviet cosmonaut, orbited in space? All he did was congratulate the Russians. Couldn't he have said, "We Americans are not used to being second best"?

Others would complain that he was bent on getting as far away as possible from his background. "The Boston Irish have schmalz," one of their number complained. "Doesn't he know he is repudiating his ancestry?"

"Nonsense," I replied. "He is the gray flannel Harvard version of his grandfather Fitzgerald's dream. He didn't grow up with schmalz."

President Kennedy held many of his press conferences in the new capacious Department of State auditorium. Being a member of the Bureau of Public Affairs entitled me to sit in on them. As I watched Kennedy flash that engaging smile, use his hands as a punching bag, deflect the mean ones with a quip, and call the top members of the press corps by name, I decided Kennedy did not need schmalz.

As Deputy Assistant Secretary in the Public Affairs Bureau, it was also my special privilege to act as greeter and briefer for the President. We would meet the President in the basement where his car and the Secret Service cars could drive in unobstructed and unobserved. On October 15 and 16, 1962, we held our fall briefing. The auditorium was full; five hundred newspaper editors had come from all over the United States. By then they knew that President Kennedy always appeared on the last day.

At three fifty-five on October 16, I went to pick up Under Secretary George Ball. The President was due any minute. We waited, we paced, and then we went back to waiting. The phone on the basement garage wall was supposed to ring, alerting us that the President had left the White House; it remained stubbornly silent. Finally the bells sounded: the President would be late. That happened twice.

I managed to get word to Assistant Secretary Robert Manning[7] to hold on: "Think of something, stall."

[7] Former bureau chief of *Time, Life,* currently editor of *Atlantic.*

The telephone rang a third time. Then two minutes later a general exodus of fast-moving Secret Service burst from four car doors. As I strained to see which car the President was in, he leapt out. In all the times I came to greet him, I never saw him step out of a car. He bolted from it.

The President, Ball, and I, plus the Secret Service, rode the elevator. Word had come through that we were drawing a very reluctant President. He looked the part.

The President asked Manning what had been said. We seemed to be stalled on dead center; no one moved toward the stage, no one spoke. I mentioned the audience's unfriendliness on the issue of foreign aid. He asked who had talked for the program. "Bill Gaud," I replied. "He was good, he did his best, but I don't think they were convinced."

In his remarks the President managed to circle all the crisis areas, new nations, defense problems, Cuba, Berlin, before launching on a stunning defense of foreign aid. Then he said he would take a few questions. Someone asked him what he thought about Ike's recent statement criticizing the Administration's foreign policy. He shrugged his shoulders: "It's that October feeling." Raising his index finger to indicate he was ready for the next question, he then added: "We all get it when election time comes round."

His timing was perfect. Everyone roared. Forty-eight hours later I learned of the Cuban missile crisis. That explained George Ball's gloomy silence, the President's delay in arriving, but not the nonchalance with which he handled what must have been, for him, an unpardonable interruption.

In the spring of 1962 President Kennedy addressed one thousand Foreign Service officers, a "first" for any President. He faced an audience of policy-level officials who regarded any outsider, no matter what his rank, with suspicion.

He told them they were fortunate. He said: "Prewar diplomacy was easier. An Ambassador merely had to attend functions and report home. But today every officer is challenged, every post is difficult, every decision vital." He talked freely about the public's attitude toward the Presidency and the State Department. The average citizen, he said, "tends to take out his frustration on us. The problems are so complex they can't understand them. We are the scapegoats. Usually it's the Secretary of State, but this Secretary has come out unharmed." Secretary Rusk flushed as he looked up at the President. Perhaps he suspected then that the brickbats were bound to come, as they eventually did.

"You have a champion in this Secretary of State," Kennedy assured his listeners. "I respect you. I hope you will continue to press hard for new solutions." He then gave statistics to prove he had appointed fewer non-career Ambassadors than had any previous President. His non-career appointees had been chosen mostly for their merit. He described Ambassador Edwin Reischauer[8] as an example. The President had never met him until the day he came to present his credentials.

"You know that every President is pressured on two fronts, jobs for Postmasters and Ambassadors. When I try to appoint a political supporter from West Virginia, the Secretary stands firm."

All the way through this unprecedented, frank, forty-minute talk the President spoke without a text, and the audience listened without a stir. As he finished, the President stretched out his arms: "Remember that we in the White House love you."

That remark brought down the house. On the way out, when I ran into Secretary Rusk, I told him I was applying for that postmastership in West Virginia.

In June of 1963, I got a call from the White House. "We need you, Katie." Ken O'Donnell, President Kennedy's appointments secretary, had a great idea—the White House would hold a seminar for all summer student interns. Different top brass would speak to them in Constitution Hall every Tuesday for ten weeks.

---

[8] Currently university professor at Harvard. In 1961, professor of Japanese history, Harvard, and Director of the Harvard-Yenching Institute.

I was to "help," a word I had long ago learned to translate as "do the dirty work."

The kickoff would be held on the south White House lawn. "We want you right there next to the President when he speaks," Dottie Davis (Ken's assistant) purred. At subsequent meetings I learned more about my responsibilities and the ambitions of others. We were covered by educational TV, there were 3800 seats in Constitution Hall and 7000 students, the hall was not yet air-conditioned.

The President did not greet the students on the south lawn. The morning of our kickoff it poured. We convened at Constitution Hall instead. Dan Fenn, a young protégé of Ralph Dungan,[9] and I were on hand to greet Kennedy. He walked backstage asking questions. Were the students all from D.C., what kind of work were they doing, real jobs or just messengers' jobs?[10]

"I'd like a summer job myself," the President began. He talked about the advantages of government service and how, if they enrolled, they would have a part to play in carrying out the intent of our founding fathers. He spoke of the Peace Corps, a favorite subject. He told the story of the Peace Corps boy who served in Colombia, South America. He climbed a mountain to call on the village chief, a dedicated Communist. The chief warned him not to preach against Communism; even when it snowed his supporters in the village walked the twenty miles to his mountaintop. Later on, someone asked the Peace Corps boy how he was doing. "I'm waiting for it to snow, so I can walk up the mountain," he replied.

Kennedy left in a hot cloud of applause. At the curb, he looked round, saw the 2000 students who had not been able to get into the hall, and set out to shake hands. Two years later Mat-

9 Special Assistant to President Kennedy.

10 Summer interns were students selected by their colleges to serve in all branches of government during July and August. Most were assigned to substantive posts. A few did clerical work.

thew McCloskey, our former Democratic National Committee Treasurer, told me a story that reminded me of this episode. As Ambassador to Ireland, Matt was on hand to greet President Kennedy when he visited there in the summer of 1963. As the President and his entourage arrived at the gate of the Ambassador's residence in Dublin, a surge of people impeded their progress. They liked Kennedy so well that they imprisoned him in the car. The President insisted on getting out and walking. Although the Secret Service tried to hold back the mob, his well-wishers almost crushed him. When Matt reprimanded the President, Kennedy remarked: "Crowds don't frighten me. It's that fellow standing on the roof with a gun I worry about."

At the end of October 1963, Marshal Tito came to the United States at the invitation of the President. Because he had come on a working visit, a stag luncheon was held at the White House. Thanks to Chief of Protocol Duke's liberal interpretation of the term "stag," Esther Peterson and I were included among fifty-odd males. (Since Madame Tito was present, Mrs. Rusk, Mrs. Fulbright, and one or two wives were also invited.)

I sat between a gentle white-haired Yugoslav General and Senator Dirksen. On his way to his seat, President Kennedy paused to chat with the Senator. They had long been friends. Over the salad, the Senator confessed that this friendship sometimes occasioned difficulties within his own party. I offered the comment that a similar situation had arisen in the Eisenhower years when the Majority Leader, Lyndon Baines Johnson, had been criticized by his own party for trying to steer his fellow Democratic Senators somewhere between opposition for opposition's sake and cooperation for the sake of legislative progress.

After the toasts and the speeches, we adjourned. The President came down to the south portico to see us off. He behaved like any other host; I watched him talk with Kay Graham, President of the Washington Post Company, holding her car door open, before he let her drive off. When Presidents act like ordinary mortals, it has an astonishingly joyous effect upon one.

When it came my turn, I told him Senator Dirksen had appealed to me for help in his campaign. Even though the Minority Leader had merely been kidding, I considered his the best political offer to come my way. The President put on a mock surprised look; he hoped I had said yes. . . .

I never saw John Fitzgerald Kennedy again. After the funeral ceremonials ended, Margie McNamara called me. Did I still have the oil painting of Kennedy that had hung in my outer office? She had told Bob what an excellent likeness it was; could they see it?

The painting was an excellent likeness. In my first days with the Department, I had found it standing on the floor. A secretary explained that the artist, Charles Fox, had left it with "someone" and wanted it hung so it might be sold. I carried it away. Later the artist called to ask me if there had been any inquiries and mentioned the price.

Walter and I took the painting over to the McNamaras, who subsequently negotiated with the artist for its purchase. Before we left the Secretary of Defense and his wife, there had been moments when we could tell that Bob was unable to speak. He sat there in sorrowful silence, looking across the room at the picture with a mixture of affection and despair. Buying this likeness, perhaps, expressed his admittedly hopeless attempt to turn back the clock.

Sometime after the funeral I translated my own sorrowful silence into a poem. I sent it to Jackie, who took the pains to write an acknowledgment by hand.

The poem identified him with the sea which he loved. We often went to Cape Cod as paying passengers on the official press plane. We would watch him get off at Otis Air Force Base. The way he waved, the haste with which he rushed into his waiting car told better than words that he was home. This was his part of the world and his sea—to return to.

A TIME TO KEEP

In Memory of John F. Kennedy

Sunken in the earth he never settled on,
he makes of space a boat to race the wind
and break the barrier back to love, anchored
in the coves of his free mind. Free of time
he sails his dream safe through the gulf between
the human hope—his hopes—and dark places
we call a day, a night, a history,
or death. Filled with recklessness, in his prime,
he sails so light the distance disappears.
He shakes the ground with the roar of his wake
and hangs his words as his starboard light.

My Lovely Country

WE WERE SEATED AT TWO ROUND TABLES AT A LUNCHEON DURING the inaugural festivities for President Kennedy. The guests of honor were Vice President and Mrs. Lyndon B. Johnson. Our hosts, former Secretary of the Interior Oscar Chapman and his wife, had separated husbands and wives. Walter was at a table with Mrs. Johnson and Speaker Sam Rayburn. Conversation turned to the traveling the Johnsons might now have to undertake. Mrs. Johnson looked over at Mr. Sam, as the Speaker's many friends called him. "You've never been out of the country, have you?" she asked, more for confirmation than for reply. "Never have." Mr. Sam nodded his round bald head, as if he had just affirmed an unusual fact—which he had.[1]

My husband recalls that a lively explanation ensued on Mr. Sam's self-imposed travel ban. "First of all, it's this business of getting somewhere and finding it's morning when you just left home at nighttime. And then that terrible, terrible food. Heavens above, it's bad enough eating at these embassies round town."

Everyone at the table laughed; Mr. Sam liked his audiences to laugh. He liked also to end a story with a stern straight-man face and then let it slowly turn into a Mr. Sam smile.

Lyndon Johnson called the House of Representatives Rayburn's great love—"he was at once its master and its servant." As a member of the House for forty-eight years, from 1913 (the sixty-third

[1] Rayburn went to inspect the Panama Canal in 1913, and to Mexico once or twice.

Congress) to 1961, he earned his colleague's respect without trying. Rayburn was Speaker of the House from 1940 until his
death, with the exception of the first two years of the Eisenhower
Administration, when the Republicans controlled the Congress.
He had the longest record as Speaker—double the number of
years Henry Clay served and longer than Uncle Joe Cannon from
Missouri. His companionship was sought after, his favors were
fought for.

When he wasn't surveying his democratic charges from the rostrum, or chinning with them in the cloakroom, he was meeting
with a chosen few in a hideaway just off the House floor where
no one could find him. After the House of Representatives had
adjourned, the Board of Education, as these private sessions were
known, would convene. Drinks would be served, mostly bourbon,
but scotch for those who were partial to it, while members continued the day's education. There was no fixed group, but those
who were welcome knew so. The meetings served as a sounding
board for the Speaker; they kept him informed on how the votes
lined up and what missionary work remained to be done. Invitations went out to the wavering or the recalcitrant; freshmen were
invited on occasion to be persuaded of the merits of pending legislation. The names of the regulars remain shrouded in mystery.[2]
Jack Garner, Franklin Roosevelt's two-term Vice President and
former Speaker, and his good friend Nicholas Longworth[3] originated the idea of these after-hours meetings. In the Longworth-
Garner days, the ice and bottles were discreetly hidden behind the
glass doors of a bookcase (lined in green felt). The reasons for
meeting were at the outset political, so the two veterans could
thrash things out, but it was their fondness for one another that
made sharing an after-work libation a pleasure.

[2] Regular members in recent years often included Louis Dechsler, from Chil-
licothe, Ohio, Parliamentarian, named to his present office by the then
Speaker Longworth in 1925, Congressmen Homer Thornberry, Texas, Richard
Bolling, Missouri, Hale Boggs, Louisiana, John Holton, legislative assistant to
Speaker Rayburn.

[3] Republican, Speaker of the House 1925–31.

On occasion members of the Senate would visit with Speaker Rayburn; among these were Senators Lyndon Johnson and Harry Truman. When President Roosevelt died, Mr. Truman was reached in Mr. Rayburn's hideaway.

The place Mr. Rayburn liked best to be was his native heath, Bonham, Texas. Just before his death on November 16, 1961, in an interview in *U. S. News and World Report*, conducted by his old friend Rags (W. B.) Ragsdale, the Speaker talked about his love of home. "When I get away from Washington, I don't want to go anywhere in the world except home, and to see my lovely country." And that was just the way he would express his very deep-down feelings, simply, tersely, without any fuss or unnecessary adjectives. "Home looks better to me than any place in the world," he added.

That phrase, "my lovely country," describes the man who used those words; he was a country boy, born in an era when the struggle with the earth had not been won, a country boy who fought for the soil tenders and menders the right to have some help in bringing the fruits of the earth to market. He used to talk about rural electrification as the single greatest act the Democrats ever passed. In his part of Texas the farms were dark, the land was sprawly and too far from the power stations. He was a land-lover; a great part of him had never left the simple life, had never forgotten how endless the struggle seemed and how the earth brought a man his reward, if you tended her. "Lovely country" for him were rich words that spoke of rough work and hardships and striving for your home, the pastures, the struggling shade trees, the dusty country roads, some mechanical power, some light in the dark, some help on the way from home to the world.

"When I was a child living way out in the country," he told an audience, "I'd sit on the fence on many Sundays and wish to God that somebody would come by, just to break the loneliness. Loneliness consumes people."

His stubborn determination was bred in his long fight against poverty and loneliness, waged for himself and others. I remember the speech he made in 1952 at the convention when he said, "I feel things deeply, for I have known the poverty that tries men's souls. An underdog in my youth in the back country of a Texas farm, the absorbing interest of my life has been the underdog, an interest that I share with the Democratic Party."

This particular underdog had a lot going for him; no one ever had more people want to show him affection than did Mr. Sam. If he had let them, all his devoted admirers and followers would have consumed him, his days and his nights. He liked the company of women, despite an early unhappy brief marriage which was never discussed. He could ride away all by himself in his big black limousine without anyone thinking him lonely.

But he had his guardians, his sisters, who came to Washington to act as hostesses and companions, and his loyal staff. Alla Clary, his secretary for forty-two years, kept close watch on his calendar. "Miss Alla," as friends called her, never would have accepted any other boss or any other assignment. She had come to Washington in World War I to work as a secretary in the War Department. Young girls, in those days, lived in guarded barracks not too far from Union Station. When it came time to go back to Texas, she went by Congressman Rayburn's office, since she came from his district, to tell him good-by. Why go home? he asked her, and suggested she stay on and work for him.

Miss Alla never did get citified even when she wore party dresses and fancy hats. She had a country look about her square frame, her round glasses, and her unlined wholesome face. She was both proud and friendly if she liked you. Her determination betrayed itself in gesture and speech. She had long since decided that she was not going to stay at home and play old maid; there was a world to see and partake of. At eighty she is still traveling around the globe to see it all. She had a rough tongue and a frankness that astonished some of Mr. Sam's telephone callers. One famous hostess, when she suggested that the Speaker come to dinner on a certain night, was met with an abrasive prompt turndown. "What are you trying to do," expostulated Miss Alla, "kill him?" That particular hostess never called again, which was precisely what Miss Alla intended.

At a luncheon in 1955, in the famous Speaker's dining room with its great gilt mirror, red brocade draperies, and very nineteenth-century air, Mr. Sam's extraordinary health became topic A. The hostess was Dorothy Vredenburgh (now Mrs. Jack Bush), the pretty Secretary of the Democratic National Committee. The guest of honor was a doctor, which led Mr. Sam into the subject.

"Went to the doctor. Hadn't been in years. Had a real checkup," he began. "Couldn't find one thing the matter with me, not one doggone thing. Weighed 176 all my life, found I weighed 176½. Went home and told my sisters, 'I'm going to have to go on a diet.'" Then he helped himself twice to potatoes and corn bread and shot at me, "Anything wrong with that steak, Katie? You seem to be lookin' off it." There wasn't a thing wrong with my steak except my fascination with what he was saying and his heaping plate. He had a brash little boy's way of bragging and a persuasive "I dare you" that made you want to heap your plate too.

"Never been sick a day in my whole life," he insisted, and went on to tell how he would go off to the woods on his farm with an ax and fell trees. "This," I thought, "can't happen too often, so there's no telling what keeps him so sound." But later he did share his secret; he took a tablespoon of honey every day, sometimes two, one in the afternoon. "You'd be surprised," he advised us, "you get as much relaxation and pickup as out of a drink." From then on, I sent him honey of all kinds for his birthday (January 6). On the card I would write, "For the sweetest Democrat of them all," and, in turn, he would send me notes of thanks that were personal and touching. The very last note struck me as almost prophetic. "Every time I have a birthday and receive such messages and remembrances [the honey, which he had described as a "thoughtful thing to do"] as yours, it makes me gladder that I have lived. To me, life has been full and satisfying, and to know that I have the well wishes of good folks like you makes me happy indeed."

Hundreds of folks got such notes, for they too were part of his largehearted appreciation for mankind.

He was blessed not only with good health but with wit and with the instinct for the right action. He liked to brag that he could walk along any street with his hat on and no one would know him. But once you had looked at that face, you could not mistake it for another. He did look very much like a small-town American; his rounded proportions suited him and he dressed as though he were unconscious of what he wore.

He kept everything he did and knew in his head: complicated parliamentary questions, some colleague's interest in a bill, a thousand and one floor actions, chairmen's and subcommittee chairmen's requests, a head count for an upcoming vote, no matter what. You could always stop him en route to the floor or outside the cloakroom or in the halls of the Capitol and get an answer. How did he know what he had previously promised or not promised? his questioners would ask. Simple, all you had to do was tell the truth. Once you did, you could never trip yourself up because your answers would always be the same. And, of course, everyone who dealt with him knew this, believed in him, and trusted him.

He liked his jokes because he made them up; addressing the teeming thousands that filled the Memorial Coliseum that night of Senator Kennedy's acceptance speech following the Democratic Convention in 1960, Rayburn began by remarking, "I am a young man" (he was then going on eighty) "and new in politics and, therefore, I am so deeply grateful that all of these thousands and thousands of people would come out to greet me this evening." A roar like breaking waves swept over the green hillsides, and for those of us within range, a marvelously low responding chuckle came from the Speaker. Mr. Sam's homemade wit was understated, it glanced off you and would catch you on the rebound. One of his favorite openers was about the man who, when asked what he was to talk about, got told: "About ten minutes." He was gently caustic about the Republican opposition: the term "Modern Republicans" could more aptly be translated to read "Modern Antiques." He never spoke critically of the Republicans' popular President, General Eisenhower, but would creep up on him with: "Ike was a fine baby, that I know. He had to have been. He was born in my district." Before the end of his talk (if we were nearing election time), he would throw in a serious line: "I've been traveling round the country and the American people are thinking. When the American people think, that's bad for the Republicans."

Mr. Sam did not like to use a text; he preferred to stand, grasp the edge of the banquet table with both hands, and begin. He knew his audiences; unlike the man whom he liked to joke about, he knew just "about" how long to talk. Invariably he would mention "his boys," as he liked to refer to those who had served in the House of Representatives and gone on to the Senate. Looking up and down the head table with pride, he would call their names. He was fond, too, of remarking that what the House needed was "more fine young men." He would turn to Mike Kerwin, senior Congressman from Youngstown, Ohio, and leader of the House Congressional Committee for Fund Raising and Recruitment, and urge him to "travel round and pick them out." He would remind the audience to beware of the "one-termers" like those washed up on the waves of Franklin Roosevelt's popularity; "we never saw them again."

He could be solemn without being preachy. No one who ever heard him speak out against bitter partisanship will forget his warning: "I have no time for hate. Hate consumes the person hating; we don't hate people, we hate things."

One of the prerogatives of my headquarters job was to sit by Mr. Sam at the 1956 convention in Chicago. The platform was well guarded: Fishbait (William M. Miller, the Majority doorkeeper of the House since 1949) would protect the back entrance where a chain kept out intruders. To our right a stairs descended to the floor of the hall. Here another of the faithful, Walter L.

Hunt, stood by a defending chain. The late, beloved Clarence Cannon, long-time Congressman from Missouri and convention parliamentarian, sat on one side with me and Dorothy Vredenburgh, the party Secretary, who called the roll of the states for the "ayes" or "nays" and for nominations. On the other side of the platform sat the late Leslie Biffle, Sergeant-at-Arms of the U. S. Senate, along with the reading clerk and the tally clerk.

Fishbait, whose miraculous bellowing astonishes TV audiences when he leads the Diplomatic Corps, the Senate, the Cabinet, the Supreme Court, the Vice President and, finally, the President himself into the well of the House of Representatives to deliver the State of the Union Message, is a familiar figure on Capitol Hill. (The Senate chamber, being smaller, is never used on these occasions.) Fishbait earned his nickname because as a fifteen-year-old boy he weighed only seventy-five pounds, thereby resembling the shrimp he used as bait for fishing in Pascagoula, Mississippi. He has developed a special affinity for ceremonial occasions: his chubby figure stands framed in the doorway of the House poised for a dramatic entrance. "Mr. Speaker," he bellows loud and clear, his words stretched out like an accordion, "the President of the United States."

Fishbait's heart is as expansive as his lung power. As Majority doorkeeper since 1949, he serves one and all the members, Republican or Democratic, with affectionate solicitude. He had long ago adopted the Speaker as his special charge. Be it at political dinners, meetings, or on convention platforms, Fishbait's two bright eyes behind his thick specs never let his charge out of sight. All Mr. Sam had to do was crook his finger or just look in Fishbait's direction and he would come charging over.

Our jobs on the platform could best be described as "keeping Mr. Sam cool." Every message, written or whispered, was screened by those of us nearest to the Speaker. We saw to it that he was not disturbed at the wrong moment and that trivia did not reach him. Telegrams voicing grass-roots opinion came in droves. At first I took them seriously until I realized that the urge to tell someone of importance what you think sooner or later strikes everyone, like the common cold. At one of the opening ceremonies, a Congressional Medal of Honor winner gave the pledge of allegiance to the flag. Unfortunately, he forgot to include the phrase "under God." I counted over a hundred wires from outraged citizens who protested in all possible variations of indignation. When I reported on this deluge to Mr. Sam he commented, "By gosh, we sure have an audience that's paying attention."

The Speaker, of course, served as permanent convention chairman. His mood was equable and serene, until someone challenged his ruling. When Mr. Sam got that dour look and banged the gavel hard, Mr. Cannon, who had his own brand of satire, would remark; "It's not the way he feels, but the wind from the stockyards is blowing from the wrong direction."

On August 15, 1956, at the third session of the Democratic Convention, the Platform and Resolutions Committee presented its report. Democratic Conventions, if not otherwise torn by strife, can always manage to get a good brawl going on such an occasion. The language presented in a minority report attempted to strengthen the platform language on civil rights enforcement. The battle of semantics was joined. The Speaker heard out all the spokesmen and called for a vote on adoption or rejection of the minority report. No sooner were the "ayes" and the "nays" heard than Mr. Rayburn's "In the opinion of the chair" was interrupted by loud cries for "Roll call, roll call."

The Speaker struck the gavel. "Well now, just a moment," he began harshly, "I have taken 'ayes' and 'nays' many times and I think I can tell which one has the most." His jaw had a look of determination. The proceedings then went forward; the minority report was rejected, the majority report adopted.

From where I sat I could sense that other annoyances were disturbing the Speaker. His instructions to the delegates to remain seated sounded bellicose. "I do trust," he continued with ill-concealed wrath, "that flags that may be offensive to anybody in the chamber will not be displayed." Turning to us, he cursed the offenders who had raised Confederate flags. The defeat of the minority report had caused extremists in some Southern states to raise Confederate flags as a sign of victory for their conservative anti-civil rights cause. Bang, bang went the gavel, and again Mr. Sam spoke vehemently. "I do trust that each and every member of this convention will have regard for the feelings of all other members of the convention." Each syllable shot forth accompanied by a deadly glare. He then introduced the next speaker. Before he resumed, just for our ears, he uttered a few choice epithets.

On Thursday, the sixteenth of August, ten men were nominated for the Presidency. That evening on the first ballot Adlai E. Stevenson was acclaimed the party's choice. Adlai then proceeded to electrify the hall by announcing that he wished the delegates to choose their Vice President.[4] In all the history of party conventions, the practice of choosing one's own running mate had been sacred to the Presidential candidate. A great scramble ensued. By balloting time, on the night of August 17, each state had been lobbied by one of the seven Vice Presidential contenders. Most states had badly split delegations.

By the time of the second ballot, it was clear that the contest lay between Senators Kennedy and Kefauver. (Kefauver led with 483½ votes, Kennedy's total was 304. The final count was Kefauver 755½ and Kennedy 589.) Although the official proceedings recount only the orderly alphabetical roll call of states, midway in the second ballot, pandemonium broke loose when the Speaker recognized Tennessee. The Speaker pointed his finger at Senator Albert Gore (a candidate for Vice President with 178 votes on the first ballot) and asked: "Does the State of Tennessee desire recognition?" After their chairman, Mr. "Hub" (Herbert Walters), had affirmed that Tennessee did indeed wish to be recognized, the Speaker, according to the official record, spoke these historic words:

[4] Roger Stevens, Chairman of the Kennedy Center for the Performing Arts, suggested opening up the Vice Presidential contest because the convention had been dull and needed some drama. Stevens, who acted as Adlai Stevenson's principal fund raiser, had a sense of the dramatic—his chief interest lay in producing plays.

"The chair recognizes the Senator from Tennessee by unanimous consent only." Parliamentary proceedings do not permit interruption of a roll call unless by unanimous consent. What the recording secretary could not hear or did not take down was, I've been told, something like this: "I ask unanimous consent to suspend the rules. Is there objection—the chair hears none," and bang, bang, the Speaker's gavel accorded him the right he had already taken. The delegates were vociferous either in approval or against recognition of Tennessee. Minutes passed before the Speaker could gavel the hall into a listening mood.

When the uproar subsided, Senator Gore withdrew as a candidate in favor of his fellow Senator, Estes Kefauver. Mr. Rayburn then recognized Governor Gary, head of the Oklahoma delegation. The Governor, following Tennessee's example, switched to Kefauver. By then, Estes Kefauver had sewed up the nomination.

The question was why, amidst a forest of banners held aloft by delegation heads screaming for recognition, did the Speaker's eye gravitate to those two states? Some maintain it was chance, others that it was premeditated because Rayburn preferred Kefauver over Kennedy. Long-time Rayburn watchers claim that, having campaigned hard for Al Smith (the first Catholic candidate for President) in 1928, the Speaker became convinced no one could either dilute or diminish the voters' prejudice against a Catholic in the White House. Others, knowing Rayburn as fair and impartial, pointed out that he had never had much use for Estes Kefauver. He considered the latter too much of a self-seeker who used his crime investigation to promote himself. Rayburn's close friend, former President Truman, had not thought kindly of Kefauver either.

Nostalgia may have prompted Mr. Sam to recognize Tennessee; he was born there and these were his folks. His choice of Oklahoma (which he recognized after Tennessee and before Missouri, Minnesota, and other states whose delegates were clamoring for recognition) may have been another personally dictated gesture. The Speaker and Governor Gary of Oklahoma were trusted old friends;

they lived only fifty miles apart across their mutual state border. But these are "fringe" explanations, offered in the rosy half-light of hindsight.

Sifting legend and fact, I have concluded that on that particular afternoon Mr. Sam was "jumpy on the Catholic issue" and annoyed with Adlai for throwing the convention open on the Vice Presidency. Any other conclusions were purely speculative.

The only event, that famous afternoon, whose origins and consequences none can dispute occurred when the electric tally board broke down. Somewhere toward the end of the second ballot its mechanized breathing choked over too many half votes and it came to a halt. There were moans and groans from the floor, but by then everyone pretty well knew Estes Kefauver was the winner.

Rumors still persist that the Speaker considered being a candidate for Vice President himself. But when supporters tried to persuade the Speaker to run as Texas' favorite son at the 1956 convention, he turned them down. "Nowadays," he told them, "a man is considered old after forty and I'll be seventy-five by 1957." Rayburn was a front-row witness to Garner's sudden descent from power as Vice President to FDR (for two terms, 1932 to 1940) and therefore would not have been tempted to reach for this office. Garner had preceded Rayburn as Speaker.

After Kennedy's persuasive Houston TV appearance (before the clergymen in the 1960 campaign), Rayburn completely overcame his fears about public reaction to a Catholic candidate. He also came round on Kefauver; after the latter's drug investigation he referred to him as a "fine Senator."

Mr. Rayburn possessed a modesty rarely found in political figures. He must have disparaged all the emphasis on his actions on that politically significant August afternoon. He lived at ease with his authority. On the Hill, his nod of approval moved mountains, even normally immovable mountains of money. When General George Marshall and Secretary of War Henry Stimson asked him for eight hundred million dollars to develop the atomic bomb they explained they could not go before a Congressional Committee and answer questions. The Germans were at work on a similar project: the secret had to be kept. Mr. Rayburn's power was such that he got the funds from the Congressional Chairman simply by telling them the money was needed for the "war."

The Speaker and I, seated together at the fashionable F Street Club one evening, watched the carefully dressed guests come through the door. When Lady Bird and the then Majority Leader Lyndon Johnson appeared, the famous Rayburn finger pointed in their direction: "There's the finest damn woman ever walked the earth." He had on many occasions spoken to me of Lady Bird, of her capacity for understanding, her consideration of others, her wise advice, and even her ability at political maneuvering. On that particular evening, he shook his head: it worried him to think of the effect Lyndon Johnson's deep-down wish to be President might have on her.

For years Mrs. Johnson gave the Speaker a children's party on his birthday. Theirs was an affectionate intimacy that grew out of mutual respect. Mr. Sam was a frequent guest at the Johnsons', and his relationship to the President was fatherly, as well as regionally and philosophically attuned. He was devoted to the tall Texan whom he had helped bring into prominence. "Lyndon," he would brag, "was one of my boys."

There were many stories, some apocryphal, about Mr. Sam's role in persuading Lyndon Johnson to take second spot with Kennedy in 1960. At the outset, Rayburn was unalterably opposed to the idea. He wanted the Majority Leader to stay where he was because he knew how unhappy and frustrated he would be as Vice President. Mrs. Johnson was inclined to agree with him. When Jack Kennedy heard of the Speaker's determined opposition, he went to see him; he convinced Mr. Sam that if Lyndon did not join the ticket he could not win. "Do you want Richard Nixon as President?" Kennedy put the question bluntly. Mr. Sam's conversion was immediate. Certain that Kennedy did need Johnson to win, he urged Johnson to accept the offer. It was well known that the Majority Leader had made up his mind not to accept without Mr. Sam's firm approval; the Speaker's urging weighed heavily.

The Speaker once told me he'd had a call from Ed Murrow asking if he, Mr. Sam, thought Ed had the qualifications to run for the Senate in New York. Mr. Sam, in his monosyllabic fashion, turned back the question with "If anyone knows politics, you do, Ed." In telling me, he concluded modestly: "What d'ya know?" The episode made an impression on me because Ed Murrow called Mr. Sam despite the fact that the Speaker had never served in the Senate. The Speaker was everybody's authority on politics and a politician's politician as well.

One January afternoon just after President Eisenhower had completed his State of the Union message, I waited with a group outside the Speaker's office. A member of the Speaker's staff was telling about a long-distance call he took during the President's message. An irate woman in Ohio requested the Speaker to please sit still so that she could get a better TV view of the President. We were laughing when the Speaker walked in. I told him about the favorable comments on his appearance the previous evening before the Women's National Press Club. "What d'ya know?" he chortled and, turning, asked, "What did I say?"

I felt like answering, "You just told them the truth and they all believed and trusted you." Instead I repeated some of his remarks. He shook his head and said, "Well, what d'ya know?"

The Tall Texan

LYNDON JOHNSON AND SAM RAYBURN HAD MORE THAN POLITICS IN common; their beginnings were modest and they both loved the land.

President Johnson earned his education, a Texas pay-as-you-go schooling. Unlike Roosevelt, Kennedy, and Wilson, he did not wear the right school ties or hold Ivy League degrees.

Lyndon Baines Johnson has been accused of many things, not the least of them that he came from the wrong part of the country. I am bored with all the talk about Texas being the land of oil-rich indifferent millionaires and nobody else but some well-bred cattle and a lot of destitute Mexicans. The President's Texas was a very modest, very real, very rural backwater with some nice smoke-colored live oak and a lot of hard white limestone caliche soil where rock deposits were as plentiful as cactus.

Mrs. Johnson described the countryside as "blue skies and white caliche." The white limestone deposit was left from an early geological age; if you dug down deep you could find patterns made by little fish. While Mr. Sam's soil was black and fertile, the President's land challenged men and aged women. When you live in an area where only 29 inches of rain falls a year, the land really does offer a challenge. But improve it he did (by means of irrigation), and in the process, improving one's surroundings became a part of his philosophy. He learned early the importance of getting the best out of everything—people as well as soil.

Lyndon was and is a man of the land and he likes nothing better than to prove it to you. Some might say he was an agrarian, or a populist, or both, but he does not like labels and they never satisfy everyone anyway. We do know he was born poor and wanted to get an education, an income, and all the other things most human beings want, including a family, some property, and some public esteem. Being a tall, persuasive, aggressive man, he went about it in a tall, aggressive, persuasive way.

One spring noon in 1967, I stood on the sloping banks overlooking the Pedernales. The President and Mrs. Johnson had invited all thirty-four of the Latin American Ambassadors to spend a weekend with them, and I had been included as a helping pair of hands. The day was fair, the warm wind blew the willows in their tender green; comfortable-looking cattle chewed their way through new grass on the other side of the river.

Johnson friends, in appropriately informal ranch-country attire, stood grouped about. The well-known barbecuer, Walter Jettson, and his minions were busily at work. A marvelously golden carcass could be seen turning round and round on a huge spit; pits of delicious-smelling ribs and other victuals perfumed the air. Performers from Albany, Texas, ordinary citizens who act out every summer a historic review called *The Texas Fandango*, looked picturesque in their 1800 costumes. In the distance one could see men dressed as Spanish conquistadors, cantering their horses in preparation for their dramatic entrance.

Young women, looking as striking as only pretty young women can in white boots, blue denim skirts, checked blouses, and white Texas-style Stetsons, supplied each of the waiting guests with a red and white bandana to be worn around the neck. We passed the kerchief through a loop made of a wooden map of Texas with the initials LBJ stamped on it. The President and Mrs. Johnson were showing the ranch to the Ambassadors while we made friends with their friends.

I chose a distinguished-looking gray-haired couple who, in true Texas style, immediately made me feel I was the one person they wanted to talk to. Harry Jersig had known Lyndon as a boy. Now president of a successful brewing company, Jersig also started out with nothing. Years back, when the President was a lanky lad of sixteen and Jersig was twenty-two, Jersig was a frequent boarder at the President's mother's boardinghouse. It cost two dollars a night to stay with Rebecca Johnson in Johnson City. Jersig was in the candy business; he went from door to door with his sample case. He hired the fine-looking boy to work for him after school and on weekends.

Lyndon's territory included every house in an adjacent area. His job was to carry the suitcase with the candy samples and open the gate for the salesman. In those days lots of folks went from door to door; you had to be good to get past the gate, the barking dog, and the busy housewife. You also needed an arresting, intrusive manner and a willingness to try, try again. Lyndon was paid the munificent sum of twenty-five cents a gate. On good days, his reward was the sample box of peanut brittle, plus a bonus.

"Not so long back," Harry Jersig told me, "I went into the ranch house and there, in a drawer underneath one of those special white telephones, was a box of peanut brittle." The President kept it hidden from Mrs. Johnson, who rationed his intake. It was still his favorite candy.

I never could make up my mind which I liked best: the story about the gate opener or the way it was told. Jersig's affection came through; he still rejoiced in the accidental circumstance that had brought him a lifelong friendship with a future President of the United States. He was just enough older, he pointed out, and enough of a salesman himself to recognize talent in his assistant.

Rarely are Americans pro-anyone. Our cynicism, particularly in Washington, is nurtured on what we describe as the lowdown. Every public figure is satirizable. Timidly, and only in safe corners of crowded cocktail parties, do we admit to being for someone. I developed an enthusiasm for Lyndon B. Johnson, years ago, and despite the stigma this awards me in various circles, I brave on happily. I cannot remember the first time I met him. James Rowe, who in the thirties served as one of FDR's assistants (a job described as requiring a "passion for anonymity"), introduced us. Later, Rowe asked my husband and me for a contribution to Congressman Johnson's campaign. In the rear mirror of my mind I see the lively, talkative young Congressman in his office, and myself, calling on him. I can remember thinking, "This young Congressman will go places."

Jim Rowe lived next door to us with a group of bachelors until he married Elizabeth Ullman in 1937, the year Lyndon B. Johnson became the Representative from the 10th District of Texas. The young couple entertained frequently. The guests, including the Johnsons and ourselves, were mostly New Dealers; we were all young and enthusiastic about almost everything that came along. Lyndon would walk around tables and chairs as if they were an obstacle race, gathering up listeners and assaulting them with events and opinions, driving them over the political road ahead with one hand on the wheel and the other gesturing wide.

In 1953, when I acceded to the title of Director of Women's Activities for the Democratic National Committee, Senator Johnson became Minority Leader. (President Eisenhower's total victory in 1952 swept in a Republican Congress, the only one during the eight years of his Presidency.) From 1953 to 1960, I watched the Minority Leader become Majority Leader and handle an entrenched power structure in the Senate. He dealt with committee chairmen as diverse as the venerable Carl Hayden of Arizona, who ruled over Appropriations; Senator Richard Russell of Georgia, the formidable head of Armed Services; the intellectual Rhodes Scholar, William J. Fulbright of Arkansas, who eventually rose to chair the prestigious Committee on Foreign Relations; the champion of fiscal responsibility, and chairman of the Finance Committee, Senator Harry Byrd of Virginia; the powerful spokesman for the deep South, Senator James Eastland of Mississippi, Chairman of Judiciary; and the respected investigator Senator John

McClellan, whose Committee on Government Operations was to expose Joe McCarthy. All these men ruled not only because their mandates were inherited by virtue of seniority but also because most of them came from one-party states.

In spite of them, Lyndon Johnson managed to get the very first civil rights bill passed, granting basic voting rights (in principle) to the disenfranchised blacks. The vote took place on the night of August 7, 1957. I sat in the gallery, enthralled, watching Lyndon and his lieutenants operate on the floor. We inhaled the first breath of what we hoped was a bright new era of race relations. At last the armistice had been broken, the eighty-year tacit truce between the two parties that had forsworn any action in this area. The bill was more of a symbol than the blueprint for the future we all wished for, but the emotion of that evening still clings to the accounts of what transpired.

Steve Mitchell, Chairman of the Democratic National Committee until 1954, felt that we must recognize the divisions in the Democratic Party but work together. Steve was a liberal on all counts, despite his unregenerate enmity toward the ADA: he disapproved of working outside the party structure. Though Lyndon Johnson held similar views, the relationship between these two men never really got beyond the necessary formalities. Steve instead dealt with Speaker Sam Rayburn.

By the time of Adlai Stevenson's defeat in 1956, the seeds of dissension were sprouting all over green baize committee tables, at political fund-raising repasts, and in the anterooms of office-holders. For all the six years Paul M. Butler, Mitchell's successor, was Chairman of the Democratic National Committee (1954-60), he and Majority Leader Johnson were at odds. Sometimes it was something tangible, more often there was no describable cause. Because the Johnsons had long been my friends, Butler threatened to replace me; he had the power, he assured me. "Go right ahead," I shot back. No matter what he said or did, the Johnsons would be my friends.

Any relationship can begin on the wrong foot; theirs did. Butler wanted a Democratic Party in the all-out liberal image. Lyndon Johnson not only inherited a Senate ruled by conservatives, but in his close 1948 race for the Senate (won by 87 votes) he had learned that the middle of the road was a reasonably safe place from which to operate. Texans attest to the fact that even the beloved Mr. Sam could never have been elected state-wide, nor could the liberal members of the Texas delegation in the House. When Johnson first ran, his supporters were only a handful of friends; some were moderately well to do, but not until he achieved power as Majority Leader did some of the new rich become LBJ fans.

When Paul Butler set up the Democratic Advisory Council, in November of 1956, on which the defeated candidates, Stevenson and Kefauver, and other liberal lodestars like John F. Kennedy, Eleanor Roosevelt, Hubert Humphrey, and Averell Harriman served, its purpose was to give visibility to a liberal philosophy. Butler felt the "image" projected by the Democratic leadership (who were dealing with an enormously popular Republican President) was far from adequate.

The Majority Leader and Speaker Rayburn politely but firmly refused to participate in the Council. The Speaker flatly told Advisory Council members Kenneth Galbraith, California's Governor Pat Brown, Senator Stuart Symington, and others, "President Eisenhower knows I turned down an offer to sit in on his Cabinet meetings." That same principle, he pointed out, would apply to any outside body.

Majority Leader Johnson would inquire mockingly of me whether the DNC was still mad at him. Not mad, afraid of him, I would say. We were both kidding; the Majority Leader was speaking of Butler, who was afraid of no one. I was talking about everyone else from Adlai Stevenson to the committeeman from a minor state who trembled at the mention of LBJ. Johnson would then give me an abridged version of his original refusal to serve on the Advisory Council: "You can't advise the Senate. Not even Eleanor Roosevelt can do that. I'll take all the advice they want to give me [they being the Council], but not via leaks or over the transom." Lyndon did not care for Chairman Butler's planted news stories labeling him intransigent and conservative.

In the early spring of 1956, LBJ's native state bloomed with brand-new effective liberal leaders. Established conservatives kept fighting this new growth. Allan Shivers, then Governor, announced he would lead the Texas delegation to the convention as favorite son. His regime represented a conservative Republican point of view. The garrulous new liberals countered with a campaign to take the delegates' votes away from him. I watched the two groups cannibalize each other and saw Lyndon Johnson work them over alternately as missionary and policeman. I should have known that our hopes for some kind of peace treaty and workable ground rules were in vain.

At the state convention in May of '56, the Majority Leader, the Speaker, two unusually competent women, Mrs. Frankie Randolph of Houston and Mrs. Kathleen Voight of San Antonio, the top AFL man, Jerry Holleman, and Byron Skelton of Temple, assisted by various friends, took over.[1] The liberals knew they could not have won without LBJ—probably all will agree except Mrs. Randolph, who, according to legend, took umbrage at a slight meted out to her by the Majority Leader when he failed to seat her on the platform after the liberal takeover at the state convention.

Both Mrs. Randolph and Mrs. Voight deserve a large share of the credit for organizing the state county by county. Frankie Randolph, a handsome, wealthy aristocrat, a chain smoker with a mannish manner, believed in labor, the rights of minorities, Senator Ralph Yarborough,[2] whom she helped elect, and in anything that would block Lyndon B. Johnson's desire to be President. She intended to stop the latter even if it meant throwing herself on the tracks of his onrushing train.

[1] Mrs. Randolph was the Democratic Committeewoman for Texas and Byron Skelton the Democratic Committeeman.

[2] Senator Yarborough was defeated for reelection for a third term in the Texas primary, May 1970.

Mrs. Randolph purchased the *Texas Observer* when it was a little-read weekly and turned it into a brilliant bimonthly magazine. Anti-Johnson, anti-oil and gas lobby, it employed bright young men, among them Willie Morris, who later became editor of *Harper's* magazine at the age of thirty-two.[3] Mrs. Randolph held integrated meetings in Houston when it was dangerous to do so. One of her followers was Hobart Taylor, a large, sympathetic, soft-spoken black leader from Houston, whose son Hobart, Jr., came to prominence ironically under President Johnson, who appointed him Executive Director of the Export-Import Bank.

When Senator Yarborough was elected in 1956, Mrs. Randolph and other of his followers descended on Washington for the swearing in and postceremonial celebration. The Majority Leader gave a lunch in his honor which Mrs. Randolph refused to attend. At a party at the Hotel Washington, I was standing beside Mrs. Randolph when Lyndon appeared in the doorway. His appearance, when he knew one of the hosts was not exactly receptive to his presence, deserved acknowledgment. I urged Frankie to cross the floor and shake his hand. "It can't hurt you," I muttered, giving her a gentle shove. But Frankie stood her ground. A cigarette hanging from her lips, she said, "Never," in her low-pitched voice and remained stationary until Lyndon left.

One liberal Texas admirer of Mrs. Randolph and Mrs. Voight claimed that they were the most impressive organizers he had ever encountered. He added sadly, "But when they played the slighted-lady role they changed character and became difficult."

At the 1960 convention, after Johnson had been nominated as Vice President, he came to the platform accompanied by his seconders. From my seat in the far corner I watched Paul Butler look at Lyndon Johnson, turn away, and refuse to shake hands. To make the distance across that empty space was perilous. If you crossed over the camera was apt to catch you, but in my eagerness to greet LBJ, I forgot the rules, clasping the nominee's hand

[3] Editor of *Texas Observer* and author of *North Towards Home*.

with all the enthusiasm I could register. After LBJ's speech the afternoon session came to a close. Mrs. Paul Butler, who had been sitting in the gallery with my husband, came to the platform exit. "My husband did not have to shake hands with LBJ. But you did." I said something harsh but it didn't matter. She was too mad to hear me.[4]

Like all public figures, Lyndon Johnson has suffered from persons whose loyalty he never questioned, as well as from friends whose political views caused them to oppose him. Senator Eugene McCarthy and Senator J. William Fulbright are classic examples. In the case of the senior Senator from Minnesota, Hubert Humphrey, the opposite was true. Had I been the betting type I could have won money on Hubert's selection as Vice President in 1964. During the 1950s, I watched the political rapport between these two men grow into friendship. The liberal Hubert and the powerful Lyndon worked well together; they complemented each other. I was a witness to a bantering conversation between them, almost a "will you, won't you" interchange, as early as March 1955.

At that time I sat between them at a gathering of Senators held by the Democratic National Committee to stir up enthusiasm for an upcoming fund-raising affair. I took in every word that passed between them. The Majority Leader was talking forcefully; knowing Lyndon well, I recognized affection underneath the proprietary tone of his voice. The conversation, without some of the four-letter words, went like this:

"Where are you when I want you?" he demanded of Humphrey. "Damn you, I want to know where you are *all* the time." This was a brand of Johnsonian flattery and Hubert knew it.

"You're either talking to the NAACP or the ADA or you're in the basement with some do-gooders," the Leader went on. Before Hubert could reply, Lyndon disarmed him. "I'm telling you, I

[4] After Chairman Paul Butler's death on December 30, 1961, his widow was given a position in the government.

need you. Where were you today when I gave you a chance on FEPC [Fair Employment Practices Commission]?"

"I had things on my mind," Hubert finally got to say.

"Damn you," Lyndon's scolding continued, "you've got six years under your belt, pay attention to the Senate."

Senator Humphrey took his Majority Leader's advice, although he still went on meeting with constituents and defenders of liberal causes, sometimes even in the basement, when all other public rooms in the Capitol were full.

After Lyndon Johnson's heart attack in 1955, I went to call on him at his home where he was recuperating. It was a warm, rainy day in August. I had persuaded a friendly volunteer from the office to drive me out in her car. I didn't mind asking her to wait for me since we had National Committee matters to talk about and Lyndon was a very sick man. I was certain the visit would last at most fifteen minutes. It lasted an hour.

Lady Bird Johnson once described their red brick, white-trimmed abode on 30th Place as a typical John Q. Citizen house: she was correct; you could hardly tell it from its neighbors. The street was tree-lined and shady; in the steamy rain that afternoon the branches gave an added protection from the elements. A straight walk led up to the door; the usual number of downstairs rooms opened off a center hall. But it was the back porch facing a happy yard of mixed shrubbery that we still talk about. Zephyr, the Johnsons' long-time cook, used to hand-freeze peach ice cream on that porch—it was often part of the menu when the Johnsons entertained.

That afternoon Mrs. Johnson greeted me and took me upstairs to the Majority Leader's bedroom. He sat on a mechanized chair that behaved as if it were double-jointed and could move or be moved like a caterpillar, expanding and contracting. There were flowers everywhere I looked. A huge TV and an even bigger hospital-size sun lamp stood guard. He wore a yellow shirt, monogrammed socks, canvas hospital slippers, and a pale yellow blanket across his lap. Mrs. Johnson perched gracefully on the bed.

The chair dropped down, and he began talking about "people" and how good they are. "They tell me this one lies and that one hates, but they never do it to me." He had been touched by gestures during his illness: the perpetual high mass which nuns attended in New Jersey, and by "old Lehman" (then Senator from New York), who got up on the Senate floor and called for a moment of silent prayer. "Mind you, he and I are friends, but not that close," he said, and added with a touch of awe, "I've been too near my Maker."

The chair swayed. He began telling me of the origins of his heart attack. As he talked I recalled a dinner Senator Symington gave at which I was seated between Lyndon and Senator Earle Clements[5] of Kentucky. The intensity of Lyndon's remarks that night about Senator Joseph McCarthy's destructive powers convinced me that his anger against McCarthy helped precipitate the heart attack.

The chair bounced. He leaned forward and confided to me that he had purposely stacked the Senate Committee with Southerners to censure McCarthy; he knew their astuteness would more than match McCarthy's. Senator Sam Ervin of North Carolina did not want to serve but Senators Richard Russell and Walter George[6] of Georgia persuaded him. Then he told about the day he had brought Joe McCarthy's anti-Eisenhower resolution onto the floor and Senator Knowland[7] of California accused him of being partisan. The chair bounced again. "Me partisan? Not any part of me. I was not going to let them do that to Ike."

That night in his office, right after Senator Fulbright and William S. White, the columnist, left, he felt "this terrible pain." He thought it came from smoking.[8]

I told him how proud we all were of his handling of McCarthy and made a move to leave. No, I must have a drink. Bird and I

[5] House of Representatives 1945–47; Governor 1947–50; Senate 1950–56.
[6] 1922 to 1951. Served 5 terms. Died 1957.
[7] 1951 to 1954.
[8] LBJ's actual heart attack occurred later, on July 2, 1955.

went down to mix them. "This is good for us," she commented on the way down. "We're used to brickbats: kindness is something new."

Back upstairs with the Majority Leader, I listened to him talk about the upcoming Senate races. He lived for politics as a farmer lives for good weather and good crops. "Now take Bill Fulbright," he said, "a Phi Beta Kappa professor operating on a slimy bottom where you can't see the knives."

We spoke of the ferment in his home state, walking carefully around the delicate questions of liberals and conservatives (the latter a dirty word in Texas liberal circles, indicating persons who today could be called Birchites). As a topic this seemed to be one we might eschew lest it cause another attack.

When I rose to leave, Lyndon sent love to his good friends Jim and Libby Rowe, enumerated who had sent all the flowers (Adlai had telephoned), and showed me the book he was reading about President Jackson, given to him by Tom Corcoran, another old friend.

I was learning that political leaders were just like ordinary folk only more so: overly sensitive, egotistical, and eager for a waiting ear.

Love That Lyndon

EARLY IN 1965 MRS. JOHNSON, LIZ CARPENTER (MRS. JOHNSON'S PRESS secretary), and I were meeting in the Queen's sitting room at the east end of the second floor of the White House. We were talking about upcoming speeches. Mrs. Johnson particularly liked this room because it had only one door; it was not a throughway or crossroad as were so many of the rooms on the family floor. Besides, it was exquisite. Each of its pieces was either comfortable or of the French Victorian period; some were both. The cheval glass bordered in gold and black could be seen in the mirror over the delicate white marble fireplace. The slight pair of black chairs on either side of the white-skirted dressing table were gilded in hand-painted touches; their cane backs and seats bespoke the loving craftsman. The walls and curtains and upholstered pieces were all covered in a piercing delft blue elaborately ornamented with a white nineteenth-century French design. A pervasive elegance closed in upon us. The hurrying world seemed far away.

But it wasn't. Suddenly the *one* door opened and the President walked in with a friend from Texas. "So that's where you are!" he began, as if one could hide in the White House. Was Mrs. Johnson accompanying him on a trip to New England? The quick questions interlarded with pungent comments brought back that afternoon in his house on 30th Place ten years previously. Then Lyndon Johnson had been totally, completely himself, as human as he liked to be, an appreciator of shrewdness and ambition, an imbiber of the strengths and weaknesses of all, and a believer in the Golden

Rule. Now, he still loomed larger than life. The question was, would he change?

Visiting with President Truman in Blair House the day of President Kennedy's funeral, I put the question to an expert.

"Of course the White House changes a man," said Harry Truman. "It will have its effect on Lyndon Johnson. But when he walks in that door, he'll do right. He knows which foot to put down first."

Part of Mr. Truman's prophecy was correct; Lyndon Johnson knew all about which foot to put down. But events were to change the President in ways none of us could have anticipated.

Lyndon Baines Johnson's measured, mature blend of skills had inadvertently won him the White House. There was only one heartbreaking flaw: the flags were at half mast when he entered. The Kennedyites had no use for Lyndon Johnson. Jack Kennedy had known his value and appreciated what Lyndon had done for the ticket in 1960. But the Kennedy coterie went around exacting disdain for LBJ as initiation fee to their inner circle. Perhaps sneering at an accidental President, when you adored his predecessor, was understandable. There was no organized campaign, unless you can call tragedy an organizer. What none of the detractors seemed to realize was that they had no choice. They couldn't *not* support Lyndon Johnson, every last one of them, until the next election. Meanwhile, the President held all the cards; he could play one hopeful against the other for the second spot, enact Kennedy's legislative legacy, and begin to set his own program in motion. When Vice President Johnson became President over that tragic weekend, a lot of Americans had no idea what he was really like. His close friends claimed that his three years as Vice President had severely wounded him. The Kennedys' sneering, the inference that he was guilty of some larger-than-life mistake because he came from Texas, all these innuendoes affected him and exaggerated his already oversized mistrust and suspicion. A friend who traveled abroad with him when he was Vice President told me that they were discussing why a certain Senator was foolish enough to vote the way he did when Johnson interrupted: "At least he wasn't damn fool enough to become Vice President."[1] As Vice President, Lyndon might have been called "The Once and Lonely Leader."

When Lyndon Johnson entered the White House, he still appeared to me to be the same as when I first knew him. He was still walking an obstacle race. Perhaps he seemed more like himself because he was twenty-five years older, and all the experience and know-how he had acquired made his original characteristics that much more apparent. He was never a man you could put on tape, or who would come through life size, mouthing a prepared text. His least finest hours were spent on TV (with one or two exceptions). He was far more persuasive in person than on the screen. He was as thin-skinned as ever, perhaps more so. The criterion always was, you were a Johnson person or you weren't. The rule seemed understandable to me; all politicians feel that way but most of them manage to hide it.

There was never anything subtle about President Johnson. If he liked you, you knew it. If he knew he was dealing with a critic he'd give you the "treatment." He would try, at least once, often twice, to overcome your prejudices. When he failed, he would admit defeat, but never happily.

His notion that cajolery and repetition were twin adjuncts of persuasion often boomeranged on him. An independent publisher with Republican convictions developed an interest in LBJ. When I encountered him later, after an interval of more than a year, he groaned at the mention of the President's name. "You can't deal with him. He's a bully. He wants you to go all the way with him all the time."

The White House press corps soon discovered the President liked to call them in unexpectedly; the hour might be late or inconvenient or both. He took them on long unannounced fast walks round the White House grounds. Some suspected him of plotting their discomfort. They were wrong. Most of his unpredictability

---

[1] "When he said yes to Kennedy, he was through in Texas," a friend of his once told me; he had become too liberal for his home state.

Majority Leader Lyndon B. Johnson and Katie Louchheim at a fund-raising dinner for the Democratic National Committee in 1958.

On August 19, 1966, at the White House, President Johnson introduced me to President Zalman Shazar of Israel, honoree at dinner. Chuck Robb, then White House Military Aide, looked on.

Ambassador Charles Lucet of France escorts author and former Senator Ernest Gruening of Alaska in to dinner.

Mrs. Edwin Reischauer (at far right), wife of the U. S. Ambassador to Japan, hosts a luncheon to introduce the wives of the Japanese Cabinet to Katie Louchheim at the U. S. Embassy residence in Tokyo.

Madame Adoula, wife of the Premier of the Congo, at a luncheon in her honor at my house attended by (l. to r.) Mrs. Robert McNamara, wife of the Secretary of Defense; Mrs. J. Edward Day, wife of the Postmaster General; and Mrs. Orville Freeman, wife of the Secretary of Agriculture.

Introducing U. S. Ambassadors' wives, received at the White House for the first time, to President and Mrs. Johnson in the Oval Room: l. to r., Mrs. Martin Hillenbrand, Romania; Mrs. William Hall, Ethiopia; Mrs. Albert Sherer, Togo.

Addressing the senior staff officers at the U. S. Embassy in London, April 1965.

Luncheon at the Senate in honor of Ambassador to Luxembourg Patricia Harris, June 23, 1965: l. to r., Senator Maurine Neuberger, Patricia Harris, Representative Frances Bolton, Katie Louchheim, the late Mrs. Dorothy Bernhard, Senator Margaret Chase Smith, Esther Peterson, Assistant Secretary of Labor, Mrs. Charlotte Hubbard, Deputy Assistant for Public Affairs, Department of State. Mrs. Walter Washington, wife of the Mayor of the District of Columbia, can be seen in the mirror.

At the Berlin Wall, Checkpoint Charlie, with German police guard.

Appointed U. S. Board Member, UNESCO, by President Johnson, I attended the spring meeting in Paris, 1969.

Speaking at a dedication of the C & O Canal, a national landmark in Washington.

At an American Field Service reception at the Department of State I got caught resting my feet before speaking.

Walter and I at home, by the pool.

Fourth of July Parade, Chatham, Massachusetts, 1969. Chairman of Selectmen Mr. Robert McNiece and Mrs. McNiece, Walter, Senator Eugene J. McCarthy.

With my daughters Judy (Mrs. Judith L. Sitton) and (at right) Mary (Mrs. Jerome Lieberthal).

My youngest grandchild, Frances Anne, in 1966.

My grandchildren: Dierdre Coulson, Frances Anne Lieberthal, and Cotton Coulson.

came from an uncontrollable exuberance, an overabundance of energy, adrenalin, and other totally irrepressible ingredients of his body chemistry. A White House staffer told me he suspected the President of secreting a dynamo in his innards. His passion for setting a scene, for personally announcing appointees, was incurable. He liked to master-mind events, at least those he was connected with. He learned the hard way that with an overexperienced press corps his way was not necessarily theirs.

I once asked the President's good friend Ed Clark, whom he had appointed Ambassador to Australia, what gave all Texans that extra ounce of exuberance.

"Why, honey,[2] it's simple," Ed said. "We're the only state that came into the Union on its own terms. And we got to keep our public lands too."[3] Although this explanation might not altogether assuage an embattled newsman or an irate publisher, it does describe a persistence that is hard to bend or break.

In the first weeks of January 1964 the press did not have to hunt for feature stories; Mrs. Johnson took her long-time cook, Zephyr, to the President's State of the Union message. In the west wing, it was discovered, Ken O'Donnell still had his same desk, but next to him sat Bill Moyers, thereby placing a Kennedy insider alongside a Johnson Special Assistant.

At the White House reception (January 11, 1964) for the Democratic National Committee the contrast between the reticent Kennedy and the expansive Johnson exploded with every flash bulb.

[2] Carrie Davis once explained the difference between the North and the South: "Those poor Northerners have to learn everyone's name. We just call them all honey." Although Ed Clark knew my name, he preferred the natural Southern idiom.

[3] Texas is unique in having the right to divide itself into more states; the joint resolution on the state's annexation to the U.S. says: "New States of convenient size, not exceeding four in number, in addition to the said State of Texas, may hereafter, by the consent of said State, etc. . . ." "In 1844, the question of Texas joining the Union was lifted out of its slavery setting and made one of national expansion and prestige" (Henry Steele Commager). Texas would have come in as a slave state (the count was then 13 free and 13 slave) but Wisconsin, Minnesota, and Iowa were waiting admission as free states.

There were fires in every room but the greatest warmth came from the hosts. The new President stood in the Red Room, TV lights playing round him and photographers jammed behind him, cameras clicking at every handshake. When I came out of the line, one of the press women dashed up to me. "What did he say?" "Hello," I answered as benignly as I could. "Go back through again and make him say something," came the request. I disappeared with what I hoped was a sympathetic look. News, even in the quantities available, still did not suffice.

In a corner of the overflowing dining room I listened to the President's remarks. No one could court and enjoin, state and implore, like Lyndon Johnson. I watched the faces expand in that way that faces do when an important person is alternatively wooing and confiding in them.

When he quoted Republican attacks on his State of the Union message, the President belted the lines in a deadpan manner that had laughs breaking all over the ecstatic audience. Even the dour, sphinx-like Ken O'Donnell wrinkled his face into smiles as Johnson declared he had to reach for Harvard when critical winds blew.

Mrs. Johnson stopped me to say: "I was surprised to find that I knew most everyone in that line by their first name." The personal touch was to have its effect. By February the political weather had warmed up and the ice of suspicion began to melt.

"No man can hold both Henry Ford and Walter Reuther, the North and the South, the Congress and the Executive forever," I heard a TV analyst say. "He can," declared the Johnsonites.

That was the month that was. Walter Lippmann, in his hour-long broadcast interview with Howard K. Smith, said flattering things about Johnson. Scotty Reston, the Chief Justice of the Columnists' Court, pronounced Johnson able: "He can make people do things, witness the farm bill, the railroad strike [settled after fourteen days].[4] He is great at moving men."

There were still—and always would be—those who disagreed.

[4] The strike began on April 9, 1964, was settled April 22, 1964.

When the President announced the appointment of fifty women, Charles Bartlett, columnist, remarked: "It's ridiculous. A President ought to spend more time on policy than on public relations stunts."

This President was different; he knew he could do both—appoint women and conduct affairs of state. Johnson's commitment to the contributions women could make was sincere. The President's admiration for his mother and his wife undoubtedly influenced his judgment. I had my own proof of his convictions.

In September of 1955, when he was recuperating at the ranch, I wrote to him, requesting that as Majority Leader he appoint a woman to the Security Commission set up by President Eisenhower to investigate government practices in pursuing possible subversives among federal employees.[5]

As I look back, asking the Majority Leader to give up *one* of his two appointments to a woman was really testing his beliefs.

In reply to my request, he wrote as follows:

September 17, 1955

Dear Katie:

It is only 8:00 AM in the morning. My Star Route Mail Carrier leaves the mail in my box across the river about 6:00, and your letter was the first one I read and the first one I am answering—just about the only one I am dictating because the doctor told me not to for the time being.

Your suggestion appeals to me greatly. . . .

There is nobody in the country who wants to help you any more than I do, and I'll do my best.

Bird joins me in best wishes.

Sincerely,
LYNDON B. JOHNSON

Susan Riley, then immediate past President of the influential American Association of University Women and President of

[5] Abuses of investigative powers, at the height of the Joe McCarthy era, had become so flagrant and offensive as to arouse a somnolent public and, in turn, a slow-to-wrath President Eisenhower.

George Peabody College for Teachers in Nashville, Tennessee, proved to be the perfect choice. Senator Stennis of Mississippi, whom the Majority Leader had selected as his government appointee, could not praise her enough.

By April 1965 a good many new appointees, all female, were sworn in by a woman, Judge Burnita Matthews. The President, in his informal remarks, expressed the hope that all the husbands in the room would find it in their heart to forgive him by next November.

The President unfortunately could not persuade all husbands to permit their wives to leave home and family for Washington assignments. The inevitable turndowns dampened his enthusiasm. He did persuade Polly Bunting, the distinguished President of Radcliffe, to take a one-year leave of absence to become a member of the Atomic Energy Commission; first Esther Peterson, and then Betty Furness became Consumer Adviser to the President (the latter commuting weekends to New York where her husband worked). Ambassadors Katharine White and Pat Harris took their husbands along to Denmark and Luxembourg, and Barbara Watson became the Administrator for Security and Consular Affairs.[6]

As Chairman of the Federal Women's Award,[7] a public service organization, I had to arrange for the six annual winners to meet with the President on the day of the banquet. Each year the President's staff and I went through a ritualistic dance. A staff member would call asking for suggested remarks for the President, another would advise me that we were to meet in the Fish Room, and a third would ask for a detailed blueprint for the occasion. Inevitably, when I arrived with my six totally terrified winners,

[6] Although many women received appointments to boards and commissions, ranking appointments never reached a total of fifty.

[7] The award was limited to career women in government service and was funded by Woodward & Lothrop, the leading employer of women in Washington. Winners were chosen by an appointed panel of judges. The program was instituted by Barbara Gunderson, a Civil Service Commissioner appointed by President Eisenhower, and greatly abetted by Vice Chairman Robert Hampton, who later was named Chairman of the Civil Service Commission by President Nixon.

still another staffer would come forward and ask me where were the awards. The awards were to be made that night; this was a purely ceremonial meeting with the President.

The President's opening remarks invariably complimented the winners for their looks. I recognized a masculine drafter's touch. For years I had pleaded with men not to talk about our pulchritude (which was rare) or about our hats (the brains beneath them were more important). Later in the speech, when he began to ad-lib, I could relax.

"If I don't watch out," President Johnson once said, "I'm outvoted three to one in this household. One of these days I'll find myself on a cot in my office instead of in the mansion."

The President recognized the value of the program and gave appointments to some of our winners. He would say: "I found some of the finest folk through the career ladder."

In the John F. Kennedy years, the Federal Award winners' visits to the White House were more informal. President Kennedy talked with them about the variety of opportunities that women had in the federal government, pointing out that no private employer offered such a choice of careers. (Award winners represented disparate skills. One had plotted Glenn's orbit, another originated the zip code, others were experts on rockets, blood plasma, air traffic control, petrography [the study of concrete].)

President Kennedy received us in his office. President Johnson, attuned to the advantages of wider news coverage for all groups that called on him, met with us in the larger Fish Room where TV cameras and news reporters could also be present. All Presidents are wary of demands on their time; the intrusion of ceremonial callers is a necessary nuisance, one they must control. But they do it in different ways.

I recall one appearance before President Johnson that revealed the depth of his concern about the war in Vietnam. He had just come from the Arlington Cemetery services for Merriman Smith's only son, who had been killed in Vietnam. Smitty, the senior member of the White House press corps, since deceased,[8] who always closed the Presidential press conferences by rising to say, "Thank you, Mr. President," had long been closely associated with Johnson. The gloom of the funeral service carried over into the Award winners' meeting with the President. He was understandably remote. He read in a monotone a plea for a new study group to be formed of Award winners to "probe deeply into the problems of working women." There was an acute shortage of nurses, he said, and the "under-utilization of American women continues to be the most tragic and most senseless waste of this century."[9] Since we already had a Commission on the Status of Women at work on these problems, some of us wondered about the need for another report. We also knew that women were less promotable than men because men did the promoting.

Though later in his Presidency you never knew what mood Johnson might be in, in the early months you could count on his exuberance and sense of happy urgency. On the Friday before election, November 4, 1964, I was called by Dick Goodwin, a Kennedy staff man who had stayed on at the White House, to produce names of women—in the next hour—to go on a TV show with the President. By the time I had the names and the women's acceptances, we had a brand-new emergency. Taping time had been reprogrammed for the next day—Saturday, instead of Monday as originally planned, and the place changed from Washington to New York City. All day Saturday we juggled meals, rehearsals, hairdos, and advisers. The time for filming climbed the clock, took place finally at 9:00 P.M., with frantic calls coming in from the rally managers at Madison Square Garden (a traditional finale to Democratic campaigns): "We can't hold the crowds any longer."

8 Merriman Smith died April 13, 1970.
9 The President's remarks had been prepared by John Macy, Chairman of the Civil Service Commission, who also handled appointments the President made. John Macy ran appointees through computers. Neither women nor blacks came out too well. He believed in adding up degrees and skills, had confidence in machines that talked like people and people who talked like machines.

They did. As a spectator I milled around dodging police, watching
the President's words break into laughter and the strong lights
shine on the platform like a prize ring. The President won a thun-
derous ovation when he marched Mrs. Johnson round the ring and
stood later, hands clasped in a victory symbol with Ethel and
Bob Kennedy, then a candidate for the United States Senate
from New York.

We traveled home in style on Air Force One. I have a fond
recollection of the President parading the aisles in a Hallowe'en
hat. On one of his rounds he stopped to give me a "good to see
you" kiss on the brow. Kissing is a facet of a political personality.
It is not by any means limited to politics. In show business, ac-
tors "darling" each other at restaurants, on sets, at high noon,
and at dawn, but none of it has significance—it's part of their
mores. One even finds kissing in suburbs, at country clubs, and
between well-known names at public events. But in politics kissing
is meaningful.

Because it takes place most often at public gatherings, it de-
notes favoritism. Some might call it a laying on of hands; to
the receiver it is a favor, especially if the person doing the kissing
happens to be the President of the United States. (Depending
on the importance of the kisser, it's not only a demonstration of
affection but an act of kindness as well.) A public kiss from a
President could, as in my case, be a reward for years of loyal service. Some might list kissing under trivia, but even those must concede it comes under what must be identified as interesting trivia.

There are those who bestow kisses without regard to partisanship. A photograph of Senator Dirksen smooching my cheek appeared in a *Look* magazine article. Senator George Aiken is a
friendly kisser, but my list, quite naturally, runs more to Democrats. Hubert Humphrey seldom kissed. Adlai Stevenson embraced one, Harry S Truman kissed only his family. John F.
Kennedy avoided any contact.

When he was still Vice President, Johnson came to the State
Department to attend Carl Rowan's swearing in as Ambassador

to Finland. About fifty of us stood in groups around the honoree. As the Vice President passed through the crowd, he paused to give me a kiss. The newsman next to me remarked, "He makes all the stops." "Not all," I replied, "only those he wants to."

When I had ideas I wanted to get to the President, I was told the surest way was to have the memos included in his night reading and placed on his pillow. I found another route. I simply gave the memos to his wife. Bromley Smith, a sophisticated White House officer who has served both parties, told me of an incident illustrating the success of my system. One noon he received an urgent call from the President's office: "Get Gronowski," came the cryptic command. Four hours and many calls later, Brom called back for further elucidation. No one knew what the President meant. In desperation a secretary called Mrs. Johnson, who could usually explain what her husband had in mind. She handed over "Gronowski," a speech given by John Gronowski, then Ambassador to Poland,[10] on "The Intellectuals and American Foreign Policy," published in the *Department of State Bulletin*, October 2, 1967. I had found it succinct and impressive, worthy of the President's attention.

Several weeks later the President detained me in a receiving line. He had read "Gronowski" out loud to Secretaries Rusk and McNamara: would I please write the Ambassador and tell him so.[11]

Lyndon Johnson's White House years can be divided into Before and After Vietnam. The Vietnam period, for me, began in the late summer of 1966. In October, I had occasion to talk with Clark Clifford about a report that he was to succeed George Ball, who had just resigned as Under Secretary of State. He indicated a re-

[10] Appointed Dean of the Lyndon Baines Johnson School of Public Affairs.
[11] My role often enough resembled that described by T. S. Eliot's J. Alfred Prufrock: an "attendant lord." On a single occasion I might be expected to act as buffer, spear-bearer, finder of lost faces, or split-second messenger ("Go get Bird" flung over the royal shoulder).

luctance to take a secondary post without any assurance whatever of moving to the top position. As I interpreted what he said, there had been no indication of how long Secretary Rusk might remain in his post. Because Clark Clifford combines the qualities of leadership with objectivity, erudition with political acumen, and because he had the President's confidence, it is possible that he might have done in 1966 what he gradually accomplished in 1968.

The Rusk-Johnson relationship remained close and devoted. They were both from the poor South, both had grit and had known hunger, picked their way through meager barren acres. Rusk was loyal, a quality Johnson quite properly valued highly.[12]

At this time, serving as senior Deputy in the Bureau of Educational and Cultural Affairs, I was caught in the cross fire on Vietnam. The President and Assistant Secretary of State Charles Frankel, who headed this bureau, did not agree. Frankel argued that both sides of the Vietnam question should be heard overseas as well as at home; he pointed out that America stood for the right to disagree. In theory, Frankel was correct; however, there was nothing to prevent any American from going abroad at his own expense to express whatever opinions he held on any subject. The President did not feel that spokesmen sent by the government at the taxpayers' expense, or official members of delegations, should speak out against their government's policies. A little over a year later Assistant Secretary Frankel resigned. In view of his strong anti-Vietnam sentiments, he wished to disassociate himself from the Administration.

The differences ran deep; the problems Vietnam raised took many forms. The Vietnam task force was down the hall from me; I had nothing to do with their deliberations or policy, but I soon learned that the differences on Vietnam had existed for some time. For instance, in the fall of 1963, President Kennedy, when he was trying on hats (he seldom wore one) for the benefit of the Connecticut hat industry and his good friend Senator Abe Ribicoff

---

[12] In his televised interview with Walter Cronkite of CBS in 1970, President Johnson revealed that it was Rusk who initiated the bombing pause.

of Connecticut, turned to his staff to ask which hat they liked best. "This one," "No, that one," came the varying responses. "You remind me of my Vietnam advisers," he said caustically.

The division was true then and truer in President Johnson's day.

On September 30, 1967, a prearranged visit with Mrs. Johnson took place. Escorting five United States Ambassadors' wives, I sat in the Oval Room in the White House at what, by now, had become a traditional meeting with the First Lady. The signals for departure had just been exchanged when a Secret Service officer announced: "The President of the United States." The President turned to Mrs. Johnson: "I heard you were having company. I thought I'd drop by."

He had just left George Brown, he told us, and Brown had supported us the day before at the UN. The President was so absorbed with the war that he took for granted that we knew the subject Brown, England's Foreign Minister, had supported us on was Vietnam.

Suddenly no one was saying a word. Fearing he would leave us, I repeated a phrase the President had used when addressing the U. S. Advisory Commission.[13] He had quoted Jefferson on the need for "spreading the disease of liberty." He nodded and repeated the line, and in the same breath he was back on Vietnam. All this talk about stopping the bombing, he said, came from people who did not have access to the information he had. He read everything on the war, his information was up to the minute. If the teachers and preachers were to run the war, he admonished us, we would be in bad shape.

When he mentioned the Vietcong lobbing mortars over to our side of the DMZ, he leaned forward and pointed to his back. "They'd get them right here," he said. There were 20,000 Marines to be protected on our side, he continued, and 200,000 Vietcong on the other. While we were bombing, we immobilized 200,000

[13] A body of scholars and other leaders set up by Congress to advise the Bureau of Education and Cultural Affairs in the Department of State.

North Vietnamese. We kept them busy repairing the damage. We bombed only military targets, never schools or hospitals, never. Many more people and many advisers wanted more bombing, rather than less. He was constantly implored to widen the bombing targets.

Talk of the bombing reminded him of how many wounded were rescued and brought back to health. With helicopters and medical service at hand, most of them went back to the front.

His tone was straightforward and compelling. He wanted these wives to have the facts. His position stated, he leaned down and patted his dog Yuki.

That evening I wrote in my journal: "The President has deeper lines. We were in the presence of a man who wants to get on with the bad news, consoling himself with the wounded saved, and getting the job done. He gives one the same sense of urgency he always did, except that now one feels events rushing him."

I heard him speak again of Vietnam in October 1967 when I was seated at his table at a White House "stag" luncheon in honor of President Ahidjo of Cameroon. The President talked across his guest directly to his friend Senator Smathers about the war. Rusk advised against bombing Haiphong Harbor because the generals admitted that by mistake they might hit a Russian ship. Then he turned to the recent anti-war march on the Pentagon; trained agitators, he reported, had taken over.

The following month the President asked me to be one of three women leaders to travel around Vietnam and report back what we had seen. Because I had been a strong advocate of sending civilian observers to Vietnam, I wanted very much to go. To my chagrin, neither my doctor nor my husband would hear of my taking the trip.

Vietnam continued to preoccupy us; it came up in the mail, in programs in our Bureau, at the State Department briefings, in conversations with visitors, and at every dinner table. One evening we were guests of a White House Vietnam expert who told us that the President was being "constantly fooled" by optimistic reports from the military. These "intravenous shots" of good news disturbed our host.

On the next night, we were told by another "insider" that the President's mood was hard to diagnose, he seemed sunk in apathy. The very next night we heard him give a rousing speech to a Democratic fund-raising affair. "So what?" said a President-watcher. "He had a friendly audience."

The President did have his defenders. Ambassador David Bruce, the distinguished and respected diplomat, told me, "Of course Lyndon Johnson is not popular. No great President ever is. Look at Truman and Lincoln."

Men like Ken Crawford, independent columnist of *Newsweek*, found other correspondents who agreed with his own high opinion of the President. "They may not like him, but they note his restraint and admire his guts."

No one was more shocked when the President announced he would not be a candidate for re-election than I. Like other major decisions, this one was kept secret. But the very next day, returning from Chicago, he talked freely with the pool reporters on his plane. A friend[14] who was on that flight repeated his remarks to me. He had felt his first job on entering the White House should be to hold the whole team together. He had spoken of taking care of President Kennedy's widow, keeping an eye on her children; he looked upon himself as one of a two-man partnership he had with John Kennedy. "I took his staff, his Cabinet, and his programs," the President had said.

He had referred to the press: "Why, I couldn't sign my name to the Lord's prayer without you-all suspecting me of some sinister motive." He inveighed, too, against the Kennedys (never the President), the intellectuals who mocked him, and the advisers who failed him. But he also emphasized that no President is in-

---

[14] George Packard, the managing editor of the Philadelphia *Bulletin*, then White House correspondent.

dispensable and that he had "no pettiness, no hatred, no vitupera-
tion, a man just collects barnacles in this job."

At an earlier time I had heard him voice great nostalgia for his
days on the Hill. In this respect he resembled Harry Truman.
Both were experts at the give-and-take of parliamentary politics,
plotting traps for the opposition, moving in a game as sophisticated and complex as chess.

If only, I told a Johnson admirer, we could order our Presidents
people-proof, problem-proof, opinion-proof. They seem so vulnerable. William S. White, the columnist, a close friend of Johnson's, remarked that the President had been good at guarding a
program, but never any good at guarding his own flank. Another
associate pointed out that his genius had been best displayed
when he ran the Senate, but that he failed to make the transition
from influencing the individual Senator to handling the public at
large. This led us to the disputed subject of his television appearances; he had been persuaded at one time to take professional advice. When the story leaked, he canceled the professionals.

Harry McPherson describes him as the most astute political
craftsman of his time. Other members of his staff claim that he
"lost the fight" in the first forty-eight hours after entering the
White House; his unilateral decision to persuade the Kennedy
people to stay on was a fatal mistake. After Johnson's announcement that he would not run for a second term, more frequent
and open criticism of his decision to keep the Kennedy Cabinet
was heard. When public opinion is divided, when polls show down-
ward trends, the hunt is on for a devil. In many a martini huddle,
the devil was Rusk, or McNamara, or the military.

Rewriting history is a favorite Washington pastime. My own
sense of what might have been is associated with *who* might have
been—at hand in the Johnson Administration. I would have had
the beloved Mr. Sam live on so that he and President Johnson
might have taken counsel together. The Speaker was the only one
who could have filled President Roosevelt's prescription: "As

President you need someone who has no ambition on earth except to help you."

Mr. Sam embodied the two most important virtues a man can have: steadiness under fire and common sense. He loved Lyndon like a son; he never spared him either affection or criticism. When he spoke, Lyndon listened. Johnson held high the advice of only three people: his mother, his wife, and Mr. Sam.

Rayburn could be folksy, a convenient disguise for his sagacity. He insisted that the most important thing any man ever said was, "Wait a minute." He might have said, "Wait a minute," to Johnson when the latter needed this kind of advice.

At the time of Dwight Eisenhower's Presidency, Mr. Rayburn said to me, "We have only one President. We elect him for four years. It is our duty to stand behind him." He would certainly have said the same about Lyndon Baines Johnson. In the last troubled days and nights of Johnson's Presidency, no Sam Rayburn was there to voice these sentiments.

Up and Down
in Herter's Hilton

THE NIGHT OF MY APPOINTMENT TO THE DEMOCRATIC NATIONAL committee, in October of 1953, I was blitzed off television by the capture of a kidnaper. The day of my swearing in at the Department of State as Special Assistant to Under Secretary Bowles on February 4, 1961, a blizzard swept the streets of Washington. Most of the friends I had invited to witness the ceremony failed to appear. Senator Albert Gore, among others, did come; he pressed a key ring into my hand for good luck.

I was to need it. After almost twenty years I was back on the rolls of the Department of State. Both the Department and I had changed. The old inconvenient, splendidly impractical building on Pennsylvania Avenue had been superseded by a modern maze of antiseptic corridors, air-conditioned auditoriums, and windowless cubicles, known as Herter's Hilton.[1]

Escorted on an introductory tour, I noted that the sacrosanct seventh-floor lounges, the suites assigned to the Secretary and his Under Secretary, reminded one of the smoking rooms of famous prewar Cunard liners. Shown the panorama of Washington from the reception rooms on the eighth floor, blanketed with eiderdowns of snow, I thought to myself, "This gives us the 'memorable marble hostages to history' that Moscow brags about." Was I perhaps a hostage to Democratic history?

[1] For Christian Herter who served as Secretary of State from 1957 to 1959.

When Chairman John Bailey (Democratic National Committee) and Kennedy staff assistant Ralph Dungan summoned me to headquarters in January 1961, I knew it must be about an assignment. Both were in a cordial mood, a state in which neither of them spent much time—at least not in public. "The President is concerned about important women who come here from abroad and whom no one pays attention to. You are to work out of Under Secretary Bowles's office as his special assistant." As I listened I grew more and more mystified; was I to be a kind of greeter, a floating hostess? "What am I supposed to do with my brains?" I burst out. My rudeness was ignored.

The Department of State, accustomed to evasion couched in suitably impressive sentences, wrote a release saying: "Mrs. Louchheim will work on a variety of problems concerned with the participation of women in international, cultural and educational affairs and with the role of women's organizations in facilitating . . . In accordance with the President's wishes, Mrs. Louchheim will be concerned with giving greater emphasis to women's activities in these important fields."

There were enough provocative loopholes in the language to drive my persistence through. But where was I going, and were women in foreign policy really a factor? A friend remarked dryly: "They do hate women in the Department, don't they?" I was to discover he had overstated the case; they ignored them.

A few days after the swearing in, Under Secretary Bowles invited me to his office for luncheon, served on an impromptu table that never quite fitted our uneven knee levels. He wanted to talk about my *not* working for him. He begged me to put my considerable talents to work for his appointee, Philip Coombs, about to become the very first Assistant Secretary for Educational and Cultural Affairs. "You can make the difference between his succeeding and failing." That noon I knew I had been robbed of the position the Kennedys had appointed me to.

Tender evidences of Bowles's solicitude appeared almost daily—flowers, memoranda, telegrams, an invitation to dinner—but the privileges of working with him were revoked. His attentions were hardly a recompense for being bounced from the executive dining room, for a down-graded office, a staff that proved non-existent, and exile to a remote part of the building.

A lawyer friend stumbled into my office one day, carrying the little map they give all visitors to the Department. "I saw your name on the door. I've been wandering for half an hour and I haven't yet seen the dogs with the brandy round their neck."

One sunny Sunday my husband and I ran into Dean Acheson. He stopped to ask how I liked working in "his" Department. Not at all, I grumbled; I spent my days taking notes from a superior who had no carry-out plans to go with his visionary blueprints. Dean Acheson has a most expressive face—even his mustache speaks. His sardonic laugh at my predicament tilted the mustache upward. "You need friends," he said. "Go see Luke Battle. He runs the secretariat."

Lucius Battle[2] transferred me to Public Affairs, where I belonged. I had spent the war years in the antecedent division of UNRRA. Thanking him, I confessed that I had been just about to advise the President that I was overpaid and underemployed.

Others became friends; men like Roger Jones, Deputy Under Secretary for Administration, who ran the place. Roger, a seasoned Republican, a bureaucrat in the finest sense of the word, would keep commitments where others promised and ran. He and I had a common problem: Bowles. An enthusiastic man, possessed of many talents Bowles had an idea a minute. I was advised by Jones to see him often, to help him select his most usable idea and stick with it without refining and changing it along the way. I did my best. At one of our later lunches (my knees were still in the wrong place) Bowles spoke eloquently of the need for a complete reorganization of the Department; he wanted acceleration of promotions, four brand-new Under Secretaries for geographic

[2] Special Assistant to the Secretary of State and Executive Secretary of the Department, 1961–62. Now Vice President for Corporate Relations at the Communications Satellite Corporation.

posts (to give underlings hope and overlings back seats), earlier retirement of officers. Obeying Roger Jones's instructions, I was about to put my foot on the idea of accelerated promotions, thereby relieving the cramp in my knees, when suddenly Bowles's subject metamorphosed into Wilson's Fourteen Points. Walking back to my office, I decided Bowles[3] could sell anything—even an old idea, a refurbished Fourteen Points, a document to settle the problems of 246,000,000 Southeast Asians.

Being "in," in the Department, meant getting off the elevator on the seventh floor. I arrived there myself in December 1963.[4] Next best was the sixth floor, where an old and dear friend, Roger Tubby, had taken over as Assistant Secretary for Public Affairs. Roger very much wanted me to work with him, but how to move me from my office on the second floor to his enclave on the sixth? We put the question to Roger Jones, who agreed that a proper title would help. Finding and laying claim to a "Deputy's" title proved as tough as explaining to my grandson what a Deputy Assistant Secretary of State did. He finally solved the problem himself: "I know Deputy Dog, he is a big shot in the Huckleberry Hound show on TV." Roger Tubby already had two Deputies; could he afford one more? Herman Pollack, Deputy Assistant Secretary for Personnel, a new friend, and author of a State Department reorganization plan largely adopted by President Kennedy, shrugged his shoulders. His shoulders said NO.

Daily reports came from all directions: the funds were cut, the title was stuck. A White House caller informed me Jones was vulnerable; he was siding with the "career types" against "us," the outsiders: the New Frontier was having its shakedown cruise. Word went out that "Jones must go."

[3] Bowles was replaced as Under Secretary November 29, 1961, and given an ambiguous title as Adviser to the President on African, Asian, and Latin American Affairs. On June 10, 1963, he was appointed Ambassador to India.

[4] In 1967, as Acting Assistant Secretary for the Bureau of Education and Cultural Affairs, I was given the ultimate privilege, the key to the private elevator for Assistant Secretaries. With it came a second key to the men's room on the seventh floor which I returned after deciding not to raffle it off.

I was to hear this ominous phrase for eight years, launched, I suspected, by those who, sensing a first tremor, set out to topple the structure. Rumors in the Department of State have a way of verifying themselves.

Jones, as prophesied, did go back to his post at the Bureau of the Budget. My White House friend who passed me the bad news about Jones came over to State. I suspected that he in turn had been unloaded by the White House Mafia.

Autumn turned to winter. Would it snow, as it had the year of the Kennedy inaugural? Would my title ever come through?

It did snow. On a cold midnight on January 20, 1962, we heard the phone ringing as we came round the corner to our front door. My shoes were caked with ice; in my haste I did a back flip, reaching the receiver from the floor. A strange voice informed me that the New York *Times* had a front-page story in their bulldog edition saying I was named Deputy Assistant Secretary for Public Affairs. The *Herald Tribune*, the stranger advised, wanted me to confirm or deny the story.

People I had not heard from in years suddenly remembered they had played tennis with me when I was thirteen, been a member of the same Girl Scout troop. Professors, newspaper friends, TV reporters, Jim Farley, old sweethearts, and older Rosemarians wrote. The pass to the executive dining room was restored. A senior officer remarked that he had seen me at lunch. "I feel just like Lady Godiva," I confessed, "with all that staring." He smiled. "Your hair isn't long enough."

My eight years in the Department took me up and down, literally and figuratively. But I always knew which floor I was on, and as Deputy Assistant Secretary I was able to get something done. In between practicing the skills politics had taught me, I could establish priorities (a habit-forming phrase) and plan. Being a woman helped: I never gave up, I persisted. Overcoming the suspicions that I was too political took another kind of doggedness. Some days I felt like Hester Prynne; my scarlet letter was a D for Democrat.

Having a staff brought results: more women joined the mainstream of our exchange programs; even Nkrumah, we discovered, had said that women were just as vital to progress as rivers and minerals. The State Department finally came round to his view. Our wives overseas had long been labeled "a strategic diplomatic resource," but nothing had been done to implement the compliment. A special training course for wives, bringing them up to date on American mores, was established at the Foreign Service Institute. Language courses, available previously only on a "space available" status, were opened up to them. Help for their invaluable voluntary efforts, especially in the developing nations, was made available. Everything from incubators and penicillin to cash and plastic bottles was shipped abroad. (In Pakistan our volunteers had not been able to dispense medicine in the clinics for lack of containers.) Members of women's organizations discovered that at last there was a State Department that could use their brains and experience. When Ethel Kennedy was asked on TV what women could do for their country, she replied, "Call Katie Louchheim." They did.

As I came to know the Foreign Service wives, I found they shared many of the same hazards the wives of members of Congress faced: frequent invasions of visitors, changes of abode, the changing preferences of constantly changing administrations.

Politics had taught me the value of wives of public officials. I could never have survived the lean Democratic years without the help of a group known as the Democratic Congressional Wives Forum. Organized originally for my benefit, ultimately it redounded to theirs and is still flourishing.

Roger Tubby fortunately understood the importance of keeping in touch with the grass roots. I joined his new program of regional briefings, first as participant and later, when Robert Manning took his place, as moderator. Also included were Washington briefings for editors from all over the U.S. and representatives of non-governmental organizations (cozily referred to as NGOs). Everyone from the President and the Secretary of State offered

advice. I learned to field the inevitable hecklers with what was
once described as ruthless femininity. On October 15–16, 1962, we
held a Washington briefing none of us will forget. Unbeknownst
to us, the Cuban crisis was breaking. Angry editors, feeling deceived by Department of State denials, wrote furious editorials
and nasty letters. When later the Cuban story broke, a special
press briefing was held. All newsmen were required to show their
passes. As the Tass representative appeared, a man from our office
shouted, "Get out." He did, with a loud "I'll tell Moscow." Stu
Hensley, of UPI, remarked dryly, "We started World War II with
less fuss."

Hubert Humphrey once said, "Foreign policy is like God—there
but rather remote." It was to bridge this gap that Roger Tubby[5]
had invented the regional briefings. He believed that the average
man should get to know the foreign policy God as well as his own.
On the road in my role as moderator I discovered that Foreign
Service officers, viewed as God's advance men, fulfill their roles
admirably. Remote, erudite, they gave well-documented speeches
and properly evasive replies to probing questions.

Someone called the Foreign Service lonely nomads, leading an
expatriate existence, often reticent, frequently afraid of making
friends who might become enemies, and vice versa. Their satisfac-
tions, unhappily, could best be described as impermanent, indirect, and impersonal. I was to become a convert to their cause;
misunderstood and underappreciated, many of them had superior
talents. Successful Ambassadors such as David Bruce, Llewellyn
Thompson, Foy Kohler, Charles Bohlen, and Fulton Freeman,
who dictated history in the pause between crises, were publicly
applauded. But a whole corps of dedicated men and women remained unknown to the public. For most John Q. Citizens, the
Foreign Service was a foreign body, a striped-pants hothouse
breed, living in luxury, waited on by immaculate servants, their

---

[5] Roger Tubby—for refusing to fire old-timers—"had to go." His departure
saddened the press corps, although he went on to Geneva to serve as Ambassador to the European office of the United Nations in Geneva.

waking hours spent at receptions drinking up free whiskey. How could this gap between the legend and the reality be narrowed; their true story of hardship posts, difficult climates, and languages be told? When I discovered that they came home—wherever home was—every two or four years, their way paid to Main Street, U.S.A., I had my answer. At no additional expense to the taxpayers, the returning FSO could meet the public. For a long while I had no backers for my idea until I met William J. Crockett, Deputy Under Secretary for Administration, a magnanimous man with a passionate concern for the Service and a confidence in new ideas that cheered me on my pilgrim's progress through bureaucracy. He helped me launch the Office of Community Advisory Services (O/CAS); once it was set up, most of the Foreign Service went through my office on their way home. Asked if they would like to talk about their experiences to local, civic, fraternal, and religious groups, they happily complied. Grateful letters from listeners flowed in. The speakers were equally enthusiastic; after they had told their in-laws all about Ouagadougou, they liked having a brand-new audience.

The Wally Byam Foundation lent us house trailers; the latter were so much in demand, especially by younger officers with families whose folks had moved into utility apartments, that the Foundation kept adding to their number. We also learned that most Foreign Service officers had never seen any part of the U.S. but their own. New Englanders shoveling Southerners out of a snowstorm was a revelation. Disneyland was a joy. TV interviews were a cinch. The officer broadened his horizon and got a chance to catch up on what Americans were thinking. Hopefully, we were destroying old myths and forming a new equation: "Confidence in foreign policy rests on confidence in the officers who carry it out."

But there remained one serious gap in our new program of communications. Top-echelon officers could seldom be spared for speaking engagements, but at the next levels, men and women of

ability abounded. Why not set up a series of community meetings
that went to medium-sized cities and university campuses, covering the same range of subjects as did the ranking officers? The idea
appealed; to moderate these groups I recruited a good friend, Charlotte Hubbard, whose own experience had also been in the communications field.[6] Only once was any question raised about Charlotte's color. Though we never tried to go into the South, we
did arrange a meeting in a border state. A civic leader called to
say, whereas he had no objection, the audience might. The hosts,
he pointed out, would like to take Mrs. Hubbard to dinner, but in
his state no white man could be seen with a black woman in a
restaurant. He suggested sending someone else as moderator. I
canceled the meeting.

When Charlotte first came to the Department, the Executive
Officer of the Bureau and I had a rather extended argument about
her salary. Knowing the Department's susceptibility to hierarchical distinction, I insisted that she be given a grade a step higher
than the low rank he proposed. His resistance and my persistence
were well matched; after a prolonged siege, he capitulated. On
March 4, 1963, Charlotte came to work with me. Barely a year
later Bob Manning asked me to release Charlotte so she might
take my place as Deputy Assistant Secretary for Public Affairs.
Her success among her fellow officers and in the field gave me
great satisfaction. At Carl Rowan's[7] swearing in as Ambassador
to Finland, Charlotte made a remark that was typical of her. Secretary Rusk officiated and Vice President Johnson attended. Charlotte observed that Rowan,[8] Rusk and Johnson were poor boys

[6] During World War II, Mrs. Charlotte Hubbard worked for the Federal
Security Agency, setting up recreation facilities in impacted areas. Her work at
WTOP in Washington, D.C., and the Community Chest had likewise taken
her into the communications field. Her father, Robert Russa Moton, was the
first head of Tuskegee after Booker T. Washington.

[7] Carl, currently a successful columnist and TV analyst, had served as Deputy Assistant Secretary in the same Bureau with me. When Bowles turned
down my request to accompany his Chief of Missions touring troop, it was
Carl who persuaded Bowles to change his mind.

[8] Rowan was born in Tennessee.

from the South: "If that's what they mean when they say the South will rise again, it's fine with me."

Breakthroughs in human rights achieved their first genuine momentum in the Kennedy-Johnson years. In politics and in my personal life I had learned how lonely it can be to espouse the cause of integration; and how few of us there were in those days compared to the legions of integrationists today. Even the early sixties demonstrated that, despite a great mountain of talking and doing, attitudes were hard to change. As one of a panel of three, I witnessed the rough cross-examination given a black applicant for transfer to the Foreign Service. When I turned the question to human rights, his answers were moving and articulate. I cast the first aye vote and the others followed suit. I wondered what would have happened had I not been present. The Department of State's record in appointments and in encouraging young blacks to join the Service subsequently became outstanding. These strides make it difficult for me to believe that the only solution to racial injustices lies in monolithic black structures; but that may very well be the way this generation chooses.[9]

I had many opportunities to hear Secretary Dean Rusk speak. His survivor's kit included both Oxford English and Georgia grit. When I presented Priscilla Abwao, M.P. from Kenya, to the Secretary, he understood at once what she meant. "We need you in my country: we have a saying, the dog goes where the bone is." The Secretary replied, "I come from a very poor family: everything we achieved we worked hard for. My part of the country was poor, very poor. I was born in a two-room house my father built with his own hands." He had a felicity of expression that came through. She got the message; the United States could help but the Kenyans would have to build their own future with their own hands.

Secretary Rusk's wife deserves a special niche in the Hall of

[9] When I resigned from the Department, a black officer, William Jones whom I had persuaded to join the Foreign Service was promoted to Deputy Assistant Secretary.

Fame of Department of State heroines. She took to public life and her role with an enthusiasm at once beguiling and bedeviling. Virginia Rusk shook more hands and held up more lines making people feel welcome than protocol required and, sometimes, than time permitted. Her hair pulled back smooth in a bun, she would look at a Foreign Service wife with an expectant air. "Now let me see, you're from Walla Walla, you were at the meeting in New Delhi." Her memory startled the wife into reverent silence.

She kept an office not far from her husband's. The office consisted of a desk in a corner by the elevator. She scrutinized guest lists; she would ask why one person was invited and not another. Her calender was filled for weeks ahead. She never missed a national day reception at an embassy and received all outgoing and incoming United States Ambassadors' wives at her home, as well as the wives of foreign diplomats. There she served coffee, tea, and concerned attention to their comings, goings, and adventures in between.

In my various incarnations at State, it was my misfortune to deal with not only routine correspondence but Congressional mail, hate mail, and other assaults upon one's time and patience. Eventually we concluded that the haters came largely from small communities where they had tired of insulting one another and taken to writing President Johnson, Secretary Rusk, and other identifiable names. Some wrote several times. My favorite State Department obscurity, used on occasion for replying to repeaters, ran thus:

> We thank you for the trouble you have taken to write us further along the lines of your former correspondence, and assure you that your letter will be added to previous communications from you for consideration by those members of the Department who are studying matters of this nature.

Next to obfuscation, the Department's most incurable addiction was the meeting. The Secretary held a meeting for thirty-five high-echelon officers every week. As "Acting" Assistant Secretary, I was included.

On Mondays, Wednesdays, and Fridays the Under Secretary held smaller meetings limited to Assistant Secretaries and what other Under Secretaries chose to be present. (There are two Under Secretaries and two Deputy Under Secretaries.) Wit flowed freely—it had to—to keep the tedious inevitable monologist from awakening latent hostilities and engendering ulcers and remorse. Of necessity, the laugh lines were brief. "We were perilously near to an agreement," reported one Assistant Secretary, "until our spokesman was run over by new instructions." Which reminded another: "Our intelligence has been overtaken by events." "That," announced a third, "is what we call diplomatic exhaustion."

Meetings at lower levels came in all shapes and sizes. At first they drove me to rhymed indignation.

> One seldom sees a bureaucrat
> without a pipe or with a hat
>> his habitat is corridors
>> he takes his exercise indoors,
>> he is always somewhere in between
>> two meetings where he should have been.
>> his favorite words are activate,
>> coordinate, evaluate.
>> he can't afford to be precise,
>> indignant, adamant, concise;
>> agendas he will implement
>> must be explored as to intent;
>> a modicum of well-phrased doubt
>> his expertise will iron out
>> attests to his prodigious craft;
>> he clarifies the final draft.
> A bureaucrat is seldom seen
> without a pen—or with a dream.

Later, I took to writing down samples of recurrent government-ese. "Conceptual-perameter" and "critical variables" tied for first place with "counterproductive" deserving honorable mention. The dangers of my preoccupation were fully realized one noon when I discovered we were on Item 4 and I was Item 5 on the agenda. My message, I knew, would be unpopular with my colleagues. The Bureau of the Budget [the government watchdog] had complained, I said. "Our 1967 report to the President is too long." The battle was on. Everyone present had written discursive parts of the report and would resist the elimination of a single word.

After such a session, my mind would return to those early days when I had obeyed Roger Jones's wise advice: "You should travel more." Fondly I recalled the solicitous Foreign Service greeter at the airport who would hand me a Baedeker of information, instructions, itinerary, and description of local characteristics and mores. At such times, Bureaucracy, I blessed your helpful verbiage. When I did face the strangers and their strange ways, I knew your caution had paid off and your careful, all-inclusive dicta had insured peace of mind as well as my warm welcome.

How I miss you, as a private citizen, now that I must pick my way through tourist traps.

The Grub
and the Glory

STANDING IN AMBASSADOR DAVID BRUCE'S LONDON LIVING ROOM, I found myself in conversation with a member of the British Cabinet, Lord Hailsham. The year was 1962. (Hailsham later gave up his title and became plain Mr. Quintin Hogg, in order to stand for election to the House of Commons.) "What do you do?" he asked, rocking gently back and forth, brandy glass in hand. I explained my assignment in the Department of State. He interrupted me: "And what *did* you do?" I produced my record as Vice Chairman of the Democratic National Committee. "Aha," he grinned, "you're one of the fruits of victory." We both laughed. At other times, when the going got rough and my feet sore from being trampled on, I have wondered if victory would have been easier if I'd been a man.

It was abysmally hot in Nicosia when I joined one of the regional meetings Under Secretary of State Bowles was holding with Chiefs of Mission around the world. There were memorable round-table discussions, but the evening I met separately with USIA officers remains vivid. Fumbling for an opener, I suggested that perhaps after days of exhaustive discussions this might not be the time to talk to them about women . . . Quite the contrary, a sharp-faced junior interposed: "Evening is just the time of day when we really become interested in women."

This was to be the first of many such cracks. Sex was the one subject men found applicable when women were mentioned. As a featured speaker at Bowles's round table, I was asked for a title to my talk. "The New Role of Women," I decided, would do. I lived to regret this innocently chosen phrase. Tom Sorensen, brother of Ted, can claim honors as the first man to laugh and ask me, "What was the matter with the old role?" Tyler Thompson, the handsome, cherubic-faced Director General of the Foreign Service, liked the joke so well he suggested his playing straight man on the line. When former Ambassador Galbraith dined with us some time later, he commented on my appearance: "They asked me in New Delhi about your remarks. I told them I had not been in the room, but I doubted that any 'new role' for women could surpass the old, and I for one was for the old one." Hadn't I seen his comments? They had appeared in "ten thousand Indian papers." I took the occasion to inform him he would have to settle for third place in order of originality, but as host he was first rank.

New Delhi came after Nicosia. The meetings were smaller, only eight Chiefs of Mission, compared to twenty-two in Nicosia. The dinner Ambassador Galbraith gave for Under Secretary Bowles was even smaller than the meeting itself, a show of good taste; only the stars were present. The Prime Minister wore his red rose, his long "Nehru" jacket, and his immaculate glossy black boots. His daughter Indira and I commiserated with one another about the education of "women as politicians and leaders in government," bemoaning our infinite efforts and infinitesimal accomplishments. Before dinner Ken very thoughtfully arranged for me to sit with the Prime Minister; searching for a mutual subject, I thought of my old friend Justice William O. Douglas. "I am certain the Justice would like to be here in his much-loved India," I said, "sitting in my place, talking to you."

"Here?" The Prime Minister turned his slightest smile upon me. "Yes, he would have liked being here, provided he was on his way someplace else."

Nehru's wit was devastating, because he never abandoned his remoteness. His distant dignity made it easier to understand India's neutralism. In a roundabout way, being neutral gives one time; one might call it a deliberate misleading of both sides, a permanent coquetting with two persuasive powerful suitors, the U.S. and the U.S.S.R. Except that one is almost within walking distance, and the other comes from afar. I came home understanding, I hoped, Nehru's relationship to his people; slightly less divine than Gandhi, he was an approachable god.

At dinner I sat between Krishna Menon and M. J. Desai. The latter was then being spoken of as possible successor to Nehru. Mr. Menon managed to be both rude and indifferent.

He scorned my proffered subject, literacy. What could I know about this deprivation the poor suffered? A good deal; we had plenty of it in America and we were struggling to rid ourselves of the problem. His comments were always whispered. He toyed with his special vegetarian dinner and, when all else failed to disrupt my composure, rattled what turned out to be sugar cubes in his pocket.

My Sikh driver was more informative. He described his fellow citizens as a people "who do not want jobs or better homes. Those at the top want to be respected, even courted, because they are Indian and represent this vast continent, and the rest want the modern equivalent of princes and pageants and Mother India on the throne."

India both attracted and repelled. I watched the pedicab driver cycling frantically forward, not showing an iota of perspiration while I clutched my Kleenex and mopped. My State Department colleagues assured me "their thermostats are adjusted to the climate." I asked a roomful of Foreign Service wives sitting under large ceiling fans whether the British had not been wise to evacuate the city in summer (this was August and the humid heat unbearable). "But they didn't have air conditioning," came the rebuke. Neither did they try to do in a decade what the combination of nationalism and Western prodding is now urging upon a largely indifferent populace. On my return, I was to tell all my friends that birth control is not the key to India's problem because it is not considered desirable or even respectable by a people who think nothing of squalor, death, and human life.

The women we met in Ken and Kitty Galbraith's drawing rooms wore their saris with more pride than a Parisian countess wears her Givenchy or Dior; the colors and textures were astounding. Their English left me feeling my repetitive vocabulary was showing; commenting on *The Rise and Fall of the Third Reich* (current reading) I referred to it as "morbidly fascinating." The beautiful young woman Deputy Minister of Finance remarked, "What a strange juxtaposition of adjectives, but perhaps most apt."

Lima, Peru, where we next convened, is a Spanish-derived city, with huge squares and carved wooden balconies on cream-colored façades. The new Hotel Crillon where the meetings were held had an unassimilated skyscraper rising out of a typical European-style rococo three-story structure. The brand-new seeing-eye door, all glass, was continuously being worked over by despairing mechanics. Lima is also modern, with free-style lush suburbs and its downtown heart beating in faceless, high-rise monsters.

At the enormous Ambassadorial residence where I stayed, there were thirteen servants with whom I spoke sign language interspersed with remnants of high school Spanish. Rosa, the upstairs maid, made it clear to me that she did not like my washing my own underwear or my gloves. There is some deep feminine urge, I find, after a long day's meeting (into night) that expresses itself in washing. I gave up trying to explain this to Rosa.

The Ambassador, Jim Loeb, and his wife Ellen were informal, congenial hosts. Jim had been the founder of the Union for Democratic Action, the forerunner of the ADA. Ellen played violin with the local symphony orchestra.

The residence was guarded by Peruvian police (who failed to notice the Loeb son when he climbed into a second-story window, having forgotten his key) and on the inside by the customary Marines.

The Indians in Peru had paintable faces; in the popular square they hawked the usual uglies in handsome native dress (the ugliest uglies were imported U.S. plastics). During our ten-day meeting a series of saints' days had native women wearing purple robes. I made the unconscious mistake of walking around in a purple dress. Was I *simpático* . . . of course I was.

The legend that there are forty rich families in Peru has not been brought up to date. One glance at the suburbs and the guests at a dinner for a hundred that the Foreign Minister gave convinced me there were many more. I drew two non-English-speaking Latin American Ambassadors; we managed to talk about the roses on the tables and the gloves on the footmen.

When Bowles arrived in Lima, the newspapers made much of his entourage and the two gentlemen of color with him (Carl Rowan, Deputy Assistant Secretary of State for Public Affairs, and George Weaver, Assistant Secretary for International Labor Organizations in the Labor Department). One exhausted evening I struck and refused to go to a large reception. George Weaver gently reprimanded me: "Come on, Katie, you know we minorities have to be represented."

On two separate occasions I met with ladies bountiful and young social workers. The first were typical; one largish leader pursued me with flowers, a silver plate, and a glossy book of self-portraits snapped with VIPs. She has her counterpart in other countries.

The social workers were young, enlightened, perplexed, and determined to modernize conditions. They raised a hundred problems, each one of which might be resolved with some assistance from the United States. I brought home more orders for help than we could execute . . . had we the funds.

Costa Rica resembles a tropical Switzerland. In the company of a woman judge of a juvenile court, I visited housing developments which an organization of women lawyers had helped to launch; they had raised the funds for the down payments, which most low-income buyers could not afford. We talked of democracy and its many attributes. "Here we take it for granted," she told me. "We do not think it, we feel it."

The President of Costa Rica drives his own car. At a reception given in his house, I took a lesson in protocol. When I can sit down, I do. A senior Ambassador's wife (our own) whispered to me: "The right side of the sofa is always reserved for the guest of honor." I have never sat on another diplomatic sofa; chairs are safe, they can hold only one person.

My travels taught me to respect diplomats and their polite precision—a necessary adjunct in handling sensitive people whose national honor, the individual feels, depends upon where he sits. Angier Duke, Chief of Protocol, thought part of my State Department experience should include the workings of a ceremonial visit to the U.S. By a great stroke of good fortune the visitor was the Prime Minister of India. Gathered in a VIP lounge at Andrews Air Force Base were all the diplomats: Africans in native dress, Indians in saris, and conventional Ambassadors in pin-striped blue suits. They stood in carefully gathered groups, their movements paced and planned. Mrs. B. K. Nehru (the Indian Ambassador's wife) questioned me. "After politics, how do you like diplomacy?" I liked the manners better. "Ah yes, I know—*dolce far niente.*"

Our pre-greeting circular included a diagram indicating just where we stood for each part of the ceremony. Like animals out of the ark, we advanced in twos (there was only one of me unless you counted my English umbrella, whose brand name was "Ambassadress"). We crossed the wide expanse of asphalt past rows of correct Air Force, Marine Corps, Army, Navy, and Coast Guard troops in gala uniform, with a special color guard at attention in the foreground. On either side of a real red carpet were pasted oversize yellow stickers with our names. Mine, fifth from the bottom, put me beside a handsome bearded Indian General. I could distinguish President Kennedy and the Prime Minister because I knew it must be they standing still in a halo of flashing bulbs. Mrs. Johnson (in pistachio green) presented the roses to Indira, hud-

dled in a black coat over her sari. The guns went off, nineteen
booms made the parade ground tremble, the band played,
and the principals descended. A surprised "Why, Katie," emitted
by both the President and Jackie, pleased me. In haphazard fashion
we transferred to the reviewing stand. Our places were marked and
again I had the bearded Sikh on my right. The sky, a pearling
pink, indicated that in moments it would be dark. The President
and the P.M. descended to review the troops. Flags flapped with a
drum roll assist from the wind; a commander barked his incom-
prehensible commands. The instructions at this point admonished
the President: "If the Prime Minister salutes, salute back. If he
does not, you need not." The Prime Minister did, and so the
President did.

After the review came the speeches. And then the miraculous
helicopters, swooping off with the official party. Our instructions
read: "A visit of ten or more minutes is expected of the welcoming party at Blair House." I sipped orange juice with Mr. Desai;
how did he manage this endless official round? "One must be
philosophical, what does not get done will have to remain in-
complete."

After a battering week of formalities that included dinners,
lunches, press conferences, we all stood at our accustomed places
at the farewell ceremony. Secretary Rusk took the President's
place. I had arranged a theater party and a luncheon for Indira in
New York. Finding the right hostess and the right guests can be as
dangerous and as delicate as a surgical operation. I've lived
through the latter, but I'm not certain I would survive another
VIP planning ordeal.

In Tokyo, as house guests of Ambassador and Mrs. Reischauer,
I discovered it was less tiring to be the person programmed than
the officer trying to arrange a schedule. Because Haru and Ed
Reischauer added in-depth briefings to each occasion, I never felt
tired. In the guise of a woman leader from the United States,
I also discovered I had propaganda value. Curiosity compounded

into candid, often critical questions, interpreters' circumlocutions, and untiring audiences kept me fully occupied. What industries could women advance in, what did working mothers do with their children, were American men opposed to educated women as Japanese men so often were? What did my husband say to my career? The leftists tackled me on our minority problems. Another favorite was the U.S. approach to women's emancipation in Japan, so legalistic, preoccupied with divorce laws, custody of children when the abortion problem is their serious concern.

In Bonn, Germany, I met with thirty-five women leaders and a different set of questions. Some were Members of Parliament, one had taken a taxi all the way from Hamburg to attend the meeting. My lapsed German came rushing back as the arguments between the feminists and their opposition accelerated. A gray-haired M.P. categorically denied the existence of women's issues: "Women don't think of themselves as women." The feminists held their ground: "Germans even educate the boys to think of themselves as superior. We should start at the cradle teaching boys that women are capable of great things." A chorus of affirmative "jas" left the men with a half dozen younger women defenders. It seemed not only diplomatic but prudent to declare that both pros and antis were needed to produce what we dearly love to call the right "climate for progress." On a return visit several years later I found the women still arguing and the cure undiscovered. In the presence of prelates, elected officials, and civic leaders, amid the old-world grandeur of a Munich flat, our titled hostess uttered a familiar cry: "Beware, women are the ones who fell for Hitler."

After these visits, I kept trying to find private means to increase the numbers of women observers from Germany and Japan who might stay in American homes and study some of our successful efforts at voluntary activities. The women who came under government programs were few and already known as leaders. We needed to discover young housewives, teachers, school principals, and other potential leaders. The foundations I contacted had other interests. We did succeed in conducting a modest program for African teachers with the help of the American Association of University Women. But with forty African countries eager to participate our numbers perforce were limited.

Fortunately both the German and Japanese governments believed in women; the Germans invited American women leaders to visit their country, and the Japanese Ministry of Education annually invited Japanese women to visit the United States. A delegation of Members of Parliament whom I had met in Tokyo were the first to come.

The required bowing and greeting took place, including a reception at my house. At a departure lunch, a month later, the hard-line leftist member of the group rose to declare herself: "If I had not come, I would not know your country. I have a different opinion now."

Eagerly I chalked up the pluses. In cooperation with the League of Women Voters Overseas Fund for Education, we developed three programs in my office funded by AID. Two were aimed at training women as volunteers in urban development (in Colombia and Chile) and one in rural development in the Philippines. These modest attempts are still creating ripples country- and continent-wide.

The care and feeding of women visitors also provided me with brand-new enthusiasms. The office visits were never long enough, so I entertained these women in my home or in the Senate, House, or State dining rooms which also made it possible to include U.S. women leaders who sharpened our interchanges.

Reading back over my journals, my respect for these women's sense of the appropriate grows and grows. There were inevitably some misunderstandings. Once in the course of arrangements for a luncheon an Eastern European embassy official misunderstood my name and thereby added a new and appropriate pseudonym to my life—Katie Lunchtime. Thereafter when unavoidable misunderstandings occurred my staff referred to them as "Katie Lunchtimes."

Madam Adoula, wife of the Prime Minister of the Congo (1963), was in the U.S. attending a Food for Peace Conference. She had let it be known that due deference had not been paid her. (We later learned that her slights had been due to faulty interpreters and intrepid press questions.) Preparation for a luncheon in her honor, therefore, included all the brass and press I could muster.

At noon of the appointed day, my assistant buzzed on the intercom: "I might as well give it to you straight. She is not coming. Her husband cabled and wants her to come home right away."

I stamped a figurative foot. Surely right away could mean right after luncheon. But the trouble was, no one could locate her, although she had not checked out of her hotel.

We canceled the press. In desperation I called on Assistant Secretary G. Mennen Williams (head of the Bureau of African Affairs). He sent his desk officer to the hotel as I went home to explain to my twelve guests what had happened.

The phone rang as I came in the door. She was on her way. A persistent Washington *Post* reporter had tracked her down in the toy department of a store buying gifts for her children.

Over a special menu she thawed. (She had lunched with me in '62 when she accompanied her husband on an official visit and I remembered her tastes.) When the re-invited press appeared, she posed happily for pictures. Her good-bys were effusive. She was driving to Kennedy Airport so as to see all she could of our lovely countryside; she might never, she sighed, return. Explanations and apologies from the Embassy flowed freely; but the real villain, obviously, was Katie Lunchtime.

Madame Chaban Delmas, then the wife of the Speaker of the Lower House and now the Premier of France, arrived on time but spoke very little English. Miss Schwarzhaupt, German Cabinet Minister of Health, who prided herself on her English, had difficulty with Mrs. Johnson's accent. Fraülein Schwarzhaupt and Mrs. Johnson talked of river pollution, and the German laws that require factories whose waste pollutes to pay for depollution. In Germany, that comes under health.

Princess Ashraf Pahlevi, sister of the Shah of Iran, toyed with a long-stemmed rose. But her delicate exquisiteness had deceived me; she was a determined woman. We spoke of her brother's giving women the vote. "He was following in his father's tradition," she told me in perfect French. "He removed the veil." In their eagerness to forge ahead, women in her country were demanding instant high office. As a personal endeavor, she preferred educating the illiterate or welfare work to women's causes.

Nepalese, Japanese, Pakistanis, Africans from every part of that vast continent, Jamaicans, Koreans, Filipinos, Australians, New Zealanders, Turkish women—and on through the alphabet of nations—passed through my office and my home, adding to my education and my understanding.

Among my most interesting guests were eight Soviet women leaders, who duly invited me to return the compliment and come to Russia. Someday I hope to accept their invitation. Meanwhile I continue to lobby for an official exchange of women between our countries, for if there is any country where we should be represented by our highly placed women leaders in all fields, it is Russia. (Present exchange arrangements require that both governments agree to the exchanges, be they women, agriculturists, scientists, etc. Private citizens on the U.S. side may, of course, visit the Soviet Union, but only official Russian women leaders may come to the United States.)

The Russian ladies arrived looking like doves and proceeded to coo. Lengthy complimentary approaches crossed the floor between us; their thanks (their delight) culminated with the presentation of a gift by a plump, matronly woman who handed me a lacquered box. She seemed motherly and genuine. I could picture her counterpart waiting for a bus or sitting on the balcony at Woody's (Woodward & Lothrop, a large department store) resting her feet, indistinguishable from other tired shoppers. Rushing in with my appreciation, I filibustered my way through their questions; what I did, where and how I did it, how important American women were, the accomplishment of our voluntary associations. The editor of the *Soviet Woman Magazine* arrived late with fresh questions and an air of superior authority; would I say a few words to her readers? Departing, they left a message: "Some think we are not friendly and we are glad to explain that although we have different systems, we must be very friendly."

In 1966, at a briefing of the Inspection Corps (a State Department group that travels constantly to check on outposts), their chief introduced me as the author of a phrase coined in my first year in the State Department. "Katie once remarked that 'women are here to stay.' I thought she was joking. Now we know she wasn't."

Flowerin' It Up

LIKE ALL HUSBANDS AND MORE PARTICULARLY THOSE IN PUBLIC LIFE, Lyndon Johnson wanted his wife to put him first. On her agenda the President always came ahead of anyone or anything else.

When asked what women should do to make their contribution, Lady Bird Johnson replied: "The great effort of women is not, I believe, to invade a man's world, or to create a woman's world, but rather to be a full operating partner in a warm, compassionate world." Translated into the vernacular, these Golden Rule words really mean: Always be a good wife.

Although Lady Bird Johnson might appear beguilingly feminine, she also is, as Adlai Stevenson described her, beguilingly efficient. During their five years in the White House she managed to put a good many activities—besides being a good wife—onto her schedule and several bright stars in her crown of accomplishments. The President both admired and resented these activities. At the last meeting of the Committee for a More Beautiful Capital, after thanking the members for their generous support, the President added: "Last but not least, let me thank you for giving me back my wife. Perhaps now I can get back on her schedule."

He was joking. But many of us had heard him speak caustically of her meetings with talkative conservationists that interfered with his taking a nap; or of her absence when he wanted her: "She's out planting a tree somewhere."

Long ago, when Lady Bird first became involved with the volatile, gifted, and demanding Lyndon Baines Johnson, she gave up

giving real slices of herself to others. Her daughters Lynda and
Luci grew up expecting the unexpected, surrounded as they were
by faces in the news. It was Willie Day Taylor, still a close friend,
who saw to it that they were hovered over and brushed their teeth.

Because I have known Bird[1] for almost thirty years, people
would ask me if she changed when she moved to the White House.
Of course she changed, but her basic traits remained constant.
She was still every bit as considerate of others, if not more so. Her
loyalty and her devotion to her possessive husband had never
been more essential and forthcoming than in the White House.

Lynda once said, "I want someone to write a book about my
mother. She is a perfectionist, a strict self-disciplinarian. She
never just sits down to read a book or take a nap, unless the book
or the nap will help her do the next thing better. My mother, well,
she's just something special." Her mother's seriousness of purpose, her incredible self-discipline, her constant striving, must have
been both inspiring and trying to her exuberant daughters. Luci,
like most second children, developed her own escape hatch, along
with her independence. Lynda stayed caught between her father's
loving insistence and her mother's determination. Lynda would
talk about Luci's pranks: "When President Ayub of Pakistan came
to visit, Daddy had a pond filled with trout. Luci went down before anyone else was up and caught them all. If I had done that, I
would have been punished. Because Luci did it, it was cute."

Lady Bird's public competence was hard-won. In the spring of
1960 when I asked her to introduce her husband at a large women's
conference (as other speakers' wives were to do) she hesitated.
She dreaded public speaking because she knew she was not good
at it. She had taken speaker's courses, but she still felt uneasy on a
platform. Finally she said yes, and wrote her own introduction:

"This is a brand-new experience for me. Usually at a dinner like
this I listen to someone introduce Lyndon with words of praise

[1] The President referred to Mrs. Johnson when speaking of her to others as
"Lady Bird," but talking directly to her, would call her Bird. Many of her old
friends also call her Bird.

and approval, all of which I underwrite and enjoy. But I want to introduce him in a more personal way—as an exciting man to live with; an exhausting man to keep up with; a man who has worn well in the twenty-five years we have been together; and, more important, a man from whom I have learned that, to put all the brains and heart and skill you have into the job of trying to make your government work a little better can be a wonderful life for a man and his wife. My friends, may I introduce my husband, Lyndon B. Johnson."

In October of that same year the Vice Presidential candidate issued a personal invitation to me to accompany Bird to Wilmington, Delaware. I watched Mrs. Johnson walk to center stage in a huge jam-packed auditorium. Her hands shook so she could barely hold her speech notes. Yet she never gave up. Her persistence and doggedness paid off; by the time she had reached the White House she no longer trembled. She had overcome her fears.

Before the Democratic Convention in 1964 she asked our reaction to a television interview with ABC's Howard K. Smith. At his very first question she had hesitated slightly: "Well, now, Mr. Smith"—that told me she was at ease—"I could tell by the lift of Lyndon's shoulders that the railroad strike had been settled." She closed with: "I have a hopeful feeling that mankind is on an upward journey."

"Spiritual," was my husband's comment.

"That's just the way she talks," I added.

When Mrs. Kennedy was unavailable for receiving foreign visitors, I appealed to Bird. The answer was always yes. The heartbroken Bolivian who had brought Mrs. Kennedy a piece of her wedding silver found consolation in having her picture taken handing it to the Vice President's wife. A lively group of young Tunisians won't forget Lady Bird's tour through the Capitol, a building she knew by heart. "There are many little things I love about this building," she told them. "It is, in looks and being, such a continuing thing, stretched from time to time to meet the new demands of a growing nation." The Tunisians later said to me:

"Such an up-to-date woman who is so wellborn just couldn't be a politician's wife. We decided she is your American Queen."

After she became First Lady, a term she never liked, Lady Bird told Maggie Hunter of the New York *Times:* "I will try to be balm, sustainer and somtimes critic for my husband." She kept her word. She insisted on seeing the critical mail so she could tell the President what people were bothered about. She spent many hours answering letters about the war in Vietnam. In the last years, when the President and some of his Senate colleagues differed sharply, Bird constantly held out hope for reconciliation. Bethine Church, wife of Senator Frank Church of Idaho, an outspoken war critic, remarked, "Lady Bird never let me feel that anything Frank said stood between us." Mrs. Johnson invited Bethine and Donna Metcalf (wife of Senator Lee Metcalf of Montana, another "dove") to be members of a speakers' group she organized in 1967 in anticipation of the 1968 campaign. She wanted to be certain the word went out on the Job Corps, Operation Headstart, anti-billboard legislation, and other "affirmative" programs she had participated in. She kept right on attending a Spanish class at the home of Mercedes Eichholz (Mrs. Robert Eichholz, formerly the wife of Justice William Douglas), where the hostess and a large number of the members were outspokenly anti-Vietnam. She kept in touch with Secretaries Udall (Interior), John Gardner (HEW), and W. Willard Wirtz (Labor), despite their opposition to the President's policies on Vietnam.

Lady Bird enlarged the President's tastes and his circle of friends. She deliberately cultivated such people as Dillon Ripley, Secretary of the Smithsonian Institution, and Joseph Hirshhorn, millionaire modern art collector, entertaining them at small dinners so the President could get to know them. She invited the conservationist Laurance Rockefeller and his wife to the ranch. And in between she saw to it that old friends were not forgotten. She watched the President's health, reminding him to swim when the pressures got too heavy, and counting his calories even though she knew he'd sneak cookies and candies on the side. Because he wanted her to have a good figure, she ate little herself.

One of her friends described Bird as a martyr. "Lyndon consumes the people he loves, his family, his old-time staffers, his closest friends. His wife is so used to giving up and giving over, she can't be human any more." To me she was astonishingly human—but I knew that every President's wife needs a protective shell. Perhaps in her case she had a shell within a shell. She never let down her guard and if anyone tried to move in on her, no matter who, she would let them know, in a tactful way, that when she needed advice or sympathy she would ask for it. I have always suspected that her inscrutability protected her and her determination saved her from importunities, even from the President himself.

In an interview, Lyndon Johnson once described her greatest attribute: "She can adjust herself to any situation and do whatever it is well." The White House years presented her with the ultimate tests and she met them as she had others, with all her laurels intact.

If she sounds too good to be true, she came near being so. "How does she do it all?" I once asked Marnie (Mrs. Clark) Clifford. "Don't you know? Lady Bird has pigeonholes in her mind that open and close at her will. That's why she never forgets anyone or overlooks anything."

At the regular Tuesday meetings of the Senate Ladies Red Cross Unit,[2] where talk often rolls better than the bandages, Bird was accorded the broadest non-partisan loyalty. The Vice President's wife traditionally presides over the group. When it came time for Mrs. Johnson to give up the chairmanship, Mrs. Everett Dirksen

---

[2] Every Tuesday from nine-thirty to three-thirty, the Senate ladies put down their partisanship and don their Red Cross headgear and matching uniforms. They meet in a quiet corner of the Capitol and bring their own lunch. The gathering dates from pre-World War I days when its purpose was purely social. When war needs arose, the group changed character (from the Senate Ladies Club it became the Senate Ladies Red Cross Unit). Talk still dominates, but the output of afghans, socks, layettes, and bandages totals in the hundreds of thousands (they now fold a small patch for the blood bank; eight of these are used per donor).

wrote: "Farewell Madame President, welcome First Lady. We miss you very much."

Republican fans like to tell the story of the letter Bird wrote to her black deliveryman when he fell ill. He told Mrs. Tobey[3] he had hung the letter in his living room because it was the most wonderful thing that ever happened to him. Mrs. Tobey said, "She treated him just as she would have a diplomat. She feels every human being is important."

In the past, newly appointed United States Ambassadors were received alone by the President. The wives stayed at home. But it made no sense to talk about "two diplomats for the price of one" when the wife of the Ambassador did not get a chance to meet the President or the First Lady of the country she was serving. The Ambassador's wife, as hostess, would sit to the left of the Prime Minister—and Prime Ministers have been known to ask very pointed questions. With the help of Deputy Under Secretary Crockett, and with Lady Bird's enthusiastic endorsement, I took the first group of ambassadorial husbands and wives to the White House on August 3, 1965. After a visit with Mrs. Johnson and a photographing session in the President's office, six couples assembled in the rose garden to hear an impromptu talk by their Commander in Chief. The President was at his extemporaneous best, weaving his own experience into the message, extolling the importance of a wife's help to her husband's success. On the way back to the State Department, Bill Crockett asked me to write up the President's remarks. I kept notes on the story he told about Bird: "Every time we'd go out, I'd notice that the most important man in the room would invariably spend the evening talking to my wife. So one evening I asked her, 'How do you always manage to monopolize the most interesting man present so that no one else gets to talk to him?' Her answer was simple: 'I just ask him to tell me all about himself.'"

Being an expert listener added up, in Bird's case, to being a great

[3] Mrs. Lillian Tobey, widow of Senator Charles Tobey, Vermont.

asset. At a meeting called by Mrs. Rusk (early in the Kennedy Administration) to discuss ways of reaching the wives of newly independent nations, Mrs. Johnson was doing some of her expert listening. The upstairs sitting room at Blair House (the President's guest house) was filled with ranking wives of officialdom, from both Congress and the executive branch. After a good hour of suggestion and countersuggestion, Virginia Rusk turned to Lady Bird and said: "None of us knows what Mrs. Johnson is thinking."

Abigail McCarthy spoke up: "Some of us have been trying for years to find out what Bird is thinking, but we've given up."

We all laughed, including Mrs. Johnson. The meeting then shed its glacial restraint and went on to produce some lively arguments and usable ideas.

One of these came from Mrs. Johnson. "When Lyndon was in Congress and we had visiting Texans in town, I would just bundle them up, take a picnic, and drive them to the home of Thomas Jefferson."

That summer, buses took the new and old foreign Ambassadors' wives (137 in all including chargés and ministers) to Monticello and points of interest along the line.

As newcomers to Washington, both the President and Mrs. Johnson had been magnetized by the New Deal and by the man who master-minded it, Franklin Delano Roosevelt. It was with great joy, therefore, that in 1964 Mrs. Johnson undertook a journey to Maine for the dedication of Campobello, Franklin Roosevelt's summer home, as an international park. Dr. Arnold Hammer, New York and California art dealer, and his two brothers had purchased Campobello from the Canadian government, restored the former President's summer plaisance, and generously presented the landmark to a Joint International Commission which was to act as guardian.

On August 20, 1964, at 6 A.M., Mrs. Johnson, the brothers Hammer and their wives, Senator Muskie of Maine, Franklin Roosevelt, Jr. (then Under Secretary of Commerce), Grace Tully

(President Roosevelt's secretary), various public functionaries, members of the press, and a few fortunate folk like myself (I had coordinated the trip for the Department of State, the agency responsible in all instances of international takeovers, boundary agreements, etc.) boarded a DC-6 for Bangor, Maine.

Good golfers, the story goes, standing on the Canadian shores of Campobello, could drop a drive across Passamaquoddy Bay into Lubec, Maine. No one has ever been too clear as to why the Canadian-American boundary treaty (signed in 1842 and known as the Webster-Ashburton Treaty) gave Canada three islands right off the coast of Maine. Campobello, one of the three, was once a hideaway for smugglers, pre-Revolutionary Tories, retired British Navy bigwigs and finally—in 1881—wealthy New Yorkers and Bostonians who bought the island and built cottages on it. Franklin Roosevelt's father was one of those. In 1912, Roosevelt's mother took him to Campobello, where he learned to sail and love the water.

We deplaned at Eastport, motored through the depressing small town that was once a prosperous sardine canning community. The brand-new International Bridge, it was hoped, would attract vacationing families on wheels. People, and prosperity, would return. We did not use the new bridge but crossed the bay instead in open fishing boats because the water route was livelier. Mrs. Lester B. Pearson, wife of the Canadian Prime Minister, crossed in yet another way. As our boat docked, we noted her carrier, an impressive naval vessel flying the Canadian flag. The diplomatic aplomb of our Ambassador, Walton Butterworth, more than compensated for our lack of a stylish boat.

Maine was at its best with fine weather—the first in weeks. (I had spent many anxious minutes talking to our Canadian friends about preparations for rain.) Campobello, with its sprawling thirty-two rooms, loomed large behind the podium. Orange and white bunting, the faded red of the shingles, and Mrs. Johnson's bright tangerine coat gave off a luminosity that cheered and warmed us. Campobello was not much to look at; like many well-loved summer homes, it relied on the view, which was startling, and the air, which was invigorating. Inside the house, one room after another, filled with faded chintz and uncomfortable wicker furniture, looked as if the occupants had just gone to the beach.[4] Grace Tully, who had never seen Campobello, remarked, "If no one had told me where we were, I would have recognized the Roosevelt family touch. All their houses had the same haphazard, unpretentious look."

In the pantry, a crank telephone hung on the wall. It was still in use. (I know because I tested it.) A folded quilt, a faded rag rug, and an open fireplace furnished the room Franklin Roosevelt, Jr., was born in. (In his remarks that noon, he moved his audience with stories of his youth and a grim account of his father being carried out on a stretcher after his polio attack.) The speeches were short; Senator Muskie's was eloquent. Mrs. Johnson linked the house with FDR's growth to greatness: "It was here among these bays and books and boats that the shaping of a President took place. In all Franklin Roosevelt's accounts, one senses the reservoirs of exuberance, strength and vitality, which summers on Campobello filled to overflowing. This island, this house, obviously had an overreaching emotional attachment for him."

We lunched in a diminutive parish hall, crowding onto narrow benches. The faces of the lady parishioners steamed with pleasurable exertion; the women had been up since dawn fixing the feast. The two First Ladies thanked them each personally.

Bird Johnson and I have a common addiction: we are both lovers of words. She traced her own addiction to a "good English teacher at St. Mary's school in Dallas." When a volume of my poetry was published,[5] Bird wrote to me: "Your book is like a pleasant drug; I pick it up and can't put it down."

4 FDR last went to Campobello August 19, 1939. He suffered the polio attack there in 1921.

5 *With or Without Roses* (New York, 1966).

She has a way of finding words to light up her sentences. Describing a visit to Winterthur, the Dupont Museum at Wilmington, she remarked, "You could just see all those sashays into history. . . . Napoleon bringing back ideas from Egypt that took fanciful shape in his furniture."

Riding out to the airport with her, after a long New York luncheon on behalf of the Eleanor Roosevelt Foundation, an affair at which there had been too many speakers (of which she had been one), she said, "Anna Rosenberg[6] was far superior. In the Agora in Greece when Pericles had finished, everyone said, 'How thoughtful and how excellent.' After Demosthenes had thundered his words, the audience left shouting, 'Let's go out and defeat the Spartans.' That's what Anna did today."

The President also has a facility with words: he coined the phrase "women doers." Bird, in turn, found ways to publicize, dramatize, and energize women doers by inviting them to a series of luncheons, the first of which took place on January 16, 1964.

The Johnsons were the first of the Presidential families to entertain officially upstairs in the family quarters. The President and Mrs. Johnson had always held more parties for more people than other political figures. Once in the White House, it was natural they would use more rooms more often. That afternoon, over coffee, Mrs. Johnson stood talking about the lovely arched windows at each end of the living quarters hall. "They frame the landscape in a pure semicircle," she said, "letting in liquid light . . . in itself an added dimension to this end of the long hall."

I was fortunate to attend many functions at the White House. My driver once jokingly inquired why I hadn't arranged to get my mail there. Each time we drove up, I looked at the vistas of lawns and trees as if I were memorizing the view. I never did get over the awe that crossing the threshold gives one. The dark of the diplomatic lobby—the President's pet economy—always amused me. I had learned where the light switches were and used them when I found guests waiting in the shadows.

[6] Assistant Secretary of Defense, 1950–53.

Despite the necessary changes to the White House for the ever expanding President's staff, and the addition of the famous Truman balcony, a great place to be seen and to see from, the preservationists have succeeded. The interior rooms have each retained their original proportions, their gracious heights, breadths, and depths.

The Johnsons' respect and reverence for the White House and its traditions were never more visible than at Christmas. The year I best remember is 1967. The President had gone to Vietnam and ended his tour with an unexpected visit to Pope Paul. He was to fly home Christmas Day. A week or so earlier, Mrs. Johnson called me at the office. My secretary buzzed loudly: "It's she—herself—on the phone." I wanted to reassure my secretary—Mrs. Johnson always called herself. She invited us to a pre-Christmas party:

"There will be a fire burning and, of course, our family tree will be up. Come and bring your daughters and the grandchildren."

I hastened to negotiate a loan of the two older grandchildren from New York (aged twelve and fifteen). When we arrived at the family floor, there, real as their anticipation, sat the Marine Band string orchestra. Inside the door of the Oval Room, Mrs. Johnson, in blue and silver, stood looking like a sugar plum fairy.

The fire, the tree lights, both in the room and outside on the giant evergreen on the Ellipse, gave sparkling reflections on windowpanes that blinked at us in blues, reds, and yellow. The buzz of people, soft music, scurrying young of all ages, the rounds we were making, gave us the appearance of a Christmas-wreathed carousel.

I saw my grandson Cotton talking earnestly with Mrs. Johnson; what about? I inquired later. "I asked her how it felt to live in such a big house. She told me you get used to it."

Savoring every sight and bauble were aunts, grandmothers, family friends, the President's soft-voiced senior secretary, Juanita Roberts, Willie Day who brought up Luci and Lynda, little Lyn in a green suit and red stockings (the Secret Service discovered him playing with screws he'd found in a drawer), Pat Nugent (Chuck had a bad cold), and members of Congress. Neither the President nor Mrs. Johnson ever set their social and working friends apart. At each White House function members of both their staffs were included. Even at Lynda's pre-wedding showers, those connected with her learning and growing-up process were invited.

Best of all the occasions with Mrs. Johnson, I liked the spring outings. When I went to Texas with her and thirty-eight foreign correspondents on a Discover America tour, we visited the ranch. The foreman, Dale Melecheck, drove us around, pointing out the sights. "This here pasture is different," he told us as we approached a tidy expanse. "Mrs. Johnson's been out here flowerin' it up." He might have used that phrase to describe what Mrs. Johnson had done for the city that had long been her home—the nation's capital. Along with a genuine love of nature, she had what some call "pride of place." She likes seeing things grow, be it education for children or grass where there were once dirt banks. She was forever reaching; in Washington she reached for citizen-wide attention to the environment, an element that had long been lacking. She taught us to look again at grim schools, playgrounds so dismal one wondered why any child would want to play there, triangles (there are 750 of these) where people might sit if there was a bench to sit on and something to look at like a shrub or a tree. And so . . . in January of 1965, a committee was put together called the Committee for a More Beautiful Capital.

Like the other members, I had served on a lifetime of committees, but never one with a President's wife at the helm. I had learned that if you have more than three members you have rivalry. Now I was to learn that if you have thirty members, outdoor excursions, and photographers, you develop what are called lens-lice, folks who appear in every picture. Because he was the Secretary of the Interior, it was almost impossible to get a picture of Mrs. Johnson without Stuart Udall. There were other camera crowders who left the less bold shuffling in the background. One day the members were divided into two groups and put on separate boats. The bashful finally got their pictures taken with their lady Chairman.

In late spring Mrs. Johnson always gave awards to citizens who had contributed to the appearance of their area. Taking Mrs. Johnson on a pre-award tour to show her the results of citizens' efforts was like preparing for a college exam. As organizer of the awards effort, it fell to me to explain why this park, this bank, this side street cleanup effort was chosen by the awards jury. To get past Mrs. Johnson's searching questions required a strenuous marshaling of facts. Sometimes I flunked the test.

In three and a half years the Committee landscaped 110 park sites, 55 public schools, 3 playgrounds, 5 libraries, and 6 approaches to the city. Four new fountains and a 250-foot-high water jet on the top of Hains Point were donated—also 1700 cherry trees and 100,000 surplus bulbs and mums for the District schools. A tulip library was planted along Independence Avenue. The Buchanan School outdoor community center, a model outdoor playground for all ages, was given by Mrs. Vincent Astor. And a mile of park along Watts Branch Creek was the gift of Laurance Rockefeller. The citizens of Watts Branch once wrote Mr. Rockefeller: "Come down, spring has come to your park." Over three million dollars were raised, new approach signs installed, roadside planting extended along freeways, and miles of daffodils and dogwoods planted—all of it producing striking visible results.

Each of us on the Committee had our favorite projects; sometimes what I called the daffodil and dogwood set won out, and again Mayor Walter Washington's educational group would score. When the efficient Nash Castro, our National Park Service member, reported that 400,000 bulbs would be planted in Lady Bird Johnson Park, the donor sat impassively by. (Mary Lasker liked anonymity as much as she liked flowers and parks.) Then the Mayor, as was his wont, rose to inquire if there were not an educational component somewhere in the program. I took up his cause. What would it cost, I asked, if the school children planted bulbs on their school grounds? By the time we had the answer, the Mayor had his educational component. Adam J. Rumoshosky, representing the American Petroleum Institute, had pledged the additional funds. At the correct season, we all planted bulbs—children on school grounds, garden club matrons, Mrs. Johnson and friends on their knees.

When my husband and I attended a small, unofficial gathering at the White House in December 1968 we never admitted to one another that this was our last party there. We had been invited to see the portraits of the President and Mrs. Johnson, painted by Madam Shoumatoff. The President's mood, as it had been since March 31, when he announced his intention not to run, was restrained and somber. But his portrait had a look we recognized—as if he were about to tell you, accompanied by broad gestures, something of great import.

Mrs. Johnson's liveliness was missing in the portrait. We liked the painting nevertheless; her coloring and her features were perfect. It was not surprising that she had chosen the Jefferson Memorial for the background. I had once heard her tell an audience that the Memorial was her favorite view.

"Because the Memorial has classical lines," she explained, "because Thomas Jefferson is my favorite founding father and four men in my family are his namesakes—my grandfather, father, brother, and nephew."

On the 1964 whistle-stop tour she took through eight states, she often ended her platform remarks thus:

"I just want to leave you with this thought. It is our privilege to choose our leader. In doing so we make conscious choice in shaping our personal destiny. Your own Thomas Jefferson said, 'Let the people know the facts and they will decide wisely.' History has proven him right."

Madam Shoumatoff was a delight, lively and impressive at eighty. Her daughter asked why I didn't let her mother paint my portrait. I was too old, had too many wrinkles, I replied.

"Nonsense, for a few hundred dollars more, Mother will take out the wrinkles."

On the way home Walter and I talked about the carefully chosen guest list, enough of the President's friends to please him, others invited for other reasons. We tried to total up the numerous times we had been the Johnsons' guests. "Sometime I hope we can reciprocate," my husband remarked as he opened our front door.

Some seven months later my husband did open the door of our house to Lady Bird and Lynda. Mrs. Johnson was in Washington helping her daughter choose furnishings for her new home. Chuck Robb, Lynda's husband, was to meet them at our house, preparatory to going to the National Theatre. Mrs. Johnson inquired where they could eat en route to a seven-thirty curtain.

Nowhere, I declared emphatically. Walter and I would prepare hamburgers. My husband gave me what is publicly called a quizzical look. Our help had left that morning for Cape Cod where we were to join them the next day. The top round arrived just before Chuck. We dealt with doorbells, plates, forks and knives, napkins, and a time limit, while our guests balanced hamburgers on their laps.

When they drove off, Chuck was at the wheel, Lynda beside him, and Mrs. Johnson, like any mother-in-law, sat in the back.

Walter commented that it wasn't exactly the way he had planned to entertain the Johnsons. I could tell by his caustic inflection that I had just entered the doghouse. I began talking fast and furiously. "You would never have thought that either Bird or Lynda had lived in recent privileged splendor. They seemed so pleased and at ease. Bird and I got to talking about—"

"You mean while I was cooking?" he interrupted.

"Must have been. She was saying that it's a very small, small town and a lot of the wonderful old houses are being abandoned. She's trying to restore the post office, and I'm looking forward to the trip."

"What trip?" Walter grumbled.

"The trip to Karnack, Texas, where Bird was born. Someday we are going."

The Power
Without a Throne

PRESIDENT KENNEDY ONCE COMMENTED IN A ROSE GARDEN TALK TO women representatives to the United Nations: "I never know whether women want to be referred to as women or as politicians." Under my breath I responded, "If they are politicians, they don't care."

Women have become the third inevitability along with death and taxes—although there are just as many holes in generalizations about women as there are in Swiss cheese. And one fact about them has become irrefutable; the world is catching up with the beautiful but dumb. Even Miss America has to have talent and a college degree.

Shortly after my appointment as Director of Women's Activities for the Democratic National Committee, I invented a slogan: "Men do the difficult, women the impossible." I kept right on smiling when a waggish male wired me: "You are so right, Katie. Men are difficult, women impossible."

Defending women, pressing their cause, is a role I never asked for or wanted. Somehow it has pursued me, even into the Department of State. Why weren't more women promoted to Class I, the highest grade in the Foreign Service? For one, too many of them dropped out, choosing marriage instead of career. But there were other reasons. Talking with Frances Willis (who never married), a career woman who not only rose to the exalted Class I state but held two Ambassadorial posts,[1] I remarked, "A lot of women would like to be in your shoes." She responded tartly, "It took me long enough to get into them!"

Promotions in the Department of State are meted out by boards chosen by the male moguls who run the place; mostly they are composed of senior career officers. Margaret Tibbetts, who with only two other women career officers, all single, reached the summit of Class I during my State Department tenure, served as Ambassador and as member of a promotion board. When I asked her to name the feminine characteristics most objectionable to men, she replied, "Lack of humor and humility." Certainly *men* without humor or humility are equally hard to take!

Which brings me to an exception to my hex on generalizations: women with faults resemble men with faults. Both exist. When Queen Victoria complained to Gladstone, her Prime Minister, that there were not many good preachers, he is alleged to have replied, "Madam, there are not many good anything."

Way down deep, I agree with Lord Gladstone. But I admire many women, particularly those with whom I have worked and most of whom have chosen some part- or full-time professional occupation.

I have many reasons for admiring Senator Margaret Chase Smith, one of which is the respect her colleagues accord her. On the opening day of Congress in January 1969, I watched the austere and much-revered Senator Richard Russell of Georgia cross the full length of the Senate floor, from the Democratic to the Republican side, to bestow a welcoming kiss on Senator Smith. He calls her "Sis," a term of endearment that combines affection with respect. When the bachelor Senator was elected President pro-tem of the Senate, an honor that includes a car and chauffeur, Mrs. Smith twitted him about the loan of his wheels and his driver. He gladly agreed. "What about the car's owner?" she teased. The Senator shook his head. "You wouldn't be getting much."

One of the very few women who can rise above chivalry and

1 Switzerland and Ceylon.

still win an argument is Senator Smith. Her famous stand against Senator Joe McCarthy—a public declaration of conscience when it was not exactly popular to take pot shots at the Communist headhunter—won her deserved national acclaim.

My own admiration for her was launched with her determined, dignified, and low-key race for Vice President in 1964. She was making a point: that women have a place in the decision-making process, a place that women like herself have earned.

In a speech to the Business and Professional Women, she spoke out freely on another controversial subject. She said "Adam's rib simply isn't the sedate sanctum that it once was. Eve's pill has changed all that." She went on to warn women that with their new-found economic and biological security goes a power that should be "very carefully exercised, lest it ultimately be the self-destruction of woman and her rightful responsible place in civilization."

Congresswoman Edith Green of Portland, Oregon, also guards her principles without raising her voice or pounding the table. As Chairman of the all important Sub-Committee on Higher Education (in the House of Representatives), she knows her opposition well and girds herself each morning for another battle. "Just think," she once informed me, "four of the members, men of my own party, really despise me!" Perhaps irreverently, I replied, "That makes you unique. How many women are there in public life who have earned the enduring hatred of four seasoned members of Congress?" She laughed.

When Edith first ran for Congress in 1954, she had a survey made in Portland to determine what effect her being a woman had on her chances. The results proved that those who would vote for or against her only because she was a woman canceled each other out.

Since that time her pluralities have steadily increased. Because of her voting strength, in 1960 Jack Kennedy courted Edith, as did Hubert Humphrey. She chose Kennedy, and his decisive win in the Oregon primary took him a long way toward the nomination. In return, there was talk of Edith's being offered the HEW Cabinet post. At the time Edith told me, "If they want me, they know where to find me. There are advantages to being on the Hill, I am my own boss."

A friend of President Kennedy's once told me that he was very high on Mrs. Green. But when others came to warn him that she could neither be counted on nor controlled, he reluctantly gave up on appointing her to his Cabinet. As the second ranking Democrat on the powerful Labor and Education Committee in the House of Representatives, Mrs. Green is still very much her own boss. When she takes on a fight the House floor fills up—her skills as a debater draw an audience.

When introducing Edith Green, the popular Republican Governor of Oregon, Tom McCall, remarked, "The best thing I ever did for education was to let Congresswoman Green defeat me." (She defeated McCall in her first race for Congress in 1954.)

With the rarest of exceptions, the women on both sides of the aisle and in both Houses of Congress have demonstrated their ability. They had to have it to get elected in the first place. Julia Butler Hansen, a Democrat of Washington, serves on that formerly all-masculine preserve, the Committee on Appropriations. Similarly, Martha Griffiths, Democrat of Michigan, was the first woman to break into another men-only habitat—the prestigious Ways and Means Committee (the only Committee elected by the full membership.)

The reigning woman in the House on the Republican side for a long span of time was Mrs. Frances Bolton of Cleveland, Ohio, who permitted no one to call her Congresswoman. She despised the feminization of the term. (I agree with her; I wince when I am referred to as a poetess.) Her stationery, her signatures, and her colleagues' form of address conformed to her wishes. Congressman Bolton, for many years ranking minority member (Republican) of the House Foreign Affairs Committee, was affectionately known to her colleagues as Mrs. Africa. When Africans came to town, I could rely on her as guest or hostess. One noon I had suggested to an African guest that our system of sending county agents to the boondocks might be one answer to the problems in her large country. Mrs. Bolton countered caustically, "Trust the Democrats to bank on the government to solve problems; we Republicans rely on the individual." Our astonished visitor was left openmouthed at the frankness of friendly partisanship.

To this whole subject of women, males—especially male politicians—react personally. They like you or they do not. I have had only one infallible yardstick: if the man is married and likes his wife, he likes other women as associates. If a state of what one calls mutual hostility exists between husband and wife, a man can be as wary of your good qualities as a rabbit of a snare. The idea that women, like men, are people—good, bad, and indifferent in addition to being homemakers, mothers, mistresses, and secretaries—hasn't crossed the threshold of his awareness.

The only women who rose to political prominence during my days as Vice Chairman came to power the hard way—by getting elected. I vividly recall my hurrahs when four women, all of them married, got elected in 1954. I referred to their husbands as "mature men." I hailed them as pioneers, forerunners of an era when women could have careers and husbands. My own did not let me forget that comment; leaving the house one morning, he turned to me and asked, "Do you think a mature man ought to go to work with a hole in his sock?" The four husbands turned out to be less mature than I had foreseen; three of them divorced, or were divorced by, their wives.

At one time the Kennedy Administration let me know that they would be happy to offer me an Ambassadorship to a certain European country. I said no without even checking back with Walter. I could not picture him as the man who came along to dinner. (My husband has lots of humor but little humility.)

Other women, however, have done well including their husbands in their entourage. Witness the successful tenure of the brainy Clare Boothe Luce, whose equally vital husband commuted to Rome and back. Nor did Eugenie Anderson have too much of a problem with husband John, a painter and an archaeologist: a man willing to applaud his wife.

Katharine White, appointed Ambassador to Denmark by President Johnson, was beloved by the Danes. But her husband Arthur, although retired when she took over, spent such an unhappy first year that she thought of resigning. As his interests expanded (he enlarged the garden, joined a bicycle club, made contacts with Danes) he settled in.

A delightful Danish reporter once told me that she foresaw a time when men would want to do the baby tending, housekeeping, and family care. "Why not?" she asked. "What's wrong with that, except that we are not accustomed to this way of life?" I told my Danish friend that my husband had long since taken over the household; he liked good food and, if our fare were left to my indifference, he would be faced with chops and baked potatoes every night.

Another talented woman, Pat Van Delden, a USIA officer whose husband was killed in the Dutch resistance, came suddenly into line for the top USIA job in Germany when the man who was her immediate superior resigned. Although the Ambassador was sympathetic and appreciated Pat's abilities, he said he could not promote her into the spot; the Germans were partial to stag gatherings, and what would they do with a woman hanging around?

I have never been comfortable with the feminists, though I concede there is plenty of discrimination. They seldom narrow the gap between letter and spirit. Their favorite stance is one of protest. Mrs. Emma Guffey Miller,[2] long-time Democratic National Committeewoman from Pennsylvania, matriarch of the original feminist group, the National Woman's Party (lobbyists for the Equal Rights Amendment), once said: "If I were a man, I might be called an elder statesman, but being only a woman, I am always called the 'old gray mare.'" She was right; but I was unwilling to join her on the firing line.

[2] Deceased 1970 at the age of ninety-five.

A reporter described me in my political heyday as the "power behind the Democratic Party." I qualified his comment: "The power without a throne." Which is perhaps some indication of the measure of insecurity many women unconsciously carry around. Brooke (Mrs. Vincent) Astor, a dashing creature with pastel good looks, a steel-sharp mind, and a good share of financial security, would agree. "Rich or poor," she told me, "it makes no difference, women are troubled." Except, I would add, those in the creative fields. "Providence has filled them with recklessness," as Yeats once observed.[3]

Every now and then, fresh proof is offered me of the way most men feel about working with women. As the lone woman in a five-day sensitivity training session, I was run through the wringer. At the final session the men were asked, "When you first met Katie, would you have been willing to work with her? How do you feel now?"

The answers were startlingly uniform; at first the nine men had regarded me with suspicion, but as the days went by they were reassured. Still, it was clear to me: a strange woman raises a man's hackles. The last man to answer the question has since become a friend. His reply was direct and unequivocal: "I not only would be willing to work *with* Katie, I'd work *for* her." I am still searching for a properly symbolic order of merit with which to reward him.

There are men like James Rowe—many a President's political Pooh-Bah—who regard all female politicians with educated misgivings. "The trouble with women," says Rowe, "is that a man feels he has to be chivalrous. He can't just have a knock-down fight with a woman." This inhibition may explain why Chairman Paul Butler chose the means he did to put me down. At the 1960 Democratic Convention he put me on the program right after

[3] "Three types of men have made all things beautiful. Aristocracies have made beautiful manners, because their place in the world puts them above the fear of life, and the countrymen have made beautiful stories and beliefs, because they have nothing to lose and so do not fear, and the artists have made all the rest because Providence has filled them with recklessness."

the keynote speaker, Senator Frank Church. When I rose, I
watched the hall empty as delegates filed out to keep caucus engagements. Happy with my text and the TV cameras, I kept my
eye on a California friend still in the hall who kept right on smiling and nodding his head. When I asked him how he had liked my
speech he said, "I couldn't hear a word! The sound went off."
Obeying my own dicta, I exited laughing.

A spare statement of Jane Austen's serves as an eloquent summation of modern women's cause for dissatisfaction. "In my opinion," the hero of *Northanger Abbey* says, "nature has given them
[women] so much more that they never find it necessary to use
more than half." The revolt, especially among the educated,
against lack of opportunity to make full and imaginative use of
their abilities is increasingly vocal and sharp.

At a recent luncheon for alumnae of Rosemary Hall, the headmistress, Miss Alice E. McBee, described the forthcoming merger
of facilities with the Choate School. Certain separations between
Rosemary and Choate would continue, she said; self-government,
for instance, would not be included in co-ed plans. "The boys,"
she added, "would get elected to all the offices and the girls do
all the work." An excellent preparation for life, I found myself
exclaiming.

After the luncheon some of the younger women expressed their
boredom and irritation with volunteer assignments. Some volunteer work, I said by way of encouragement, is important; the rest,
frankly, is just a waste. Like all continuing efforts, large areas of
government and of volunteer programs become stagnant. They
should periodically regroup, reorder their priorities, and start anew.
WICS (Women in Community Service), a newer group composed
of existing organizations which grew out of civil rights effort, now
supplies the volunteers for Operation Head Start and other poverty
programs.

In England, women serve along with men as lay justices of the peace,[4] the lowest court, to hear cases involving adults and young people up to seventeen, except in cases of homicide. They are unsalaried and must have had experience in some form of social work, although they need not be lawyers. The court consists of one man and two women, or the reverse. The clerk, a lawyer, is there to advise on legal questions that arise. It is considered a great honor to be appointed a lay magistrate. After serving for ten years, they qualify as chief magistrate. Many women hold these posts. Because of our overcrowded courts and particularly because of the enormous juvenile problems in our big cities, qualified women could certainly act in voluntary capacity to speed the work of the court. Women would not only add a missing ingredient in the handling of juvenile cases but would also serve as catalysts in initiating essential reforms and improvements in educational, preventive, and penal institutions in their communities.

All of us today are faced with evidence of failure, particularly as parents, if not as citizens. Frustrations are very real in government, in public and private life. These are only in part due to "bigness," overpopulation, pollution, and other currently culpable phenomena.

The talents of women remain hidden under clouds of prejudice, not only of men, but of custom. The more I look at the dilemma of split-level creatures (like myself) with husband, children, home, and career, the more I am grateful to the journalists, poll takers, sociologists, and critics who constantly label and advise us. By giving us the needle, the ambition, or the compulsion, they have handed us the inspiration we need to use up all our energies and insights, to carry out our convictions and earn the wisdom that comes with experience outside of the home and hearth. More and more of us want to lead meaningful existences and still make a home for a man and children. Women's Lib are telling us something important; we need safe abortion laws, day-care centers,

---

[4] Over one hundred women serve in London alone. They are appointed by the Lord Chancellor. In other areas, they are selected from a panel elected by the justices.

equal pay,[5] and, above all, opportunities (more medical schools, more law schools) so that we may use our talents and enrich the lives of those we chose as partners and progeny—instead of serving them gourmet recipes with frustration sauce.

The intelligent woman volunteer, the ambitious professional both have learned that shifting gears gives men a wider view, a greater range, an inner strength that makes their own lives and those of others sometimes blessed, often productive, and generally satisfactory. Women are not against men, nor are they against women, as they are so often accused of being. Most of them would agree with the comment by the talented French musician, Nadia Boulanger, in response to a review that paid more attention to her sex than to her performance. "I have been a woman for over fifty years," Mademoiselle Boulanger said, "and have gotten over my initial astonishment."

[5] Women's Lib ought to rectify one little noticed but intolerable injustice: in order to insure passage of the Equal Pay Act the sponsor (Congresswoman Edith Green) had to exempt executive, administrative and professional positions.

The Tough Brother

THE 1960 DEMOCRATIC CONVENTION IN LOS ANGELES WAS ALL BUT over. John F. Kennedy and Lyndon Baines Johnson had been duly nominated. Senator Henry Jackson, one of several unsuccessful candidates for the Vice Presidency, had been named Chairman of the Democratic National Committee. Senator Stuart Symington, still another Vice Presidential hopeful, was asked to introduce Lyndon Baines Johnson to the sixty thousand people in the Los Angeles stadium—and to a whole nation watching on TV. Adlai Stevenson, who had hoped for the top spot himself, had agreed to set the stage for John F. Kennedy's acceptance speech.

Each one of the above, except for the nominees, had shown the loser's traditional good sportsmanship in accepting his lesser role. It was to be my turn next.

At precisely midnight the telephone in my office rang. My assistants Barbara Luther and Geraldine Sohle and I had been working all evening packing up files for the return journey to Washington the next day. We had, as happens on such occasions, looked back at some minor and a few major successes, and found it possible to laugh over the catastrophes.

Barbara, who had answered the phone, said, "It's for you, Katie." Bob Kennedy, in what could best be described as politely authoritarian tones, without any prefix or preamble, announced, "We're going to give your job to Margaret Price [then National Committee woman from Michigan]." As the harsh words hit me, I made two discoveries: being a good sport was not going to be easy, and the Congressman who had warned me that politics was "ruthless" had been right.

Later, Bob Kennedy and I became friends. But that night on the telephone we talked tough.

"You'll regret this," I said, feeling and sounding like a harridan. "I've got friends everywhere; I know the territory; I've got the workers with me, I've trained them. You're making a mistake." Bob growled back, "We don't like to be threatened."

It took us a good three minutes to realize we weren't making any sense. When I mentioned my disappointment at not being able to help elect his brother, he said, "That's different." He sounded almost pleased. He was certain his brother would be glad to have me pitch in.

Adlai Stevenson, whom I found at Senator Symington's head-quarters, where they were presumably commiserating with each other, gladly offered sympathy. But he added, "You've come to the wrong two men for help. We haven't exactly won any prizes."

If only, I kept telling myself, I'd come from a proper state instead of from the voteless District of Columbia (we did finally get the vote for President and Vice President in 1961). But after I had voiced all the excuses I could dredge up, I had to admit that as an Adlai appointee I was both vulnerable and expendable. Besides, I held the only title left to swap.

On Saturday, the very last day of the convention, the change-over was made official at the customary Democratic National Committee meeting. Appointed to a greeting committee to escort the new nominee into the meeting room where a hundred expectant National Committeemen and -women waited, I became the beneficiary of an offhand remark: Jack Kennedy tapped me on the arm and said, "We're glad you're going to work with us—with my brother." This comment, quite naturally, changed my outlook and, as events were to reveal, my future course.

The actual ceremonial takeover, from Chairman Butler to Chair-

man Jackson, and subsequently from me to Margaret Price,[1] over-
flowed with kind words. Senator Jackson gave cheerful thanks that
"Katie is staying with the troops." I praised Margaret, which
prompted Jack Kennedy to give me a grateful glance. Margaret
duly praised me. The Presidential nominee, looking far sharper
than he should have after five days of tension and backstage maneuvering, made a short speech, which left us all cheering. He had
a genius for terse prose and understated wit, and his sincerity had
a plausible ring. When he publicly offered me an official welcome,
elaborating on his private remark to me before the meeting, I
decided I was a lucky loser.

After my mother died, in December of 1960, a terrible sense of
loss, of wounds that would not heal, pervaded me. I started a
poem (finished much, much later) and discarded it; I could not
seem to do her justice.

Among the messages of condolence was a hand-lettered card,
telling me that at the request of Bob and Ethel Kennedy a high
mass was being said for "Mrs. Adele Scofield," my mother.

One day Bob called; how was I? We talked of the victory; I
congratulated him on his share in that auspicious event. Would
I like to come back to work? It might do me good, I replied. I
had not found a way to resolve my mother's absence. He suggested I come to the office and take charge of all the notes of
thanks that must be written to those who had helped in the campaign.

I suspected him of creating a make-work project, motivated by
an instinctive sense of what sorrow can do to one; but I found a
very real accumulation of unassorted confusion that was crying out
to be dealt with. I went to work putting different categories of
people together, drafting sample letters that might be used. I
recognized the friends that the President would want to handle
himself and put their names to one side. My only regret is that it
went so fast there was little time to keep records, and yet it was

[1] Margaret Price served devotedly as Vice Chairman until her death in 1968.

all part of the John F. Kennedy story, the hundreds who helped at all levels, and who came from varying backgrounds.

After we returned from the Democratic Convention in Los Angeles, I moved downtown into a building where the Citizens for Kennedy-Johnson operated. At that time Bob moved into my old office at the Democratic National Committee. After the campaign I would visit with him there, checking on the latest appointees, reporting rumors and reactions.

The day his brother decided to announce Bob's appointment as Attorney General, I happened to be in Bob's office. He was standing behind his desk, looking not unlike a boy who had lost his way—except that he was never uncertain, his feelings were never moderate, they were either far out in favor of, or equally far out against. He never outgrew that boyish look and tension gave him a glazed, bewildered expression.

I asked him if he had had lunch. He didn't want any. Nonsense, I would go down to the cafeteria in the building and get him some. He settled for soup and milk.

He drank the milk and toyed with the soup, giving me a grudging grin between swallows. There was no time for conversation. That evening on television I watched the President-elect invest his brother with the office of Attorney General. They stood, as had other appointees, on the steps of the Georgetown house Jack and Jackie Kennedy still called home. What a contrast in these two brothers, one so urbane and unflappable, and the other so fiercely proud and "uptight."

Once in a while we would meet on the Washington social-political-benefit merry-go-round. Ethel Kennedy often prompted and always participated in everything in Washington with a New Frontier label. The Administration took special interest in the newly emerging nations, so Ethel gave teas at her Hickory Hill home for new Ambassadors' wives. I watched them steal surreptitious glances round the room as she poured tea and chatted with them. There was plenty to see at Hickory Hill—walls and tables full of framed photos, surprising dogs, and the forever erupting, always enchanting children.

I remember going with Ethel to a post inaugural fund-raising luncheon, full of good will, bad food, and indifferent speeches—the normal fare at any do-up-the-deficit clambake. The snow of inaugural week still pursued us; we had trouble finding her black car because all big black cars look alike. Ethel finally identified her car when she spied a large-sized papier-mâché lamb left on the seat. She opened the window: wasn't it warm? Would snow hurt a fur coat? What a splendid idea I'd had using the National Gallery of Art for the Distinguished Ladies Reception. Where else could you have put five thousand women? Could we use the Gallery for the 1964 Inaugural Ball?

Her cheery hoarse voice delights one; she's all outgoingness and "Next question, please." We talked about the 1960 campaign and her heavily accented Hungarian secretary. I reminded her of the time in Bob's office when she had remarked, "That secretary is getting the Hungarian vote. Every day she makes a new goulash of her *s*'s and *z*'s."

After President Kennedy's death I finally gathered up my courage in February of 1964, and went to pay a condolence call on Bob Kennedy. At first neither Bob nor I mentioned the grotesque, macabre tragedy, but talked of trivial, mundane matters.

He made a point of telling me, once again, that he continued to receive good reports on me from the Department of State. Suddenly he switched topics to inquire if I didn't miss politics. I admitted I did. We walked backward for a while, reviewing the 1960 campaign, our mutual experiences, his brother's victory.

Of course, then it was easy to talk about Jack. Bob had helped me across that difficult bridge. I talked freely, told him of the witticisms Jack had pulled off—at my expense. I even told him about the friend in Dallas who had implored me not to let the President come to her city.

In her large, legible hand, Lillian (Mrs. John) Kilgore, a senior

long-time supporter of Democratic liberal causes and Lyndon B.
Johnson, had written me several letters emphasizing the dangers.
The city had spat on the Vice President and his wife, had roughed
up Adlai Stevenson. On neither occasion had the police offered
proper protection.

In response to Bob's questioning, I told him I had sent relevant
portions of her letter to Dick Donohue[2] (a White House staffer),
who had promised to be in touch with the President's advance
men.

That night, that black Friday, I had called Lillian Kilgore. She
was almost hysterical—talking constantly of the harm the Dallas
Morning News had done with its editorials. We reviewed a lot of
disconnected facts, just to keep talking—as if talking could change
anything. Lillian had been one of the hundreds at the Merchandise
Mart waiting for the President to arrive; as the delay grew longer
and longer, something told her that what she had most dreaded
had come to pass.

There had been many such warnings. Bob and I talked about
them for a while. Little did we know then of the nightmarish
proportions the insane acts of distorted minds would assume.
When I rose to leave he insisted on taking me to the door. His
giant dog, Brumus, walked beside him. They made a strange pair.
He asked me if I wanted to work in the '64 campaign. My enthusiastic yes brought a big grin and a responsive "If I have anything to do with it, you'll be there." In a muffled voice he asked
me if I wasn't going to kiss him good-by.

He could be affectionate, but for Bob Kennedy to show this side
of his nature in public would have been difficult. He would shy
away from such a role; for most of his life he had portrayed the
tough kid brother and the part suited him. The sensitive side of
Bob belonged only to his family, very close friends and, on rare
occasions, a few political associates who had shared some of
those epoch-making events on his brother's way to the White
House.

2 Aide on Lawrence F. O'Brien's legislative staff.

The last time I saw Bob, then Senator from New York, was at the State Department on February 28, 1968. He had come to attend the swearing in of a constituent, Edward Re, a law professor who had been appointed Assistant Secretary of State for Educational and Cultural Affairs. I had been delayed at a White House tea given by Mrs. Johnson for the officers of the National Council of Jewish Women. Walter and I were hurrying through the entrance when a voice boomed out: "Hey, Katie, where are you going?"

His eyes looked bleary from fatigue, his hands, when I shook one, were rough. We rode up in the elevator to the eighth floor where these ceremonials took place. I mentioned that some of the officers of the National Jewish Council had related their meeting on the Hill with him: "I hear they mobbed you." He hoped, he replied, I had not told that to anyone in the White House. I had not, I reassured him. We talked about the telethon he and Ethel had just staged to raise money for a D.C. swimming pool.

"Your mother was right, you do need a haircut," I said as we got off the elevator. Jack Paar, alternately fatuous and funny as M.C., had relayed to Bob an offer of five hundred dollars from his mother, if he'd have a haircut.

We were startled to find our way impeded by an overflow crowd. Taking him in hand, I wove my way round the perimeter of the room, over and around people, saying, "Please," and having them fall back when they saw Bob. We reached a point where we could see just as the last part of the swearing-in ceremony was taking place. Ed Re and his wife and eleven children were being photographed with Secretary Rusk. Finally I managed to move Bob forward. "What do we do now?" he asked. "We'll think of something," I said, laughing. But it was Secretary Re who thought of something. "Senator," he began, "if I'd only known you were here, I would have mentioned your name in my remarks."

When I left the reception, he was still being surrounded by people who wanted to shake his hand. "You're on your own," I called out over their heads. He smiled and waved back.

Later, after he had announced his candidacy (March 17, 1968) and entered primaries, I watched the televised processions with some terrible sense of foreboding. He was forever seated on tops of cars, being clutched at, pulled, paraded into crowds.

Muriel Humphrey told me at this time that when the advance men for Bob went into South Dakota (the state where she had been born) they told the police they wanted no protection. Their orders were, let the crowd break through, let them come right up to the ramp of the plane. Foolhardy, we both agreed.

We spent Memorial Day weekend at the Homestead in Virginia with our older daughter, her husband, and three grandchildren. Walter and I walked the flowering woods we loved; I wanted so much to speak of my apprehensions, but hesitated. The thought of all the frenzied howling crowds chilled me. I mentioned Muriel's report to Walter; he shook his head. "What has happened to campaigning?" "Television," I replied.

Tragedy is rarely bearable, especially when it befalls one so young. Why did he take these risks? I kept asking myself. He owed it to Ethel and his children whom he adored to guard his life.

Much later, when I mentioned to Ethel that I thought Bob had risked too much, she replied so spontaneously that one wondered at her courage, "Oh, Katie, if he hadn't run, he would have been miserable."

Was Bob avenging his brother's death when he ran for President? His anti-Vietnam, strongly pro-black convictions could not have been the sole factors; had his intense dislike of President Johnson provided the main motive in his decision? His feelings went deep, back to a boyhood where to compete was the law of the household, and to win, the tribute one could offer a brother who had been cut down in his prime.

Mark van Doren has written that "the years permitted to any man are beautiful, perplexing and few." Perhaps that is where one must let Bob rest. He surely found the years perplexing and yet he had been part of more of the beautiful—his brother's triumph, his years as Attorney General, the capture of a prize Senate seat and a joyous family life that the media never tired of describing and their viewers, readers, and gazers never tired of consuming —all these beautiful things had been his, a far greater share of them than is granted to most.

Perhaps what most distinguished him from a good many of his contemporaries is that the emotions he evoked in others were much like his own; no one dismissed Bob with a shrug. They despised him or liked him a lot. Some, like Alice Longworth, who has sat in judgment over several generations of leaders, would say, "He was moody and determined, but I loved Bobby."

Congressman Frank Thompson, of Trenton, New Jersey, knew Bob well. In 1960 Frank and I plowed into Bob's registration drive, Frank commandeering the troops Bob set up, whereas I went out to places where there were no troops. Frank liked to remind me that early on I had said of Bob, "He's a very determined young man, rather frightening. I don't know how much he knows about politics." I was wrong, of course, about his expertise, but his fierceness ran deep.

It ran deeper in relation to his brother Jack, it turned him into an avenger. He had convinced himself that he alone could carry on for his brother.

Some Moldy Laurel

HUBERT HUMPHREY'S HUMOR, MUCH LIKE ADLAI STEVENSON'S, IS self-directed. Standing once on a podium on the State Department's plush eighth floor, he pointed to the Presidential seal splendidly emblazoned on marble in gold and said, "See that eagle, his wings outspread, his quiver full of arrows, and the laurel in his right talon bursting with greenery?" Then he described the Vice Presidential seal: "My eagle's wings are down, one miserable arrow and some moldy laurel, and you have the distinction clearly defined."

It was 1966 and the Vice President was talking to a large group of foreign students, many of whom were African. "We are a pro-people," he reminded them, "and not a pro-dollar country." Hubert's message, delivered from a prepared text, as usual, was too long. Despite his windiness, he is rarely excelled as a lay preacher, rallying-cry rouser, and optimist. With Hubert one always gets the sins and the salvation. I can close my eyes and see him on a variety of platforms, from drawing rooms (he could make a dining-room table quiver) to distinguished formal diplomatic rooms, and hear him end the moralizing with a chuckle: "Will all those who have not sinned meet me in the telephone booth in the hall?"

The force of his preaching is founded on a kind of homespun candor; he means whatever he says. Preacher, professor, but a deviant from the traditional characteristics of both, he holds on very tightly to the moral side of his chosen profession—politics.

Because I come from a long line of Humphrey fans, I found his defenders' defection in 1968 ironic. They liked him fine when he was on the hustings against the Republicans or pleading a liberal cause (promoted by the ADA or some other do-good organization he had christened or founded or both), but when he became part of the Establishment they pulled away. They even found him discursive, weak, dull, boring, repetitive. The man who was once "forceful, gripping, fiery" was now despised for not having turned on his President and that President's Vietnam policies.

Doves of both parties insist that Vice President Humphrey could have won the election in 1968 if he had come out against his President on the war in Vietnam. Although Hubert occasionally put a toe in the water, he remained safely on the banks.[1] Most of Hubert's critics, it should be noted, had never had to take an unpopular stand. Some had been his colleagues. Others had been the first to cry, "That's the man I'd like to see President—someday."

There is a very American story in the pursuit of personal happiness by the Humphreys, an objective seldom attained by prominent public figures. Public life and family happiness often do not mix well. But the Humphreys have done better at attaining their goal than most.

I have known both the Humphreys well. They are *very* American; they really are as small-town, unsophisticated, and un-Establishment as they look and talk. By 1959, Muriel had accepted Hubert's Presidential aspirations and had begun to prepare herself. One day she consulted me: "I just had an interview with a nice girl from the New York *Post*. I told her I made my own clothes. Was that all right?"

When folks, mostly Democrats, began talking about Humphrey for President, in the middle and late fifties, he had already electrified a good many Joe Doaks. Beginning with his civil rights siege of the 1948 Democratic Convention, he went on to stand in the center of posed pictures and his words made the lead stories on many front pages.

[1] Richard Nixon, who won, never came out against the war either.

The years of public limelight wore Muriel down; she had four children to bring up and very little help. She would ask: "What can I tell all these folks who come up and say they want Hubert to run for President?" "Tell them," I would reply, "that this is the open season for hopefuls." She would shrug her shoulders and look at me as if I'd just handed her the wrong key.

"Hubert is a good Senator. He belongs in the Senate," she would protest. "Why won't they let him be?"

There wasn't any cure, then, for her shyness. But she got through it and at the right moment, when her husband had to be carried round on the rocky shoulders of his supporters and be acclaimed, Muriel's worst fears had vanished. She no longer remembered a letter she once wrote me refusing to be Chairman of the Democratic Wives Forum (an organization I invented) because she was timid about handling this kind of administrative assignment. In fact, by the time the 1968 close-shave defeat was history, the reluctant, harassed wife had turned into a tiger! "I'm for him. I want him to be President. I hope he runs again."

In 1962 a very young, promising Senator was elected from Indiana—Birch Bayh. I had followed his career and admired his pretty wife. I tendered them a "Welcome to Washington" luncheon. Hubert, who sat at my right, kept the table awash with his usual Dr. Humphrey political patent-medicine utopianism. In between he dispensed free advice. "Young man," he admonished Birch, "don't let anyone tell you that your Senate vote does not count because there's a power bloc in the Senate. Every Senator has one vote and no more. Remember that. Don't let anyone tell you that oldsters must be called upon. They're fading out." All Birch Bayh needed was pad and pencil, the prescriptions kept right on coming. "What is needed," Humphrey continued, "is a great big tax cut. It's like the man told by his doctor to take penicillin. When the patient finds out how expensive it is, he decides to take half the quantity. But nothing less than the full measure will do." (Since then Senator Bayh has written several of his own prescriptions in historic ink as leader of the opposition to the Haynesworth and Carswell nominations for the Supreme Court.)

The pharmaceutical analogy was appropriate. Each man has his own familiar analogical terrain. Hubert had been a druggist, he knew all about quick remedies and mislabeled cures. Going down the Potomac, I listened one night while he held a whole boatload of sophisticates spellbound spinning yarns of olden days in his father's drugstore, describing the ingredients for Humphrey's Stomach Powder, which he mixed himself, and the signs he and his father put up on the bulletin board to cheer the depression aches.

Hubert's opinions have always ranged over all the Washington spectrum. In September 1962 he sat in our garden, telling us what was wrong with the Telstar program, the State Department, the spectacle of a do-nothing Senate and, prophetically, the destructive force of the media, forever preoccupied with disputes. (After the 1968 defeat he described TV coverage of the convention as disgraceful, provocative, and purposely in search of sadistic scenes to keep their audiences fed on blood and hostility and glued to the set. By then, his was not the only voice to be heard inveighing against the Box. Criticizing TV was to become a Vice Presidential habit.)

In the doorway he paused to wrap up Khrushchev: "He's in trouble. It all started with the U-2. When Khrushchev asked Ike, 'Did you do it?' hoping for a no he got a yes. Ike should have gone to Russia, he would have been acclaimed."[2]

One day in 1962, in his Majority Whip office, I got the full story of what was wrong on the Hill. To listen to Hubert by oneself is an awesome experience; he has the attention-getting powers of five normal people—it seemed a shame to waste them on just me. He first sermonized on the press: "I'll be sitting in a hearing room when some eager TV reporter will hand me a slip of paper suggest-

[2] Averell Harriman would agree. The U-2 episode occurred while he was attending a Democratic Committee Platform hearing. The press, totally uninterested in the hearing, bore down on Governor Harriman; should Eisenhower have admitted the plane had been on a spy mission? "Never. All you do is embarrass the Soviet."

ing I challenge the witness' statement so he can put the cameras on me." The answer was no. Hubert had grown mellow and expansive. "We always have trouble," he said, "when we're in power. The President runs on his own. We are not like the British, elected with our leader. We're not pledged to support him." (He should have added, "I will support him, even if it means my defeat." But that was yet to come.) "I accept our system," he continued, "but I find the lack of discipline here in the Senate horrifying. The other day I went looking for a bill to bring up; all nineteen of them were being held up for Senator Capehart to introduce, a man we are hoping to defeat." (We did, in November of that year.) "Just some more of that Senate Club spirit." He did finally find a bill to bring up, only to discover that meanwhile a Democratic colleague was trying to adjourn the Senate. Looking about for something or someone more recent to inveigh against, he pointed to a pile of telegrams on his desk: "My staff act as if there were no hurry about answering these. I'm going to tell them a thing or two!" Suddenly his good humor broke through: "What am I getting all wound up for?"

By June of 1965, I knew very well why I was getting wound up about Hubert Humphrey. My husband was just getting over an operation when, to surprise him, I invited Hubert to come for supper one evening. Muriel was at their summer home in Waverly, Minnesota. Hubert's faithful appointments secretary, Pat Grey, promised he'd be at our house at eight. Knowing Hubert's predilection for tardiness and respecting Walter's stomach, we ate lightly at seven. By then I could no longer keep the secret from Walter. All evening the calls kept coming from the Vice President's office. I knew from eight thirty-five on, when he had started into a meeting, just what he was doing. At ten I was window-watching, merely to get out of Walter's sight. At ten-fifteen my husband went to bed. At ten-forty Hubert rang the bell, looking harassed and rumpled. Had Walter gone to bed? he inquired. He had but we might still visit with him. In the bedroom, Hubert expostulated on his delays, describing the turmoil of a hard day. "I won't stay for supper," he explained, "I'll just say hello."

My irate mate had turned into Prince Charming. He got up, remarking: "After all, Katie has supper waiting for you. I'll sit with you while you eat."

Walter did just that while Hubert consumed two portions of lamb stew, a salad, a glass of milk, a shot of his favorite Canadian Club, and a piece of peach pie.

At eleven-thirty the Vice President was still going strong. How had the story of his interview with DeGaulle in Paris leaked? The Department of State headed the suspect list. State must be reconstructed from top to bottom (this was 1965), President Johnson must have a new Cabinet. Important and influential Washington-watchers were to complain that LBJ's loyalty to the Kennedy appointees cost him dear, but Hubert was the first to articulate these ideas.

We touched on finance, Walter's favorite topic, and the long hours Hubert keeps. "I am no sooner settled in my uptown office," Hubert said, "than the President decides he needs me right away on the Hill."

Leaving, he told us how happy he felt, how fulfilled. "The boys [his Secret Service agents] must be somewhere in the street." Out of the shadows they would appear. He thanked us as if we had fed him ambrosia, and later we received a warm note of appreciation.

On that night when he might have been described as "the man who almost didn't come to dinner," he seemed very sure of himself. I lay awake thinking about his indefatigable enthusiasm and how infectiously convincing he had been. And about how far, then, he was from the White House. Would the clutch of lonely laurel leaves ever come within his grasp?

There were many such evenings; Muriel would arrive on schedule and we would wait for "Humphrey," as she always referred to him. Finally we would sit down at the table, and once in a while she and I would play duets at the piano, both of us exclaiming at our rustiness, wishing we had more time for practice.

After Humphrey had arrived he would say, "I thought you were going to play duets." And Muriel would reply, "You are much too entertaining." That was so; we would gather round him while he dined. He pretended, perhaps purposely, that he never ate vegetables but these were the best damn peas, thereby delighting our maid, Frances, who had waited for these moments when she might watch him eat.

Inevitably, we got on to current legislation; beautification, I recall, occupied us one evening. Mrs. Johnson hoped we might succeed in banning billboards from certain highways. From highways to the poverty program, to a possible sales tax, we galloped through persistent concerns and their possible cures. Meanwhile, Frances would have brought in the coffee to hear the Vice President say, "This coffee is as fresh as a teen-ager's kiss." Teasingly we would ask, "How do you know?"

Our daughter Judy, hearing him tell how votes were obtained, would insist these deals sounded too much like a travesty of democracy. Patiently, the Vice President would explain: democracy deals in trades, not in bullets.

Hubert, like others whose skills have won them all varieties of audiences, prefers small groups, heated arguments that give him an opportunity for expansive replies. Muriel, a teacher at heart herself, explains that Hubert wants "people to understand before they vote." One evening, faced with an audience of brand-new junior Foreign Service officers, Hubert talked about his poverty-stricken youth. Both antique clocks on the State Department's eighth floor struck ten (within seconds of each other), and although Hubert had been talking for an hour, no one stirred. The faces of these young people were so still, so rapt, one might have thought they had stopped breathing.

His discourse took us on a travelogue, from Huron, South Dakota, to the nation's capital; it was a very American journey, full of heartaches, regrets, and success. He told us how poor his family had been, how he'd dropped out of the university to help his father in the drugstore, how Muriel had supported him by taking a job as bookkeeper so he could go back and finish his education. In their early married years they had dreaded debt so much that they owned nothing. "Now I have three cars, but I cannot drive any of them, two homes and I am never in either of them." He admonished them to enjoy life while they were young—they *were* young—and went right on to point out the promise of science and the need for anti-pollution, interlarding the global ideas with the advantages of a good wife. He quoted Muriel, who liked to idealize their hardship years: "My wife likes to reminisce; she remembers that when we were young we believed everything was possible. One must never lose that belief."

When he left he remarked, "Katie worries about my not eating, especially when Muriel is away. I am glad to be one of those she pampers." I forced a roast beef sandwich, hastily wrapped in a paper napkin, in his hand as he went out the door. VIPs and their staffs seldom find time to eat. The Vice President's Secret Service detail sometimes grabbed a bite in our kitchen, thereby providing a special in-house excitement for the cook.

During the first years of President Johnson's Administration there was continual talk about providing a permanent residence for the Vice President. The Humphreys' house was really too far away from the Capitol and the White House to be reached in a hurry. The newspapers produced yards of both probable and improbable solutions. One young matron, a brass-hearted self-promoter, told a wealthy builder that Mrs. Humphrey would like the builder and his wife to move out of their newly furnished duplex and give it to the Humphreys rent-free. Muriel, who had been making discreet and, she hoped, off-the-record efforts to find a home, was horrified. "Someone tell her, please," she urged, "to leave us alone." They would not have accepted a "rent-free" home; no important public official could afford to.

But Washington had discovered a brand-new topic and was not about to let go. The realtors and the rash, unsolicited helpers were locked in a gigantic struggle to solve the residence problem, not only of the Humphreys, but of all succeeding Vice Presidents whose means did not permit large living quarters. There were in addition all those historic houses whose owners would gladly deed them over if the government would restore or refurbish them.

Muriel, fortunately, had a strong determination that took her directly to her objective: she found a home, within their means, within quick reach of the Capitol and the White House, and moved in. After the Humphreys were settled in Harbor Square, the new, sprawling southwest Washington apartment house that rests on stilts, we were invited to visit them. From the exterior, the balconies stare at one like predatory giants. On entering, one is overwhelmed by courtyards, drive-ins, underground garages, and at that time, of course, the vigilant Secret Service. Once we had been cleared and admitted to their apartment, we found the view from the glass-walled living room astounding. The sunset reflecting off the Potomac dappled each of us in rose.

The Vice President toured us from the view to the kitchen via the dining corner, pausing to question, "Mama, where is all our silver that's been packed away?" Muriel gestured all about us, indicating the silver in between her favorite Royal Copenhagen blue and white plates. Everything was utilitarian and functionally located. The kitchen sang of handy mechanical helpers that pleased the Vice President.

We "did" the library with its open fireplace and went on to "my room," as the Vice President called his combination study and dressing room. An open closet exposed neatly hung suits and shelves of boxes. "All these shirts I'll never wear," he said, shaking his head. Verbally he completed the furnishing of the room. "There'll be a desk there and a fold-away bed for the kids when they visit."

Three balconies, all carpeted and protected from peering eyes by box trees in tubs, were duly noted. On the bedroom balcony carpet Hubert Humphrey spotted leaves: "I must come out here later and vacuum, I must have missed this one," he muttered. We glanced at Muriel. She nodded. "He will. He likes things to be right."

We sat down and began to talk politics in the drowning sunset. "People are like my family," Hubert Humphrey said. "You can't give them anything for Christmas; they have everything." We elaborated on the electorate, discussed the economy, the farmers' plight, Minnesota's internal politics, and the gnawing preoccupation with Vietnam.

My husband complimented the Vice President: "You think things through. You are good at clearing up a situation."

The Vice President nodded his appreciation but he looked glum. "I sit here sometimes at 5:00 A.M.," he said. "I don't even hear when Muriel is trying to get me to go back to bed. Believe me, I think. I think all the time. The President should put this country on a war basis; the Vietnam pace requires some sacrifice from us all. People would understand and accept this conflict if they were asked to pay a tax, if their gasoline were rationed, if . . ."

In the car going home I commented, "Hubert is right about the war. But will the President consider his ideas?" My husband remarked, "It's not a question of whether the President agrees with Hubert but of Hubert getting through to him." We shook our heads, almost simultaneously. In an effort to be cheerful, I remarked, "Right now I'll bet Hubert is vacuuming that balcony."

One could marvel at Hubert's ebullience in tackling everything from domestic chores to running for President. When his candidacy for the Presidency was first discussed, way back in 1958, he rejected a friend's insistence that he hire a manager. He laughed. "The only person that can manage me to my liking is Hubert Humphrey himself." He was being humorous but, to those of us listening, his words had the ring of unhappy truth. The unhappy truth seemed to pursue Hubert. Whether it was the intraparty strife on Vietnam, or the young militants who refused to recognize his earlier achievements, he seemed to be pursued by the political furies.

After the 1968 convention, in the grandiose office of the Secretary of Labor, Willard Wirtz and I talked about the decompression process. And of course, about the convention and the candidate, Hubert H. Humphrey. Bill defined mistakes he felt had been made at the convention. "The majority should have adopted the minority plank, and all Hubert would have lost would have been Texas. The TV takeover was outrageous and, as for the police, their takeover was criminal." The Humphrey people, he felt, should have stopped it. A good many others agreed with his analysis.

In the innermost party circles, it was now Hubert's turn to serve as punching bag. He talked too much, he huffed and puffed, but the White House remained standing and the keys went to Richard Nixon. As for his inability to say no, one intimate remarked, "If he'd been a woman, he'd be pregnant every nine months."

It had been a year of hostility, a time for strife, for pitching out loyalties, and praising dissent. Hubert knew this. For long years he had been the dissenter. He had tried to keep both sides happy and ended by isolating himself.

Who knows what the future holds for Hubert Humphrey? He might just pull another Richard Nixon.

Part of the Main Text

BECAUSE WE ARE CLOSE FRIENDS, FELLOW POETS, AND POLITICIANS, in that order, I am frequently asked to explain Senator McCarthy. Anyone who lives happily with Aristotle, Aquinas, the Scriptures, and Robert Lowell is not to be pinned down, like a butterfly, with a label. He is a man whose attitudes and actions may often be inexplicable but whose soul will always be uniquely his own. He is full of duality, which by my definition means he can be both humble and arrogant, basely political and spiritually pure, selfishly indifferent and unselfishly kind. Mostly he is cerebral; at times he is vain, sipping adulation with a connoisseur's refined appetite, and often he is just as petty, mean, and unpredictable as are any one of us.

In the winter of 1959–60 we were both on the road: he was campaigning for Hubert Humphrey and I was fulfilling my duties as Vice Chairman. Candidates were descending on available banquet tables like homing pigeons. The Detroit Light Guard Armory, far out of town, was noisy and full. The acoustics were inadequate and the crowd roaring and restless. I sat beside Senator McCarthy. The long head table stretched out on either side of us. Two chairs away sat Senator John F. Kennedy, surrounded by a milling mass begging for his autograph. Gene turned to me and said, "Pay no attention. The meat is so bad they had to find something to distract them."

Gene was the third speaker. He cut out with a display of deadpan wit that left nothing unmocked: candidates, Republicans, and

By the Political Sea

what he referred to as homogenized issues. He came back to his seat clutching some scratched notes which turned out to be illegible. I know because I tried to read them. His face was white and he was blue about the lips; it had sounded so effortless, but it took all he had. Even Kennedy, the man of the hour, failed to recapture the audience.

After another inedible repast, this one in Albuquerque, Gene and I went looking for food. A state trooper drove us past several quick-and-dirties, cautioning, "You wouldn't like those, ma'am." I finally turned him around. "I would like anything edible." After we had eaten, Gene and I decided that oratory, as we had known it, was out and that he and Kennedy, with their dry, unstressed, flat delivery, represented the voice of the future. "The new soft sell," I said, "puts it up to the listener; he has to get in there and catch the flies."

We rode the plane back to Washington talking of the different kinds of truth: the only certain thing, I suggested, was that the world asks questions of us we cannot answer. Gene proffered that the only sin was the denial of the Holy Ghost, of faith. Later we spoke of Kennedy; he had twice quoted history in his Albuquerque speech. "All those years in the House," Gene remarked, "I never heard him quote history."

Gene and Jack Kennedy were never *not* friends; they enjoyed sparring, face to face, or before others who would print what they said. Inevitably Gene found a way to get quoted. "Why not me?" he asked. "I'm more liberal than Hubert and more Catholic than Jack."

By 1967, I could count on regular press queries about McCarthy. A morose, brainy reporter from the New York *Post*, Jerry Talmer, described me as an Administration loyalist "deeply fond of Gene McCarthy." I was willing, he added, "to play the new national game of psychoanalyzing Gene McCarthy, but like most people encountered on this beat, please keep her name out of it."

I had told Talmer that Gene looked like an El Greco, that he was never as shy when talking about someone else as when talking about himself; that he was extraordinary, had a kind of inner ambivalence, and was a very spiritual man in a very delightfully mortal way. I said further that it was not in his nature to be President, that at times he didn't seem to want to be Senator. My description seemed accurate. Perhaps now I would not be quite so dogmatic about his nature in relation to the Presidency.

E. W. (Ned) Kenworthy of the New York *Times*, who covered his campaign, characterized him as a "strange man" in a "strange campaign." Ned and I have spent a lot of time analyzing this man you cannot analyze. Gene, Ned affirms, visualizes the President's role as that of a kind of philosopher-statesman. Gene played at both roles in his public life, taking side excursions into the Scriptures as well as the pleasure palaces, the "fun houses" where mirrors aggrandize and distort.

Hubert Humphrey, a forgiving man, never made the mistake of underestimating Gene McCarthy. They talked to each other and about each other. Hubert, at Lynda Bird Johnson's wedding in December 1967, described Gene as "unreachable. No logical approach," he said, "will get through to him." His estimate was correct. I tried and failed.

Gene was a frequent guest at our house. He would simply call, asking to come by for a swim, to bring or carry away a book, to show me some poems, or share an impromptu meal. When he walked through the door he reminded me of a winged creature with a way of moving that is nearer to loping than walking. If invited guests were already present, he was never surprised or ill at ease: give him a roomful of people and he would bounce his wit off them.

He saw analogies in everything. A certain politician was like "Enoch Arden at the window." Senators were like the football coach of whom it was said, "He's smart enough to understand the game and dumb enough to think it's important." Doves on Vietnam who would talk but not stand up and be counted were like Nicodemus, "who came to the Christians by night." He frequently used this image. Some of his followers were like Nicodemus; he spoke of forming a Nicodemus Society for them.

Reading all the watch ads became a new fascination. "Now they make a watch that tells you when you last saw your wife or when to put the roast in. They make another you can see through to the works." We agreed we saw through enough already. Wouldn't it be awful if someday we were to find out what others were thinking? "That is what hell will be," he replied.

He also had thought about a heaven. There would be a place for me in it . . . he smiled as one would at having invented a new reward. "Who else is there room for?" I wanted to know. He named no names. "A small select company!"

One noon, over coffee, someone asked that cliché question: "Are we going down as a country?" Gene thought not. We were merely moving too fast, getting our technical progress in gulps. Turning from technical progress to highways, he remarked dryly: "Deaths on the road are more effective than Vietnam. They get all ages of victims." I kept my eyes on his half-smiling, half-questioning glance—waiting for the laughs. He always got them.

"Strange," Walter mused one evening when he had stayed with us until late, "he is always remote, always sparkling. But when he's gone and you try to distill him, he slips away from you."

Back in 1965, Walter and I went to a reception Gene and his wife Abigail gave. As we came through the living room we noticed an unusual flower arrangement, almost the duplicate of one we had received that same day from the President and Mrs. Johnson. It turned out that the McCarthys and the Louchheims had joint wedding anniversaries. In 1966, on the occasion of our fortieth, I staged a surprise dinner party for Walter, including the Mc-Carthys, the Willard Wirtzes, Liz and Les Carpenter, and the Humphreys (who at the last moment were called to a higher cause, the arrival of King Saud). The event went off with predictable sparkle in champagne and talk. Abby and Gene McCarthy, Liz Carpenter, and I had each written a poem for the occasion. That fall, Liz gave a poetry party in honor of the appearance of my first published collection of poems: *With or Without Roses*. The guest list was considerably larger and each guest contributed a verse. Gene wrote:

> *Poetess of unclear spaces*
> *Drawing lines—Pointing*
> *But leaving free the sacred places.*
>
> *Poetess of the high ridges*
> *Running their edges—sharp*
> *   above the dark valleys*
> *But stopping short of roads or bridges.*
>
> *Poetess of what is left to till*
> *   with hope and love*
> *When men stop short for ignorance*
> *   or want of will.*

Another poet, James Dickey, became a devotee of Gene McCarthy's soon after becoming Poetry Consultant to the Library of Congress in 1966. Jim's long poems are familiar to readers of the *Atlantic, Harper's,* and *The New Yorker*; they have a troubadour's lilt and—some—a preacher's hell-fire. Jim is a Southerner, in speech and astuteness. He measured Gene with a savage, still youthful yardstick and announced, "I'd vote for him any time." Much later, he was to complain, "He's running around with the wrong poets," meaning Robert Lowell. Jim was possessive, but Lowell was too. Jim's assessment of Gene the candidate was sharp: "He isn't cruel enough. He isn't politically attuned. Like Adlai, he is too sensitive, too intellectual. Presidents either are, or become, cruel. Political animals, they fight for their corner of the political jungle. Gene is just playing, like a collector. He collects adherents. But the masses won't stop to listen."

He was wrong about the masses and right about Gene's superficial resemblance to Adlai. In one single thaw, in New Hampshire, Gene turned on the young. Masses of them. Adlai and Gene could both be described as intellectual and sensitive. But Gene was a loner. With his persistent aloofness went an unwillingness to reveal himself, and an undisciplined capriciousness that disregarded all advice but his own. He did collect people; he always will.

The three of us, Jim Dickey, Gene, and I, on occasion had lunch. In 1968 we were seated at a window table in the dining room of the Cosmos Club. It was summer: we faced the garden, light streamed in all around us. A young gardener was hanging geraniums, intermittently staring at us. I remained fixed in my listening, catching Jim's and Gene's word war.

"It's not how long you live but what you do with the time left you." The words belonged to Dickey, but they could have been Gene's. Gene seized on the time theme, weaving in politics. "Abba Eban had the advantage at the UN [he referred to the Mideast crisis]. He could talk about four thousand years of history. The poor Syrian was badly bested. He had only sixteen hundred years to claim."

They talked about death and immortality, then about the ages.

"I am a man of my own time," Dickey affirmed. He would not have wanted to be a Roman or an Elizabethan.

"I don't know," said Gene mischievously, "what about one of those Assyrian Kings who rode chariots with swords in the wheel spokes? Pretty thrilling!" His face had the mystical look it wears when he is pleased—half satyr, half god-glee.

Time . . . death . . . history. It was not the first occasion we had met to brood over these subjects. With Gene, they were part of the woof of politics as well. He mulled over the thought of eternity on time payments—and used it again and again: "Between the plush animals and the travel insurance, they sell eternity on time at airport newsstands. I intend to rescue the Church through political power." Politics reminded him of the new faiths belonging to new faces in the Republican Party: "Mormons [Governor Romney] don't believe the things that are true, and Christian Scientists [Senator Percy] believe the things that aren't true. Matter of fact," he went on, "no one believes in death any more, except the Spaniards. They demonstrate their belief in death by the bullfight.

In Spain death is both present and real. . . . We can never win in Vietnam," he said, "because we have lost belief in death, and the enemy have not."

After he had gone, Dickey commented: "He talks like he's conducting a seminar," and added, "I love that man."

For Christmas, in 1968, Gene gave his friends a collection of his own poems under the title *And Time Began*. I knew them all, had watched them take shape and meet the growing recognition they deserved. He would talk with me about his subjects, often in mystical terms. The difference between infinity and eternity—a favorite topic—he illustrated with a story from his childhood. In Watkins, Minnesota, where he grew up, there were two hardware stores, which supplied their customers with nails wrapped in the kind of paper boys make kites of. One store used orange paper; the other blue. In the spring one could always tell from their kites which store the boys' parents patronized. What intrigued Gene was that both stores also served another function—as undertaking establishments. His underlying theme was the lack of interest in infinity to a child, with eternity becoming a recognizable, arguable proposition only to a man.

In the title poem of the collection he speaks of kites; in the last two stanzas, he writes:

> *One day the string broke.*
> *The kite flew over the shoulder of the world,*
> *but reluctantly, reaching back*
>   *in great lunges*
> *as lost kites do, or as a girl running*
> *in a reversed movie, as at each*
>   *arched step, the earth*
> *set free, leaps forward, catching*
> *her farther back,*
> *the treadmill doubly betraying,*
> *remote and more remote.*
>
> *Now I lie on a west facing hill*
>   *in October.*

The dragging string having circled
*   the world, the universe,*
crosses my hand in the grass. I do not
*   grasp it.*
It brushes my closed eyes, I do not open.
That world is no longer mine,
*   but for remembrance.*
Space ended then, and time began.

When on rare occasions during his campaign he would call, I would ask if he had written anything. Between primaries, he told me about the day in Nebraska, trying to get away from the press, when he had stopped at the side of a road, found a deserted train track, and wrote a poem. Old railroad ties, he remembered, had previously preoccupied him. He'd wanted to talk about the "right of way," a riot of colors, with wild flowers blooming in stubble, now vandalized by people who had thrown rocks and taken up the ties. Not unlike the way, it occurred to me, he had been taken up by campaigning.

On the morning of November 10, 1967, when the Washington *Post* ran a story about Gene entering the spring primaries, I called him at his St. Paul hotel. As always, he was responsive, except that with Gene you may get only a quip for an answer. That day he was serious. He had not seen the story in the *Post*, but he had seen a wire service story the night before. He denied having made any decision. Since I had not even heard that he was thinking about it, I was astounded. Was he in earnest? Oh yes, he was: "You cannot be effective unless you offer a choice."

Suddenly I remembered having received a message that he had called me from the Washington airport. I was sorry to miss the call, I said. Sensing my thought, he said, "Oh, it was just to talk poetry." That evening I told Walter, "Some people seem bound for self-destruction," and silently I wondered whether we would ever talk poetry again.

But we did, and politics too. He joined Walter and me for a long breakfast and talked about his intentions. I'm certain he recognized my concern for what it was, honest and genuine. I repeated what I had said to Abby, his wife, that I was motivated not only by my loyalty to President Johnson and the party, but also by my fears that what he was about to do might fail. I was wrong. I had also warned that his candidacy would unleash Bobby. I was right about that.

He credited me with sincerity. Walter and I, and Geri Joseph, the Democratic National Committeewoman from Minnesota (an exceptional person, intelligent and fair), he told me, had all expressed the same thoughts. He knew all three of us to be his friends. He drove me through the northwest gates of the White House (where I was bound) and dropped me at the door. He said good-by affectionately.

He later wrote us a note, one that only he could have written:

> I appreciate very much your counsel and concern, and will weigh both carefully. I am something of a fatalist with reference to politics, if not to life, a little short of Dylan Thomas, via Vernon Watkins.
>
> > *"My immortality," he said,*
> > *"now matters to my soul*
> > *less than the death of others."*
>
> Politics is something short of this.

Misguided perhaps, but wondering what I might do to stop him, I hit on the idea of seeing Senator Gaylord Nelson of Wisconsin. Gene had once said he would not take on the primaries should his Senate "dove" friends oppose it. Gaylord was an outspoken dove and his state had an important primary coming up.

Gaylord was frank with me. "It will be murder," he said. He summed up his position: if he came out for Gene, he'd be opposing his Administration and his President. If he came out for LBJ, he'd be betraying his own dovish sentiments. If he were silent, he would be tagged a coward. He saw no point in talking to Gene. By that time Gene had decided on everything but the timing of his formal announcement.

I was nonplussed. I had really not envisaged this solid holdout. But Walter suggested, "Gaylord may have thought you were sent by the Administration to help persuade Gene to get out of the race."

Sometime later Gene and I lunched. He acknowledged that matters had gone too far; he could not withdraw. Did he know what he would do to people like Gaylord? He did. It would be rough. But even his wife, he admitted, had given up trying to stop him.

Primaries can be dismal and dreary, I reminded him. Would he take a new staff? He spoke of traveling simply. But I could picture him as he was to be—in a press-packed airplane, well-wishers in all shapes and sizes waving him on and off at the stops. I was sad for him, and for myself who counted him as a friend. My gloom was wasted, as was my concern. The New Hampshire primary turned out to be a political love-in, complete with dazzling young boys and girls, all with high IQs, who knew what to do and how to do it. And the company Gene kept, his extraordinary entourage made up of inspired writers, dedicated stage and TV stars—some of them the only real "beautiful people" of our times—would never leave him disconsolate, at least not for long.

Shana Alexander,[1] in her lucid legato prose, wrote: "Off and on through that long last day [Chicago Convention], as the tensions in the city grew, the McCarthy clan stayed loose and the oranges flew" (the Senator and his brother had been playing baseball with an orange). Later there would be bitterness, and tragedy. But I knew then that Gene's footnote in history would be written very large. As he himself said, when leaving Chicago, the footnote "may well become part of the main text."

His was a new style in politics and his followers, who stayed "clean for Gene," were a new generation: radical converts, possessed by this unpredictable quixotic man whose religion blended with his politics, as his poetry did with his life.

Before New Hampshire, I asked him if it was as much fun as it seemed. "Not when you tell them what you know they want to

[1] *Life*, September 6, 1968. Vol. 65. No. 10.

hear," he said. "You just stand there and feel cold." This from a man who was hearing the most intoxicating applause, the adulation of a "concerned" people.

At another time, I asked if it was true he was going to found a fourth party. He told me I'd solved his problem. With that magic mockery in his voice he said, "You've saved me. I always said I wouldn't start a third party, but a fourth—now that would be different."

The day Walter and I returned to Washington after the convention, he phoned. "This is a time for poets," he said. Not for me, I told him. I could write nothing. I still felt sick, a kind of permanent nausea that came from watching the convention on TV. We talked of the Chicago police who brutalized his kids. Over and over he paid tribute to the students' diligent devotion, and spoke of his own horror and the shame of those who would not intercede with the authorities when trouble first began.

Shortly thereafter, at a dinner before they left for a holiday in the south of France, Abby described her treatment by the convention police. They held her at the gate, harassing her and demanding her pass. Gene suggested she might have resisted and gone to jail.

"What, spend the night in the Cook County jail while you and Lowell debated dactyls and spondees?" she asked. We were relieved to find we could laugh; there was more than enough of suffering, horror, and hate.

That evening I asked Gene what would have happened if Bob Kennedy had lived. "He and I together would have turned Hubert around. I would have given my delegates to Hubert."

Introducing the Greek poet, George Seferis, at a poetry reading, Gene remarked that he wasn't quite ready to be just a poet.[2]

[2] December 2, 1968.

Hostility and Hope

A KEEN POLITICAL OBSERVER ONCE REMARKED, "POLITICS SEEMS TO attract so many terrible people, and yet so many wonderful ones." All kinds of people do get into politics. But we are all kinds of people. And if the last decade has taught us anything, it is that we ought to get to know one another and our institutions better.

I believe in politics, and in participation, in being active in the party of one's choice. If I had not believed that the individual mattered and could change things, I would never have done what I did. And if I were a Republican, I would say the same thing. My unshatterable belief in the two-party system, with its strengths and weaknesses, has never been in need of shoring up.

I agree wholeheartedly with the poet Karl Shapiro, who says:

> I hope they will find us guilty of facing
> the age we helped to construct.[1]

In this—"The Age of Hostility"—two things have to happen soon. The young have to make up their minds whether they want change or anarchy, and the old have to make room for the young in the political structure. If we want youth to become involved in the political process, we must also make it possible for them to earn the titles. At too many meetings, at the national level, I have watched the usual cliques take over, some of whom have held power too long.

[1] From *The Trial of a Poet*.

Copping out is easy and it is understandable, but it changes nothing. Eugene McCarthy, in his book *The Year of the People*, writes: "Despite all that happened in 1968, the year revealed that there is within the people of this country a great reservoir of good-will as well as ability and energy." His faith is not unfounded. Let us hope the young will respond. Those who worked for Senators McCarthy and Robert Kennedy surely learned that believing in a cause can compete for satisfaction with any twentieth-century experience.

They also learned that in order to win they needed to organize and that an organization calls for self-discipline. If any of these crusaders do join up, they will discover for themselves the paucity of people in the established ongoing political organizations. The title holders are there—there are many chiefs but few Indians. After the 1956 campaign Adlai's sister Buffie wrote me a plaintive letter pointing out these facts—facts that are partially remedied every four years with the formation of the Citizens for X. What holds most people back is the dreariness of precinct work: keeping forces together when there are no elected officials to come and pep up the troops, bringing precinct lists up to date, getting people registered and to the polls. By the time a Presidential election rolls round it is too late to bring in new stalwarts; most Presidential candidates therefore develop their own leaders in the state to run their campaigns.

Even more serious is the problem of election-year turnouts. In 1968 only sixty per cent[2] of the people in the United States who were eligible to vote actually did so—the lowest proportion since 1956 when President Eisenhower ran for a second time, and the American people also ran up only a sixty per cent total. (That was the year many an American who loved the General cast a vote for him as a kind of get-well card.) There are reasons, of course, for the low percentages; this is the age of mobility. Millions are disenfranchised because their companies move them, and

[2] Seventy-two million votes were cast, out of 120 million of voting age.

they arrive too late at the next destination to comply with their new state residence requirement.[3]

Many young intellectuals came home from World War II determined to change their lives by changing their government. I talked with one of these, a professor at the University of Chicago, and urged him into precinct politics. He showed up at several meetings in his area at which nothing comprehensible—to him—occurred. Drinks were served and fraternizing remarks were exchanged and he was ignored. He quit. Which was precisely what the local pros wanted him to do. After they'd mocked him, pretending to do nothing, and otherwise humbled him, they undoubtedly met to celebrate. "I can't take it," he wrote me. "My time is too valuable." Like all eggheads, he wanted to start at the top.

If I had walked out on all the meetings at which I'd found myself irritated, bored and/or ignored, my attendance record would have fallen pretty low. This was especially true of the early days, when my friends and I struggled with the power structure within the Democratic Central Committee of the District. The conservatives were combative and the liberals soon fell to quarreling among themselves (as they so often do), but a few of us sat through the fights, knowing that our only chance of winning was to be present when the votes were counted.

In the sixties I gave a commencement address at Athens, Ohio, a lovely old Greek Revival town. I had spent the morning with a group of young professors and their wives who had asked to see me. They had recently been outwitted by the local city council on a zoning change. Concerned lest commercialization spoil their unusual surroundings, they had hired a city planner. His report was presented, voted down, and the rezoning from residential to commercial accomplished before they could raise a hand to voice

---

[3] A recent Voting Bill (H.R. 12695) has finally become Public Law 91-285, signed by President Nixon June 22, 1970. "To enforce the guarantee of the 14th Amendment, it is necessary to completely abolish the durational residency requirement as a pre-condition to voting for President and Vice President."

an objection. What could they do? they asked. "Run for office," I replied. I later learned that one of the wives had done just that and had been elected.

The professors had full-time jobs, so their wives took over the civic responsibility. Too often, one finds the non-salaried local offices held by businessmen whose livelihood depends upon their being pro-business and anti-conservation. When I see the members of the League of Women Voters and other organizations out clutching petitions, collecting signatures opposing an action after it has been taken, I wonder, Why weren't these women candidates for local office?

Local office can be compared to family life—often predictable, petty, and dull, but yet at the right moments absolutely vital in its response to challenge. It is still up to the people who use our institutions to make them into viable bodies. Any officer nowadays, at any level, has to recognize that, to make democracy work, he has to do more than hold down a job. When I was in the Department of State, I noted a tendency on the part of all Americans who traveled abroad or attended meetings in the United States with other nationals to disparage our country. No society as rich and powerful as ours can behave without blame, but every now and then we ought to take time out to be glad about something. For instance, our system works when most others do not (under stress, strain, racial strife, the kind of anti-everything revolution the young are verbalizing); it does show more concern for the individual, it does pay heed to divergent points of view, and when it becomes arrogant, the people rise up and reassert themselves. And let us not forget that democracy gives a larger share of responsibility to more people at the federal, state, and local level. I trust the American people, their common sense and their judgment, and their ability to redress their mistakes, for they do make them.

Anyone can tell you what's wrong with everything, from the government, the Congress, and on down. My own hair shirt is fitted carefully, and remains, I trust, invisible. Congress, for instance, doesn't do enough about the nation's over-all problems and the federal government doesn't do enough about the growing threats of bigness. Both the Congress and the federal establishment are too big and too reliant on their staffs. Running from meeting to meeting, officials must depend on the memos handed them by men and women with—naturally—a bias or a determination, either for or against change, for or against the subject, the procedure, and the solution.

Meetings these days are as compulsive as doodling. I've created superstructures listening to dreary speeches. I have always been a meeting goer. I've been to so many I've become allergic to badges. But I've never been able to kick the habit, not even on those occasions when I feel like the young woman who asked, "Should I surrender in a Dior or slug it out in stretch pants?"

I go, I listen, I learn something. During my Department of State days, I heard Joyce Hall of greeting-card fame announce that Walt Disney had done more to create good will internationally than either President Eisenhower or Winston Churchill. A fleeting vision of Disneylands, greeting cards, and marvelous machines that sold happiness crossed my mind. But Mr. Hall was right; foreigners do extol the wonders of Disneyland.

I am almost always astonished at meetings, because Americans have a remedy, a cure, for every problem on the agenda. A favorite relief from frustration for the average citizen is the new idea—his. Citizens who CARE CRITICIZE. I have listened to more eager men and women, thoughtful Americans, some with a bias, some without, all of whom are going to solve our dilemmas with their particular brand of miracle.

Today we tend to structure our problems too much—name them, study them, and write a report about them. Sometimes the meeting techniques help us along a road we need to go, but too often they do no more than produce another report or another motion. Many meetings have become ends in themselves.

I want us to grab a neighbor or a friend and get on with the job. Cooperative efforts, in turn, must be decentralized. Large organizations are important forces; they influence the Congress and public opinion. But to meet today's urgent needs, we need to localize and to work in smaller units. I count on the young for ideas, for imagination, and for muscle.

If dirty politics exists (and it does), remember it is due to citizen apathy. Reform is part of our essential process of renewal, almost like going to church on Sunday. Every citizen ought to set aside Sunday to think about God (I did not say go to church, though that probably helps), and every other day to give some time to his or her duty as a citizen. The petition and the protest are not enough—one can stand outside forever. One must really get involved.

Joyce Cary wrote that "What is startling to anyone who has done a real political job is the naïveté and cocksureness of popular slogans about government, which is the most difficult and uncertain job in the world." Too little credit is given the politician. And the United States Government. Despite the fact that it has grown big and cumbersome, it runs steadily on a rough track. Furthermore, it is full of dedicated civil servants who know what they are doing. Many a bureaucrat knows how to make things happen, but the political appointee is also needed to guide and steer the bureaucracy in the direction of his administration's particular goals. This is especially true in diplomacy.

The Department of State is charged with making the most important decisions of our troubled times. It desperately needs the idea men, the evaluators and innovators to reorganize, redistribute responsibility, and revamp the ways of a necessarily cumbersome bureaucracy. Most Foreign Service officers will confide that to serve as Assistant Secretary of one of the regional bureaus (a political appointment) is to put one's future on the firing line. But the career men do often take these jobs, and serve ably. The Congress accepts the politically appointed Secretary of State as a representative of his party, as well as for his expertise. The new appointee sometimes rejects the past, which is as it should be.

There is every reason for politicians and diplomats to serve together. Both have learned to get along with others, to handle the intransigent and the unconvinced. There is undeniably politics in diplomacy and diplomacy in politics.

My husband once asked Averell Harriman to what he attributed his continued success. "To my willingness," he said, "to take any job offered no matter how low or high." Because of early experiences, I had followed, perhaps unconsciously, Averell's philosophy. When I was fired as Vice Chairman by the Kennedys, I could have gone home and sulked. It would have been easy; but I kept on telling people I was going to help in the Kennedy campaign and would manage no matter where they put me. I went from my large office to a cubbyhole, from two secretaries to a part-time one, from a staff of seven to a staff of nobody. I learned that I could adjust and enjoyed the challenge.

Being deprived of office can be a great boon. When the petty inanities disappear, it clears the air of dislikes. A man who knows what this means is Steve Mitchell, the former Chairman of the Democratic National Committee, and my friend and mentor. Steve once told a reporter, "I started at the top and went down and down." He was right: he left the Chairmanship to go back to his native Chicago. He challenged Mayor Daley and lost. Steve believed in citizen participation. He moved to New Mexico and started all over again. He put his considerable political acumen at Eugene McCarthy's disposal during the 1958 convention. He is a man of strong convictions; when someone once asked his wife Evelyn if he were moody, she replied, "Heavens no. He is the most even-tempered man I know, he's always mad." Their enthusiasm exhilarated me.

Steve's tigerlike urges for reform delighted me, horrified others, and discomforted Adlai, his sponsor. Steve deserves a special laurel, but the liberal Establishment seldom gives them away; they keep them for themselves. Certain in-house liberals are so often people who believe only in their own kind. Arthur Schlesinger is one of these. He himself has written of the ferocity with which they enshrine themselves.

The worst of the liberals are institutional, not elected. When a liberal wears out his welcome in office, as some have, the electorate gets rid of him. The unelected liberal is forever.

There are, of course, wonderful liberals as there are good and bad reactionaries. But the inflexible liberal and his counterpart, the reactionary, each in his own way lacks faith in the system of checks and balances we have so carefully guarded. To me, being a liberal means to be open-minded, at least to the point of questioning myself and admitting I don't have all the answers.

Some liberals can't seem to rise above the past; they remind one of Winston Churchill's prophecy: "If we open a quarrel between the past and the present, we shall find that we have lost the future." The young have little use for the preaching liberal, and the snobbish attitudinizing he indulges in has alienated the middle class—which, by dint of its sheer numbers, is the American power structure. I admit that I read what the liberals write; because of my weakness for good prose I cannot resist them. But I can see through their verbal virtuosity to their basic ineffectiveness. Because they are my friends—at least some are—I deplore their decline, but they have held center stage for too long. Perhaps, too, they failed in the most important respect, according to my doctrine: most of them never joined a precinct organization.

On the hustings, I invariably suffer an attack of chauvinism. That's one reason why politics is good for one. The same thunderclap of enthusiasm for my country struck me whenever I toured the United States or returned from a visit to some other part of the world. I enjoyed the people, their egos, their prejudices and great zeal for joining and listening. I even fell in love with the scenery, the confusion, and the variety. Washington is a great place to live, but it's an even more insular post than the farthest outpost of the British Empire in its heyday. There are of course minuses as well as pluses, wherever one goes. Not the least of the detractions is the bad weather one encounters. I used to wish for the power both to ameliorate the elements and to conciliate the factions. My success on both fronts was predictably limited except for one occasion in Wyoming. We arrived in Casper during a bad drought. While I was speaking in a community hall, rain suddenly began to fall in hail-sized drops. A man's voice in the back of the hall bellowed:

"Lady, if you can do that, you'd better stick around!"

I appreciate his belief in my supernatural powers. If I had them, they could be put to good use; but even without them there's always something one can do.

Index